THE SHADOW™

DANCE

&the Astrological 7th House

(Marriage, Partnership and Open Enemies;
i.e., the Shadow in us all)

WORKBOOK

Rebeca EIGEN

Edited by Ann Bugh

Libra26 Press, Houston, Texas

First printing January 2009
Libra26 Press, Houston, Texas

Second printing, 2016
Third printing, 2021

ISBN 978-0-9709258-7-9

shadowdance.com

I dedicate this book
to my loving son, Kevin,
who kept reminding me
to write my book,
and
I couldn't have done
any of this work without
my best friends,
Terri Barnes,
Patricia Wilson
and the
love of my life,
God/Goddess.

Acknowledgments

It always takes two who are committed to get the most value from doing Shadow work. With grateful thanks to all of my dear friends and family who have polarized with me, and then were willing to come back to a place where we could be REAL and love each other, including our Shadows, because I couldn't have done any of this work alone. I also sincerely appreciate those who willingly shared their experiences with me, in order to help others understand themselves. They will remain anonymous.

Very special thanks to Ann Bugh, who hung in there with me for five years editing this workbook as a trade if I would teach her astrology. She was a skeptic at first (about astrology — doubting it all until I read for her one-on-one because of a twist of fate). She was not only a gifted editor, she is a spiritual advisor and a generous angel sent to me to help me put this all on paper. She made great suggestions that improved the readability and content, and I will forever be grateful for her patience and hard work. Thank you also to Amanda Perry, who has the voice of an angel; Alan Holt, who lives in two worlds, and I'm glad he's part of mine; Gail Best, whose talents are many; Sharon Wallingford, who enthusiastically gave of her time; Maree Hubbell and Marcia Zelinksy, two of my spiritual sisters in this life, for their input as well.

Thank you to my teacher and mentor, J. Pittman McGehee, D.D., who helped me understand what Jung was saying and how to relate it to my everyday life, by his example and his humor that kept me hooked.

Thank you to my friend Jenny Grier, who was the owner of Centerpoint, a community center in Houston, for a very long time. She was the one who encouraged me to teach others about this subject.

Thank you to my astrology teachers and there have been many from all over the world, but I especially want to thank Liz Greene, Ph.D. for her outstanding books and psychological reports; my first teacher Kimberly McSherry, owner of the Houston Institute of Astrology, where I took classes for five years; Glenn Perry, Ph.D. whose teaching methods as a psychological astrologer are invaluable; and Jan Spiller and Michael Lutin, whose work on the Nodes I found of primary importance for healthy relationships.

On the production end, I want to thank Millie Barnes and Robin Beckham for proofreading, and Matt Welsh, David and Victor Lu, for making the printing of this book a dream come true.

And last but not least, my deceased ex-husband Ed Eigen, who never stopped being my friend. And Austin Cater, I appreciate you for being a mirror of my 7th House. Thank you for everything.

Contents

Part 4. Symbols, Correspondences and Key Words

Part 5. Astrological Consultations on the 7th House

Foreword

From a Feminine Point of View
by Terri Barnes

Knowing Rebeca for over two decades, I have heard countless discourses on "the Shadow." I can honestly say I've been trained to look at things quite introspectively now, whether someone appears to cause an upset in me, or the opposite, when someone has my awe. It brings home the philosophy that there is just one of us here; we are all reflections of some aspect of ourselves waiting to be owned and integrated. It's a beautiful way to live your life, for there's no space for victimhood, as we accept our wholeness, through the courage to look at all parts of ourselves that seem out there but are really within. For years Rebeca has counseled hundreds (thousands?) through her comprehensive study of astrology, Jungian psychology and metaphysics, searching for answers and insights, supporting others to create healthy and conscious relationships. I have no doubt that from the first chapter a healing journey will commence for the reader, who will be awed at what will be uncovered in the light of Shadow work.

What Rebeca teaches takes discipline and is often uncomfortable. Who wants to tell the truth about the nasty thoughts and feelings we harbor but deny? And by the same token, who of us is willing to proclaim our divine heritage without a shred of guilt that we're worthy? I've often remarked to Rebeca that I think her life path in teaching is quite challenging, as it takes great courage to face our demons and encourage others to do the same. The beautiful thing is, if we are daring enough, the demons are revealed to be the illusions they always were and the love that was always there becomes apparent. That's the miracle and healing that comes from doing Shadow work.

This book is filled with personal examples of Shadow work, and Rebeca is so graciously allowing me to go first. Not long ago, I had my 50th birthday. I knew it was going to be a difficult one, as it was my first birthday after my husband John's death. I left town to be with my son, Andrew, in Boston, and family in New York. I woke up missing John a lot that morning, but was also mindful of my many blessings, particularly, my son. As Andrew was driving us back to Boston that afternoon, I noticed feelings of disappointment, sadness and anger stirring in me, directed at my son. He had not given me a present, not even a card. Just a "Happy Birthday, Mem!,"* which left my heart unfulfilled. I had helped him out considerably financially the last few months when it was challenging for me to do so, allowing him time to compose and complete his master's degree. Surely he could have set a little aside for a card or a token gift when he knew this would be a tough birthday. I depended on him! I saw him as selfish, uncaring and not as conscious as I expected him to be. As I was having these thoughts, I was feeling increasingly guilty for having them. After all, he was still struggling financially, and I should have been grateful just for his being with me, driving me to and from Boston and New York, and not expecting more.

---

*"Mem" is what Andrew calls her.

As I went back and forth between being angry with Andrew and guilty for feeling so, my upset grew, but so did my determination not to start this new decade without healing it. I owned that yes, I was the one being selfish and ungrateful and unconscious and projected that unto Andrew. At the same time, I value my relationship with my son dearly; we've been through a lot together, and I owe our relationship the honesty it deserves. I told him I felt disappointed that I received no card or gift, and that I did not like having these angry, upset feelings toward him.

He apologized for not giving me his card sooner, but waited until we were back in Boston. His card included a letter proclaiming how much our relationship meant to him, how much it made him evolve. In the letter he said he was composing something for me, but he was not complete with it yet, and to please be patient. The love I felt through his words was immense. No gift from a store would have the value of his music for me, and he knew that. He was giving me the greatest gift he could, the gift of his love, through his music. All feelings of anger, sadness, selfishness, and guilt either blamed or owned were replaced by a gratitude that filled my heart to overflowing.

By being willing to tell Andrew the truth and risking more upset, I received a healing of something wounded within me, and allowed him to be the instrument of that healing. I was also a teacher for him that it's all right to express your feelings, especially to those who matter the most. He has always been pretty good at that, but I think as we get older we get more conditioned to respond in ways that are not authentic. I went to bed that night with a heart full of gratitude on a challenging day, even more mindful of my blessings, and even closer to Andrew. Months later, Andrew summoned me back to Boston for the debut performance of a string quartet he composed in dedication to the journey of love, passion, grief and surrender he witnessed with John and me.

There is a quote from *A Course in Miracles* that says, "In my vulnerability, my safety lies."

This is what Rebeca's life's work is all about: having the courage to be vulnerable, to tell the truth and to own our part of what we're perceiving. And in so doing, healing happens and the presence of love is what we know. I love you, Rebeca, for the awesome role you have played for me and countless others. It is holy work, indeed.

Foreword

From a Masculine Point of View
by Austin Cater

A Hindu walks up to a hotdog vender and the vender asks him, "What would you like?"
The Hindu answers, "Make me one with everything." We are one with everything. Let
me say that again, "We are one with everything." Our free will, or the concept of it,
along with a healthy dose of individuality and self determination give us the ability to
turn a blind eye to everything around us and our part in this universe. That perception
of reality leaves us living in blissful ignorance, being a mere victim of the calamity that
happens to us. The perception Astrology can give you will show you the clockwork of
the universe and how you are a part of it. Science is the observation, description and
explanation of natural phenomena as they relate to the human existence. Again, that's
HUMAN existence. What human being cares about Martian algebra? That doesn't affect
us, we know nothing about it, and it's not our problem. Astrology is arguably the first
Science.

Long ago when man (and woman) first started gazing at the stars at night, they
noticed that not all the stars were moving across the sky in the same manner. They gave
names to these celestial objects and began plotting their courses. With their scientific
minds, humans noticed that there was a correlation between the position of these objects
and their effects on mankind. People born on certain dates, in certain places, with certain
planets present would have certain characteristics, good, bad, or both — mostly both. In
understanding this, generations of humans have come closer to understanding who we
are, and why we are the way we are. It is a scientific glimpse into the "clockwork of the
universe" and where we fit in it. We are stardust, and so is everything else and everyone
else. (So why is it so hard to get along with one another? We are all connected, right?)
Astrological knowledge is our human understanding, our science.

Rebeca Eigen is an astrologer who specializes in relationships. Rebeca incorporates astrology with "Jungian Theory" (i.e. the duality of man, the Shadow self, projections, etc.).
She will introduce you to your Shadow. Getting to know your "Shadow Self" will open
your eyes to the things that you don't like about yourself. Those things are reflected back
to you in your disdain for that certain person whom you loathe. We all know those people, right?

This workbook will help you to recognize your characteristic traits when it comes to
relationships with others, through your understanding of astrology. As you know yourself
better, you will better understand what it is you need to learn to share with a significant
"other" to form or improve your relationships. If you are in a relationship, it can help
you to better know your partner as well. It will become clearer to you what it is that they
need in their relationships. Astrology gives you a tool to better understand one another.
Wouldn't that be nice?

The workbook exercises at the end of each chapter will help you to gain further clarity
and understanding into your total self. Don't skip these; they are not only very helpful
but also fun.

And remember, we are one with everything.

Introduction

To confront a person with his shadow is to show him his own light.

Once one has experienced a few times what it is like to stand judgingly

between the opposites, one begins to understand what is meant by the Self.

Anyone who perceives his shadow and his light simultaneously

sees himself from two sides and thus gets in the middle.[1]

CARL GUSTAV JUNG

Relationship Patterns

What is it that constitutes a good relationship? Is it getting along harmoniously, being loving, truthful, honest, supportive? These are certainly virtues and ideals that we all strive for. Yet, despite our most valiant efforts, few of us maintain these virtues and ideals in our relationships for long. In fact, despite our best efforts to make relationships work, most of us continually come across problems and situations that puzzle us.

A very interesting thing about relationships — like life — is that they all start repeating at a certain point. If we're honest with ourselves, we will recognize that the person we fell in love with when we were in our twenties looks eerily like the same person we were attracted to and fell in love with at thirty — or even at forty. If we start to examine our relationship patterns, we also soon notice that the same kind of person keeps showing up, even if we decide to leave or try to distance ourselves from their presence. They might be in our life as our mate, our boss, our siblings or maybe even a coworker or a friend, but sooner or later, we will all face difficult or challenging relationships. Those of us who are willing to live a reflective life have to ask ourselves some very important questions, like why did I attract him or her, what is this about, and why is this repeating in my life?

We can choose to resolve the issues we encounter by leaving one relationship and finding another. We can also leave a job or a friendship, or even a sibling or parent who we have decided is causing us pain. We can continue to blame others for our negative relationship experiences — or we can muster up the courage to take a long, hard look at our own Shadow.

Shadow Work

In this book you will learn about a part of yourself you may have never seen before. "The Shadow," a term coined by the eminent Dr. Carl Gustav Jung, is a part of all of us that we badly need to know about. Through his experiences, knowledge and practice as a psychiatrist, and his courageous self-honesty, Jung encountered a darker double, a *doppelgänger,* residing in all of us that can be a valuable asset to us once we learn about it. You will learn how your Shadow side formed, and how it operates in your relationship with yourself and your relationships with others. Reclaiming this lost part of yourself is important for long-term relationships to be loving, healthy and real.

Finding and integrating the Shadow doesn't happen overnight. It is a lifelong retrieval process. For those who are willing to do the work — because it takes work to retrieve this lost and hidden part of yourself — it is a boon like no other. Dr. Jung has given us all a precious gift — the gift of truly accepting our unique *selves*.

Shadow work is not solely for couples. In fact, ultimately it is the relationship we build with ourselves that will help us break free of old patterns, embrace our Shadow and learn about these hidden parts that were there begging for our acceptance all along.

In this book, there are many anecdotes from my own life and the lives of others who have shared their own experiences with me while confronting their Shadow selves. These stories illustrate the complicated theory of the Shadow for anyone who wants to understand himself or herself better. Even after years of doing this work, I am still in awe of the profound ways the Shadow content comes to our awareness and of the challenge it poses for all of us.

Dr. Jung was a brilliant psychiatrist who was way ahead of his time. Once we become familiar with his theories, Shadow work can be done with our partners, a very close friend or a sibling, as well as by working with a therapist. I have written this workbook to make it useful and practical on a daily basis.

The power of Shadow work, however, is far from simple. Dr. Jung believed that this task — owning and integrating our Shadow — was the single most important work for the evolution of the collective consciousness of our planet. Near the end of his life, he wrote a book called *The Undiscovered Self,* in which he explained the importance for each individual to do this work in order to heal the collective.

It takes an investment of time to reflect and honestly look inside ourselves. I have provided a place for you to take notes and record "AHA," light bulb moments. I hope you will keep this book as a journal to come back to time and again when you remember or experience something later, so that it will become an ongoing part of your life long after you read it.

The reward for being willing to do this work is what we all want most, deep inside — an experience of real and lasting LOVE — love for ourselves, love for God/Goddess within us and love for each other.

Love has no desire but to fulfill itself.

To meet and be like a running brook

that sings its melody to the night.

To wake at dawn with a winged heart

and give thanks for another day of loving.

KAHLIL GIBRAN

Filling the conscious mind with ideal conceptions is a characteristic feature of Western theosophy, but not the confrontation with the shadow and the world of darkness. One does not become enlightened by imagining figures of light, but by making the darkness conscious. The latter procedure, however, is disagreeable and therefore not popular.[2]

CARL GUSTAV JUNG

*Love? Do I love?

I walk within the brilliance of another's thought.

As in a glory. I was dark before,

as Venus' chapel in the black of the night.

But there was something holy in the darkness,

softer and not so thick as other where;

and as rich moonlight may be to the blind.

Unconsciously consoling.

Then love came, like the out-bursting

of a trodden star.

THOMAS LOVELL BEDDOES

*(When I started writing this book, this poem by Thomas Lovell Beddoes came to my mailbox in a pink envelope addressed to an unknown person with no return address.)

NOTES:

1)   C.G. Jung, Collected Works Vol. 10 - *Civilization in Transition, Good and Evil in Analytical Psychology,* Princeton University Press, Bollingen, 1964, par 872, pg 463

2)   C.G. Jung, Collected Works Vol. 13 - *Alchemical Studies, The Philosophical Tree,* Princeton University Press, Bollingen, 1967, par 335, pg 265

1 Recognizing Our Shadow

Have you ever met anyone you couldn't stand? Conversely, have you ever met anyone you instantly fell madly in love with or put on a pedestal? Well, say "Hello" to your Shadow.

The Shadow

The Shadow is a psychological term. It describes everything about us that is unconscious, repressed, undeveloped or denied. The Shadow describes the person we would rather not be and don't want to know about either. The curious thing about the Shadow is that it includes both dark (negative) and light (positive) aspects of our being ***that we know nothing about.*** These are parts of us that we've been missing. This is the gift of Shadow work and one of the main reasons why we badly need to acknowledge our Shadow. We need these parts.

When I first learned about the Shadow, I was amazed to find out how much was actually unconscious. We go around thinking and believing we know ourselves, but that is a very sad misconception. We are all so much more than we actually know.

Our Shadow characteristics are often primitive and infantile, mainly because they are undeveloped and hidden from our conscious ego. Jung called the process of retrieving hidden (unconscious) parts of us in order to be a whole person ***individuation.***

Everyone has a Shadow. This is not something that just some people have. We all have a Shadow, and a confrontation with it is essential for self-awareness. Because it's impossible to truly learn about ourselves if we do not learn about our Shadow, Jung tells us that we are going to attract it through the mirrors of other people. These people can be a marriage partner, a friend, a sister or brother, a coworker, even our parents. Really, anyone can bring to our awareness a part of our own Shadow.

Archetypes

Another way to think about the Shadow is as an archetype. The late John Sanford, author of *Evil, the Shadow Side of Reality,* gave the best and most simple definition of an archetype.

Archetypes are our psychic equivalents to instincts. They are inherent, predisposed patterns of thought, prototypes of behavior common to every one of us.

To paraphrase Sanford, he said that an archetype is an essential building block in the psyche typical in consciousness for everyone. It is an innate pattern, or an imprint. The word "archetype" comes from *arche,* imprint, and *type,* pattern. Jung first spoke of archetypes as ancient primordial images and took the term from the *Corpus Hermeticum,* an alchemical manuscript. The ancient discipline of alchemy, a mystical version of Christianity, had numerous descriptions in symbolic form of these archetypal dimensions of the human psyche. Plato called them forms, and St. Augustine called them divine ideas.

There are as many archetypes as there are typical situations in life. Endless repetition has engraved these experiences into our psychic constitution, not in the forms of images, filled with content, but at first only as forms without content representing merely the possibility of a certain type of perception or action.[2]

CARL GUSTAV JUNG

Notes to Myself:

_____
_____
_____
_____
_____
_____
_____
_____
_____
_____
_____
_____
_____
_____
_____
_____
_____

Jung described archetypes as being like riverbeds waiting to be filled with experience. Each of us comes into this incarnation not as *tabula rasa* (blank slates) for our parents and experience to mold us, but already imprinted with these archetypes at birth.

Jung also said that archetypes are to the psyche as instincts are to the body. Instinctually, we all know when to fight or flee a situation, because we all experience these raw, gut feelings. Immediately our body responds. Everyone experiences instincts in the same way. Archetypes are our psychic equivalents of instincts. They are inherent, predisposed patterns of thought, prototypes of behavior common to every one of us. They result in specific actions, events or situations that will have a common thread or meaning.

Astrology is a study of the archetypes inherent as patterns of psychic life described in metaphors of gods, using Greek mythology. Throughout Jung's work, there are references to his knowledge of astrology as a symbolic system. He emphasized the importance of symbols, metaphors, myths and images. He felt that we all had access to this primordial information through what he called the collective unconscious, a substratem of psychic activity. This is the underlying archetypal structure of consciousness connecting us all to each other. In his autobiography, *Memories, Dreams, Reflections,* Jung explains his own journey of discovering the collective unconscious within man, which came to him in a dream. This book was instrumental in helping me to relate to my own unconscious and to find and relate to my Shadow, which resides in what he called the personal unconscious — the part of the unconscious unique to each individual.

There is no better psychological system for recognizing our innate archetypal psychic structure and individual needs than through the study of astrology. Archetypes as described by astrology are universal in their content and basic to each human being, as we all share certain patterns of behavior. For example, archetypes describe psychological needs and experiences we all have, such as the need to nurture, to be needed or to belong. Nurturing needs correspond to the archetype of the Mother (Moon) in astrology. The need to take action or assert ourselves, forge our own way, is represented by the Hero-Warrior (Mars) archetype. An archetype can describe an event as well, for instance a fire, a war, a football game or an object or a place. A weapon, a fire truck, a red chili pepper and a martial arts studio all correspond to the archetype of Mars. Some additional archetypes that Jung called attention to include king and queen, wise old man *(senex)*, father, crone or wise woman, lover, divine child *(puer aeternus)*, hero, trickster, witch and more. Even professions like teacher, doctor, preacher, sailor, police officer and lawyer have archetypal meanings we can all relate to.

Jesus Christ and Buddha are examples of the archetype of the savior or the healer. As Jung said, the life of Christ was archetypal. "What happens in the life of Christ happens always and everywhere."[4] Deep inside us, we are all predisposed to want to save, to rescue, to help, to be compassionate and to want to heal the suffering of others. Metaphysicians teach that we all have Christ within.

Innate within each individual are these archetypal structures or themes. Our astrological birth chart shows which of these archetypes are more dominant in our character than others, but we all have them all. Therefore, astrological symbols are metaphors for the psychic constitution of man. Part 4 has a chart for correspondences as described by the zodiac, as well as keywords for the signs.

Establishing a relationship with our Shadow can help us learn of this archetypal world within our being, waiting to be discovered. Its discovery not only introduces us to our own personal unconscious, but holds the key that unlocks the door toward becoming whole and complete.

How I Learned about My Own Shadow

By midlife, most people begin to notice that many situations in their lives have repeated. Without any psychological training, most of us find these experiences completely puzzling and disheartening. We wonder about ourselves and why these experiences with others keep repeating. I was really glad I had kept journals, because it became interesting to me at midlife to go back years later, reread them and acknowledge these patterns in my own relationships. That said, I'd like to begin by telling a personal story of how Shadow work came

Our astrological birth chart shows which of these archetypes are more dominant in our character than others, but we all have them all.

Notes to Myself:

_____

_____

_____

_____

_____

_____

_____

_____

_____

_____

_____

_____

_____

_____

_____

When I first read my astrological report, I remember being amazed that a computerized report could be so accurate.

Notes to Myself:

_____

_____

_____

_____

_____

_____

_____

_____

_____

_____

_____

_____

_____

_____

_____

into my awareness. I truly believe that by telling each other our stories and communicating honestly about our experiences, we can begin to see how this wisdom of Dr. Jung can potentially help us all in our everyday lives.

My story combines life experiences with a love of astrology and the study of Jungian psychology. In 1985, I started studying astrology, and in 1988, I ordered a "Psychological Horoscope Analysis" report from a famous British astrologer and Jungian analyst named Liz Greene. Her reports give a psychological description of our inherent, predisposed character based on our birth information — the time, place and date of our birth. When I first read my astrological report, I remember being amazed that a computerized report could be so accurate. The words were not vague or fuzzy; they described me clearly. This report also included a description of my Shadow. When I read this part, I could not identify with any of the character traits described at all. I ignored this part of the report and told myself, "That's not me. I'm not like that." Eventually, I just plain forgot about it. I continued studying both astrology and psychology, but it would be two more years before I really understood how both would lead me back to an understanding of the description of my Shadow in that report.

Most people who read daily horoscopes or "sun sign" columns have no idea just how complicated astrology actually is or what it is really based on. When people first begin to study the art of astrology, *it seems as if* the planets are causing us to behave in certain ways. While there is tremendous accuracy in the planetary character descriptions, through a more thorough understanding, students find out that this is a misconception. It is not until you actually study astrology for years that you find out its depth and benefits. Rather than being about planets out there in the sky doing things to human beings, astrology is actually based on an ancient worldview that postulated signatures and correspondences between lower and higher orders of life. The ancients believed that the universe was alive and that everything and everyone in the cosmos is part of one unified organism. Whether we know how or why it works, our individual astrological chart describes the blueprint of our psyche. We are born at a particular time and place, and who we are is reflected by the energy present at that moment in time. The planets themselves are symbolic of the archetypes that we are all made of regardless of race or gender. Just as we all have the same body parts, we also have these archetypal forces operating within us.

Liz Greene, in her book *The Dynamics of the Unconscious, Seminars in Psychological Astrology, Volume 2,* cowritten with Howard Sasportas (who was a very influential teacher in my life), in her chapter on alchemy states:

So the principle Mars is not only a planet, it is also found in the earth as iron, and in the human body as the adrenal glands, and in the psyche as the aggressive instinct and so on. Saturn is not only a planet, but also lead in the earth, and the human skeletal system and the impulse for self-protection. The Sun can be found not only in the heavens but as gold in the earth, and as the human heart, and as the capacity to love. The vision of a unified cosmos with interconnections via a finite number of archetypal lines was fundamental both to alchemy and astrology, so the two were never separate. The metals upon which the alchemist worked were not only actual substances, subjected to cooking processes; they were also seen to be the planets themselves, and the great cosmic principles behind them. So if you were transmuting lead, you were transmuting Saturn, and in turn working on the defensive, dark, depressive and barren aspects of nature and of yourself in order to release the solar gold of a loving heart and a joyful vision of life.[5]

You will be surprised by the detail involved and the profound accuracy in describing your own psyche.

Combining a deeper understanding of the symbolic system of astrology with the wisdom of Jungian psychology brings insights into your life that are truly enlightening, because you cannot deny who you are. So much can be revealed to you by studying your own birth chart. Our chart is a map of our soul. All you have to do to prove it to yourself is to study your own chart and those of the people who are close to you. You will be surprised by the detail involved and the profound accuracy in describing your own psyche. I have studied the subject now for 20+ years and know it will be a lifelong study as there is so much to it — which brings me back to my story.

Two years after I received my "Psychological Horoscope Analysis" report by Liz Greene, a friend of mine gave me a few cassette tapes of some Sunday school classes taught by an Episcopalian priest, the Reverend J. Pittman McGehee. I started listening to these tapes and found his thoughts about life very intriguing. He really made me think. For several years, I had been heavily involved in the New Age metaphysical movement, or what some might call the power of positive thinking. This priest's views were quite different from my own in this area; however, what made me want to go hear him in person was that he also made me laugh. I absolutely loved his sense of humor and his ability to synthesize such complicated subjects by telling personal stories that were entertaining, as well as informative. He is an exceptional storyteller and has a way of making profound ideas easy to understand.

One Sunday I decided that it was time to put a face on these tapes I had been listening to. I accompanied my friend to the Sunday school class that Rev. McGehee was teaching. Afterward we attended the mass. As I sat watching him, I began getting more and more uncomfortable, fidgeting in my chair. Finally, I turned to my friend

Notes to Myself:

9

I obsessed about him (which I later learned is one of the surest ways you find out about your own Shadow — it won't leave you alone!).

Notes to Myself:

_____

_____

_____

_____

_____

_____

_____

_____

_____

_____

_____

_____

_____

_____

and said to her, "That man is so cynical. He's depressed." It was overwhelming to me. I became so uncomfortable listening to him that I wanted to get out of there. My friend actually intuitively sensed what I was feeling and asked me if I wanted to leave. We left the church that day before the service was even over.

I went home that afternoon and could not get this priest off my mind. I obsessed about him (which I later learned is one of the surest ways you find out about your own Shadow — it won't leave you alone!). At first I thought maybe I should try to uplift this man by giving him a positive-thinking tape or book. Then, as I sat there in my room pondering this experience, I remembered something he had said on one of the tapes which I had listened to during the prior weeks. He had said the word "Shadow." That word triggered a thought in my mind, and around four o'clock that afternoon I went to the closet to get my "Psychological Horoscope Analysis" report by Liz Greene and reread it. There it was — a description of my own Shadow. It said that *I was a cynical and depressed person in the Shadow,* a person who didn't believe anything would ever work out. This part of me believed that life was just plain unfair. The report went on to say that I held these views in my Shadow in order to compensate for my conscious, overly optimistic view of life. This report had been tucked away in my closet, and I had not looked at it in two years. On this day I remembered it because my emotional reaction to this priest had had such a strong impact on me. I decided then and there to go and learn from him. He was teaching classes at the C.G. Jung Center in Houston, Texas, and I became very interested in understanding more of what he was talking about. He became the most influential teacher I have ever had in my life.

The first course I took from him was a 12-week course titled "Basic Concepts of Analytical Psychology." What I found out from studying under him was that Jung's concepts of sensation, thinking, intuition and feeling were almost exactly the same as the descriptions of the elements I had been studying in astrology — earth, air, fire and water. Everything I had studied in astrology became more alive and even more useful after I began to study Jung. His theories explained so many previously unanswerable questions. What I was learning was so valuable that the teacher archetype (Jupiter) — which is strong in me (in my 10th house of career) — wanted to get out and share it with others. A friend of mine, Jenny Grier, who ran a community center called CenterPoint in Houston encouraged me to teach a class, and that is how my passion for teaching others about the Shadow began.

Jung's Theory of Opposites — a Compensatory Factor in the Unconscious

Jung postulated that there is a compensatory factor in our psyche designed to compensate when we are out of balance with ourselves. This theory of opposites explains that whatever we believe about ourselves, *that is, whatever we are highly identified with, the exact opposite is also true* and will be building up in the unconscious in direct proportion to our conscious attitudes and beliefs. These opposing characteristics and qualities he called our Shadow because they are hidden from our awareness and our ego consciousness. Psychologically, our Shadow stands hidden behind us, just like our physical shadow. The Shadow is everything we cannot tolerate about ourselves. Whenever we become lopsided in our view or whenever we overdo any part of our character, our Shadow will begin automatically compensating for us by taking the opposing view. This is nature's way of keeping us in balance with ourselves. Jung describes it as the counterbalancing, self-correcting instinct within us.

The presence of my unconscious, compensatory Shadow was exactly what repulsed me when I first heard the priest speak and saw his cynical, depressed state, so much so that I wanted to get out of there. When we see negative parts of our Shadow in others, there will often be a repulsive element to it. Although what I was seeing outside of me was a part of him (as he was going through some major life changes), it was also in me or it wouldn't have bothered me so much. As I was going around trying to be loving, positive and optimistic all the time by following the New Age philosophy, I was getting darker and darker in the unconscious without knowing it.

As I began to understand Jung's theory of opposites, I realized that this was definitely one of my relationship patterns. I couldn't stand being around people who were negative, cynical and depressed. I remember telling myself, "Don't they understand that if they just think positively, they can change their lives?" That was my guiding philosophy at the time. If I couldn't somehow enroll them into my upbeat, positive way of thinking, I would automatically find a way out of the encounter as quickly as possible. I had very little tolerance or patience for anyone who was stuck in a pessimistic rut or going through a crisis, which we all have from time to time. I wanted them to snap out of it, and if they didn't, well, I just wasn't going to stick around for very long. My aversion to them would be intense. If you can describe what you are feeling about another person as an "aversion," this huge reaction is the first clue that you are seeing an aspect of your own Shadow side.

That first day that I discovered my Shadow by seeing it outside of me in the mirror of this priest, I was overwhelmed with emotion, and I started crying. Memories flooded my thoughts, and I realized that Liz Greene's report was true. There inside me (in the Shadow) were all of the dark moods and all of the hurt and anger I had felt over past disappointments and had denied and repressed for years.

If you can describe what you are feeling about another person as an "aversion," this huge reaction is the first clue that you are seeing an aspect of your own Shadow side.

Notes to Myself:

_____

_____

_____

_____

_____

_____

_____

_____

_____

_____

_____

_____

_____

Most of the relationship choices we make will be shaped unconsciously by what is repressed within us, and we won't even know it.

Notes to Myself:

_____

_____

_____

_____

_____

_____

_____

_____

_____

_____

_____

_____

_____

_____

_____

My inherent and naturally optimistic temperament would look for the lesson in everything. I would go into my head, tell myself everything would be OK and completely ignore my dark feelings. That day, those dark feelings washed over me, and I cried and cried all afternoon. I literally stayed in a black funk for days.

As I got in touch with a lot of my repressed feelings, I was able to see that it's actually OK to be in a bad mood sometimes. I was finally able to acknowledge my dark feelings and thoughts. I found out that not everything is going to be immediately explainable, so I couldn't just jump right into my usual upbeat *modus operandi* of "What can I learn from this?" Sometimes things happen in our lives that are not understandable or are depressing, and it's human to feel these negative emotions. Stuffing those real emotions and denying our real feelings doesn't get rid of them. Too much optimism and idealism needed to be balanced with an equal amount of the exact opposite ingredient. Cynicism and depression in myself were the result of not embracing the opposite qualities of healthy discrimination, realism and caution in moderation. These were some of the parts I was missing and badly needed.

Religious and metaphysical teachings that focus only on the positive can at times divorce us from our authentic selves as we all try to live up to ideals we cannot keep 100 percent of the time. Like many others who have become overly idealistic in our strongly Christian culture, I had become lopsided in the unconscious in my attempt to live only by my highest ideals. I was so focused on being "good" that many of my healthy instincts and natural responses to life were being shut down and denied. Unfortunately, whenever we repress and deny half of our true nature, we are no longer able to objectively supervise or monitor our decisions because half the information we need is no longer available to our conscious ego.

Most of the relationship choices we make will be shaped unconsciously by what is repressed within us, and we won't even know it. That is the scary part. We attract these relationships to ourselves unconsciously.

Whenever we are unwilling to acknowledge and create balance for ourselves, this other side of us will show up in the outer world in our relationships as the exact opposite of what we would want. Without an understanding of our Shadows, most of us will attract negative people, situations and events that are inexplicable.

People Who Are Our Opposites

While they automatically create problems, people who are our opposites are also a vehicle for growth and self-awareness. Opposites need each other to complete what is incomplete in themselves. These characters and situations that come into our lives will repeat over and over. Once again we will experience firsthand that there are no accidents. We have attracted this "other" to ourselves as an opportunity to learn and to become aware of our darker side, our "Shadow."

Don't be afraid of the term "your darker side." I know it sounds sinister and foreboding, but "dark" just describes what is hidden from view or awareness. It's impossible to meet this aspect of ourselves in any other way. As we strive more and more toward wholeness, we will be mysteriously drawn only to those people from whom we will learn about ourselves, even though at times that can be rather painful.

What he meant by an individual relationship is one in which both people become aware of the opposites within themselves.

Rationalism and superstition are complementary. It's a psychological rule that the brighter the light, the blacker the shadow; in other words the more rationalistic we are in our conscious minds, the more alive becomes the spectral world of the unconscious.[6]

CARL GUSTAV JUNG

Jung said, "Seldom or never does a marriage develop into an individual relationship smoothly and without crisis. There is no birth of consciousness without pain."[7] What he meant by an individual relationship is one in which both people become aware of the opposites within themselves. They strive to acknowledge and own them consciously and then make an effort to find a place for the disowned parts of themselves in their everyday lives. This may sound easy, but it is not. It takes courage and a willingness to change. It can occur only when two people are willing to make a commitment to their relationship and are dedicated to communicating authentically, even when it hurts. By doing Shadow work together, they can help each

Notes to Myself:

_____

_____

_____

_____

_____

_____

_____

_____

_____

_____

_____

_____

_____

_____

other grow. When we blame others and see every problem as being only in them, then we are back to square one.

We may unconsciously choose the same kind of partner, friend or boss several times before we begin to recognize that we are the common denominator in these challenging experiences with others. You will know you are headed toward healthier relationships when you begin to reflect on just what these opposites are doing in your life and what the Universe and your own unconscious wants from you. Especially take note of the things that start to repeat. When we're in our 20s, and maybe even in our 30s, we may not be consciously aware of these repetitive patterns, but by the time we're 40 or 50, we know this has happened to us before.

Opposites are not just about marriage partners; we all have relationships. Relationships are happening with our banker, our friends, our siblings, our bosses, etc. Even though we are not married or in a significant relationship with the opposite sex or same sex, we will be experiencing relationships, and these, too, will act as messengers. Give yourself a chance to learn more about yourself by engaging more closely with others.

Psychology and metaphysics both say that there are no accidents. There is an order in the Universe, whether we can see it or not. We must trust that these meetings are purposeful and not by chance. Jung said there is a teleology to life. Teleology means that events are purposeful. They are leading us somewhere. We have to ask ourselves when we recognize yet another pattern, "What does this experience want from me?" Only then can we begin to see what part of us got projected out and is seeking our acceptance.

It can sometimes be painfully slow, but with conscious effort you will see improvement in your understanding. Shadow work is a process that will last your entire lifetime. Jung described these changes taking place in the psyche as circular. Every time one of these patterns comes around, it does get better if you can own it. You may still have to go through it again and again, as it's a part of your own energy. Nothing comes into anyone's life that is not also a part of his own pattern. As you strive to become conscious, you will see the meaning, and then transformation and acceptance can occur.

In the book *Owning Your Own Shadow,* Robert Johnson says that the first sign of maturity is to be able to hold a paradox in consciousness. He says to stay loyal to paradox is to *earn the right to unity.*[8] Indeed paradox shows us that two statements are equally true and neither is more valid than the other. Everything in the universe has its opposite. We can see for ourselves the many pairs of opposites. Here are a few:

Male/Female	**Dark/Light**	**Up/Down**
East/West	**North/South**	**Left/Right**

Black/White	Good/Bad	Do/Be
Hot/Cold	Morning/Evening	Go/Stop
You/Me	Us/Them	Push/Pull
Play/Work	More/Less	Reject/Attract
Enough/Lacking	Move/Wait	Holding On/Letting Go

Nothing comes into anyone's life that is not also a part of his own pattern.

Now add some of the characteristics that we see all around us:

Love/Hate	Aggressive/Passive	Happy/Sad
Giving/Receiving	Rich/Poor	Energetic/Halfhearted
Helplessness/Strength	Courageous/Weak	Confidence/Self-Doubt
Self-Love/Guilt	Considerate/Inconsiderate	Liar/Honest
Responsible/Irresponsible	Ethical/Crooked	Together/Apart
Genuine/False	Growing/Stagnant	Forgiving/Resenting
Kind/Mean	Loving/Hostile	Altruistic/Selfish
Belief/Disbelief	Trusting/Cautious	Outgoing/Reserved

Now add some opposites yourself:

_____	_____	_____
_____	_____	_____
_____	_____	_____
_____	_____	_____

Notes to Myself:

_____

_____

_____

_____

_____

_____

_____

_____

_____

_____

_____

_____

_____

_____

Gradually, you begin to see that each of these pairs of opposites lies within us all. ***Whenever we take a stand on one side, the other side will automatically project out.*** That is the profound paradox in life. We have to get to this understanding to really do our own Shadow work.

Positive thinking, optimism and living a spiritually aware life are all very important ingredients for a happy life, but they are not the totality of our earthly experience. Creating balance and taking responsibility is where Jung's theory of opposites offers an important insight to help us as we strive for a more conscious understanding of ourselves and our relationships with others.

Taking Responsibility for Our Lives

The first step in creating balance is to recognize that we have a Shadow in the first place. In order to do that, we have to take responsibility for our lives. This is a very difficult and long process, and no one does this overnight. We have to be patient with ourselves and others as we do this work.

Being in the human experience, we have all had painful, difficult experiences where it clearly looks like it is the other person's fault, or bad luck or whatever else we want to call it. Taking responsibility for what appears to come to us is no easy task, but it is well worth the effort. When we take responsibility for what happens to us, we can then learn and grow from experiences and make new choices for ourselves. Changing our attitude from one of blaming others to one

This axiom is saying that what is within us will also be outside us. Inner states of consciousness will be reflected in outer situations time and time again.

of taking responsibility will change what happens next in our life. Whatever we are afraid of facing in ourselves we will constantly see paraded before us. The more we are unwilling to see this as part of us, the stronger and more painful it will become outside of us.

I am very fond of an ancient axiom given to us by the alchemists of long ago: "As above, so below; as within, so without, so that the miracle of the one can be established."[9] This axiom is saying that what is within us will also be outside us. Inner states of consciousness will be reflected in outer situations time and time again. If we are willing to look at the significance of these repeating patterns, we will see the synchronicity of events and situations. Ultimately, once integrated, the miracle of the one is established as we become one with ourselves.

So What Does This Look Like in Real Life?

We have all had experiences with other people who really irritated us. Whenever we overreact emotionally to a quality or characteristic in someone else, especially if there is a repulsive element to it, we can be sure that we are reacting to a part of our own Shadow. We may not be able to stand this person or be around them at all. Our reaction is usually extreme distaste, as the characteristics or qualities that we despise or hate in others are also our own but usually operating outside of our awareness. They are in our unconscious, and usually they will be the exact opposite of what we believe to be true about ourselves.

Conversely, we will be very drawn to a person carrying a light part of our Shadow. We may even "fall in love" with them. This is the "Gold" part of our Shadow. I will explain this in more detail in Part Two. We can also project our own positive qualities onto someone we truly admire. We will say to ourselves, "I wish I could be like them. They're such a neat person. They are so bubbly and outgoing, or they are so smart." Whatever the quality is that we are drawn to in another person can also be a part of our Shadow. Jung said the Shadow is 90 percent gold. The Shadow hides both positive and negative qualities or characteristics.

Projection and Denial

Whatever we wish to hide from others, as well as ourselves, will remain unconscious. We place these characteristics or qualities onto others by a psychological mechanism known as projection. It is as if we "project" out onto a movie screen or a mirror a reverse image of ourselves.

Jung says, "Experience shows that the carrier of the projection is not just any object but is always one that proves adequate to the nature of the content projected — that is to say, it must offer the content

Notes to Myself:

_____

_____

_____

_____

_____

_____

_____

_____

_____

_____

_____

_____

_____

_____

a "hook" to hang on."[10] Usually the person who carries the projection is what Jung called "a hook." We are not imagining things. These people will be expressing certain characteristics or acting out behaviors often in an extreme form, and that is why we can easily see it. It looks as if the quality we are seeing is outside of us because this is a real human being. Usually we do not identify with the projected quality or characteristic at all. It appears to be only in them, not in us.

Usually the person who carries the projection is what Jung called "a hook."

Projections change the world into the replica of one's own unknown face.[11]
CARL GUSTAV JUNG

Often, an objective observer, our spouse or a good friend who really knows us could tell us that sometimes we behave exactly the same way as what we perceive is only happening in our fellow human beings. We can remain completely unaware, as it will be the unconscious that is doing the projecting. Projection is one of the best ways to see our Shadow. It happens spontaneously. We have no control over how it happens. It just does. An example would be to see someone as being very hypocritical, dogmatic, manipulative, selfish, greedy or egotistical and be repelled by what we see.

We will feel highly uncomfortable when we are around someone

We will feel highly uncomfortable when we are around someone who is carrying a part of our Shadow.

who is carrying a part of our Shadow. Sometimes this takes time to see, and it will be a gradual experience. As we are repulsed by that person and whatever they stand for, it will feel like whoever they are is totally against our principles, moral values and ideals. We will be highly critical of their actions or way of being in the world. We will even start to pick on them if it is someone we are around a lot such as our significant other or a coworker or a sibling. Suddenly they can do nothing right. The feeling is intense. We may have really liked this person at the beginning of our relationship, and now we cannot stand them. These huge shifts in emotion are usually a good clue that Shadow projection is taking place.

> Closer examination of the dark characteristics — that is the inferiorities constituting the Shadow — reveals that they have an emotional nature, a kind of autonomy, and accordingly an obsessive or, better, possessive quality. Emotion, incidentally, is not an activity of the individual but something that happens to him. Affects occur usually where adaptation is weakest, and at the same time they reveal the reason for its weakness, namely a certain degree of inferiority and the existence of a lower level of personality.[12]

The psyche is a closed system. This means that all of our emotions, affects and beliefs are still there even if we decide to ignore them in the moment. They don't leave us. They stay within us but become invisible to us. In mythology, this is represented by the Greek god Hades, or the Roman god Pluto, who wore a helmet that made him invisible to mortals. Hades, god of the underworld, represents our darker thoughts, obsessions, compulsions and beliefs about ourselves which are hidden from consciousness until we resurrect them and bring them into the light of awareness.

Whatever we deem too negative to express, whatever goes against our highest ideals will be conveniently projected out into the world. Our energy is like a magnet, and the unconscious is profound. It will draw itself to itself, over and over again. So remember what the 12-steppers say: *"If you spot it, you got it."*

Sometimes, people mirror for us not something we are doing, but a quality that we actually need to develop. This offers potential for improvement in our own character if we express it with some temperance. Maybe we are too humble and self-sacrificing and need to develop the quality of confidence. Maybe we need to toot our own horns a bit more or to be more self-focused if we are sacrificing ourselves all over the place. Unconscious Shadow parts, once brought into our awareness, can actually become helpful and productive aspects of our character.

Notes to Myself:

_____

_____

_____

_____

_____

_____

_____

_____

_____

_____

_____

_____

_____

There is often fear around these unconscious parts. We fear that if we were to behave this way, we would go overboard, so instead, we denigrate the characteristic and overdo the opposite quality. Usually our biggest fear is that we'll find out that we really aren't ok and we are all just pretending to be nice. When we hear the words "dark side," they conjure up feelings of guilt and shame. A good friend once said to me, "If people really knew me, they wouldn't like me." We all remember only too well our compulsions, our weaknesses, in short, our secret selves that we hope no one will ever see. These hidden selves have to be examined and made conscious because this is where the gold actually is.

> *You have to live the life you're given*
> *And never close your eyes!*
> *You hold on and stare into the skies*
> *And burn against the cold*
> *For any moment you might find the gold!*
>
> LYRICS IN A SONG CALLED "GOLD" SUNG BY LINDA EDER
> MUSIC: FRANK WILDHORN AND LYRICS: NAN KNIGHTON

In alchemy, the ancients called this hidden part of us the *prima materia* — the base part of us. In our dreams we will have symbols that describe a buried treasure that is hard to find. The alchemists talked about the fact that they were looking for gold, but it was not ordinary gold. To quote Liz Greene,

> The Alchemist is therefore not engaged in changing something into something else; he or she is releasing what was always there, shrouded in a darker and more primitive form. This makes nonsense of the idea that one must leave behind the baser aspects of one's nature in order to reach the spirit, because the spirit IS base nature, transformed in its manifestation rather than its essence through the magical power of consciousness. Put in more ordinary language, it is not the strong, developed and well-adapted aspects of the personality which yield the greatest inner rewards, but the despised and infantile parts that we spend so much time trying to hide from others and from ourselves.[13]

To do Shadow work, we have to be willing to be **real** not only with others but especially with ourselves. That means becoming conscious of our real feelings and motives for "niceness." Anything denied, but not truly felt, will go directly into the unconscious, where it will fester and eventually create havoc in our world when we least expect it. Denied thoughts and feelings will leak out in either overt or passive-aggressive ways, and we will end up hurting others and ourselves. Passive-aggressive behavior can be forgetting you have

Unconscious Shadow parts, once brought into our awareness, can actually become helpful and productive aspects of our character.

Notes to Myself:

_____

_____

_____

_____

_____

_____

_____

_____

_____

_____

_____

_____

_____

Repressing or denying our Shadow can also lead us into experiences where we are over- whelmed as the Shadow takes us over.

Notes to Myself:

_____

_____

_____

_____

_____

_____

_____

_____

_____

_____

_____

_____

_____

_____

plans with someone, not returning phone calls, constantly being late or even procrastinating — always putting off what one says they are going to do. They just never get around to doing it. One woman at a workshop I taught who was able to reflect on this information about the Shadow realized a Shadow quality in herself. She told the group that whenever she felt neglected, she would make selfish choices and passive-aggressively punish her partner by withdrawing. She was not aware of this behavior until I talked about it. This is what can happen. We won't be aware of our motives and reactions; therefore, they will be much more charged and destructive than if we had been willing to suffer the acceptance of our real selves and relate to others honestly. We need to say yes when we mean yes and no when we mean no. Like everything else in our lives, this takes practice because many of us are accustomed to shoving our real feelings out of our awareness.

Repressing or denying our Shadow can also lead us into experiences where we are overwhelmed as the Shadow takes us over. Then we often end up with egg on our faces, acting in the very way we have denied or condemned in others. When we least expect it, we say or do the wrong thing. These are the experiences that all of us in the metaphysical or Christian movement can attest to when we behave in a way that is contrary to our higher ideals. After we have completely embarrassed ourselves and our Shadow goes back into hiding, we say to ourselves, "Why did I act like that?"

*Denial is pushing something out of your awareness.
Anything you hide in the basement has a way of burrowing
under the house and showing up on the front lawn.

HOWARD SASPORTAS

*(I heard Howard Sasportas say this at an astrological conference.)

A Blind Spot

Working with our Shadow is very much like working with a "blind spot" in our character. Because Shadow qualities are repressed, we are completely unaware that we even act this way. When a friend criticizes or points out to us something about an unknown part of our character, we say to them, "I am not like that!" Our first reaction is often resentment. We don't want to have anything to do with them anymore because we feel misunderstood. Whenever you catch yourself saying "I'm not like that" and it gives you a huge emotional charge, know that you are like that. Your Shadow has just given you a chance to see another part of you. We hide these personality traits from ourselves, but everyone else can see them.

Have you ever said something or behaved a certain way and then asked yourself, "Who was that in there who acted like that? Was that

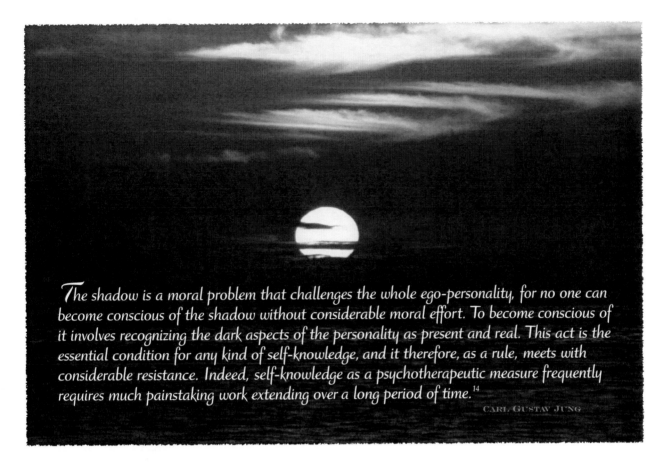

The shadow is a moral problem that challenges the whole ego-personality, for no one can become conscious of the shadow without considerable moral effort. To become conscious of it involves recognizing the dark aspects of the personality as present and real. This act is the essential condition for any kind of self-knowledge, and it therefore, as a rule, meets with considerable resistance. Indeed, self-knowledge as a psychotherapeutic measure frequently requires much painstaking work extending over a long period of time.[14]

CARL GUSTAV JUNG

really me? What got into me?" We can really doubt ourselves and feel bad because we are not living up to our ideals. A week or two will go by and we'll forget what happened for a time, but, like anything repressed or denied, the same behavior will be triggered again and again in our outer experiences because it wants to be known. Our Shadow will jump out compulsively and startle us. In his book *The Undiscovered Self,* Jung says, "Since it is universally believed that man is merely what his consciousness knows of itself, he regards himself as harmless and so adds stupidity to inequity. He does not deny that terrible things have happened and still go on happening, but it is always 'the others' who do them. And when such deeds belong to the recent or remote past, they quickly and conveniently sink into the sea of forgetfulness, and that state of chronic wooly-mindedness returns which we describe as 'normality.'"[15]

When Two or More People Say the Same Thing to You

It's also good to pay attention if two or more people say the same thing to you about yourself. Two or more people pointing out something that is unconscious is no longer chance. A good exercise is to purposely ask two or three close friends to describe you on paper. In this way, learning about our Shadow can be a rather humbling experience. We may realize we are not who we thought we were, but we'll also find out about good qualities we may not have known about either.

Remember, Shadow qualities are not what you already know about yourself. We all know our faults. The characteristics in our Shadow are completely unconscious.

We need to pay attention, as there is probably a gift involved if we can learn to use these parts consciously and with some balance. It really takes a lot of moral courage to admit these things to ourselves. Remember, Shadow qualities are not what you already know about yourself. We all know our faults. The characteristics in our Shadow are completely unconscious.

The Shadow personifies everything that the subject refuses to acknowledge about himself and yet is always thrusting itself upon him, directly or indirectly — for instance inferior traits of character and other incompatible tendencies.[16]

CARL GUSTAV JUNG

If we are in a long-term, committed relationship with a friend, they are going to notice things about us. We will bump up against each other's humanity. It's inevitable, as no one can go around for too long being totally wonderful every single minute of every day. As the saying goes, we all wake up on the wrong side of the bed sometimes. We all make dumb or childish mistakes. These are called *faux pas.*

If we are hurting ourselves by not knowing something about our own behavior, we hope our close friends will say something to us. When we cut them off from being honest with us, we are shooting ourselves in the foot, because we need friends who care enough about us to be honest with us. This is a true friend. Of course, it all greatly depends on how they say it. If that friend is being emotionally abusive by pointing out everything that they see is wrong with you and is harshly condemning and shaming you, then it's likely also part of their own Shadow that they may be seeing in you. Remember that we are energy and like does attract like. In this case, it would be more like what Jung called "Shadow boxing."

In Shadow boxing, both parties usually get their feelings hurt, making it counterproductive and not the same as when a good friend in a caring way points something out that we might not know about ourselves. This is done in order to help us, not hurt us. You'll know which one it is by how it feels energetically and by their tone of voice. It will not be sarcastic, teasing, hostile or caustic.

A good thing to remember is that e-mails are not a good venue for criticizing a friend. If you are going to point anything out, it is best to do so in person and ask the person if they would like some sincere feedback. If they say no, then honor that. If you find yourself wanting to criticize a person, a good idea is to go inside first and ask if you are projecting something before you speak, especially if you know that you are upset with the person and that's really why you are being critical of them in the first place.

Notes to Myself:

_____

_____

_____

_____

_____

_____

_____

_____

_____

_____

_____

_____

_____

_____

_____

Another special instance of Shadow boxing is when two people are arguing and they are both sure they are right. Both people are usually projecting the very same quality on each other. It takes a lot of ego strength to admit it. Many religions talk about getting rid of our egos, but Jung advocates strengthening our egos first. We can't get rid of something we do not possess. He says a strong ego is required to not flinch when seeing a Shadow quality that has been projected. A person with no ego can be flattened by the vicissitudes and complex situations that occur in our lives. They will not be able to deal with being honest with themselves or critically looking at their mistakes either. So developing an ego actually allows us to then be able to let it go when we are clearly at fault. Only a strong enough ego can humble itself and admit a mistake.

You Do Your Work; I'll Do Mine.

As I started doing my own Shadow work and talking to my friends, I started to see the Shadow side of the people in my life. I had a friend I will call Jill. She told me about a woman named Sandra who was in a dream group with her. Jill couldn't stand Sandra. Sandra seemed to have no boundaries. According to Jill, Sandra kept asking personal questions she shouldn't be asking and was intruding psychically. She took over conversations and was rude. The more Jill talked about Sandra, the more there was to say. Jill went on and on and on about Sandra, and everything she said was giving her a huge emotional charge. Nothing good could be said about Sandra.

After hearing her go on and on and on for a while, I pointed this out to Jill. I suggested that maybe Sandra was showing her a Shadow quality in herself. Had she thought about that? I knew Jill was familiar with the terms and had studied Jung for several years herself, so I wasn't at all expecting what happened next. Jill could not go there. She turned and snapped at me and now would hardly speak to me. Sadly, our relationship was never the same after that. Now I was the enemy, too!

If a person cannot face that they too have a dark side, it can cost you their friendship if you try to point it out to them. Of course, a friendship that cannot contain that kind of honesty isn't very solid, and we can't lose something we never really had. A true friend will never tell you about a Shadow quality that they see in order to hurt you or humiliate you. When sharing observations of others' Shadows, we do have to be compassionate about their boundaries or walls. Those walls are there for a reason and have to come down slowly and in their own time.

I deeply regretted confronting Jill, as she was an interesting person, and I'd grown to care for her in the year and a half that we had been friends. She then refused to see how angry she now was at me

He says a strong ego is required to not flinch when seeing a Shadow quality that has been projected.

Notes to Myself:

Notes to Myself:

for pointing it out, and our relationship basically ended shortly after that. She insisted that it had nothing to do with her Shadow and that the girl she was describing had no boundaries. She then began to point out everything she decided was wrong with me and crossed me out of her life. Now I was this totally awful person also. I learned a lesson. It's best to do your own Shadow work and let others do theirs in their own time.

Healthy Boundaries vs. Projection

As it turned out, Jill wanted me to look at the fact that I made no mention of boundaries in my workshops, so I did some research about boundaries. Shortly after that, I went to hear a lecture she recommended to me on boundaries to see what I could learn, and I found it to be helpful. There are many times when we need to establish boundaries with others. Projecting our Shadow and having boundaries (about something you will not tolerate) are very different. With boundaries, you will not like a certain behavior a person has exhibited at the moment, but you will not condemn the entire person.

For example, I hired two friends to do some bookkeeping work for me. One of my friends is a very lively, talkative woman. They both sat at the same table, each working on separate bank accounts. One of them said to the other, "Have you seen such and such movie? What did you think of that movie?" I was working in the next room and could hear the conversation clearly. After a few minutes of chit-chat, I felt it was cutting into the time I was paying both of them to work on my bank accounts. I said to her, "I have hired you to do this work, so I expect you to concentrate on it. These are my bank statements, and it's very important to me that they be accurate or I wouldn't have asked for your help with them." This was a clear request, and I was expressing what I felt. Yes, it was awkward and uncomfortable for a moment for both of us as she adjusted to my confrontation, but she respected me and our friendship. From that point on, it was not a problem, and she apologized and got back to work. This was uncomfortable for me, but I had to have my boundaries honored to get the work done that I had hired them to do. Because they are both real friends, they, in turn, respected that and both continued to work for me after that experience.

When you just need to preserve your boundaries, you will have no need to go on and on to others about problems with that person. A good way to double-check yourself is to notice whether you have to bring that person up and complain about them to a lot of people. This is a clear indication that your buttons are being pushed. You will want everyone's opinion or advice about the person. It is constantly present on your mind, and you can't drop it.

When a relationship is important to preserve and problems are only a matter of boundaries, you will talk to them. You will make your personal wishes clear to that person, acknowledging that we are all different. Sometimes we hurt each other or bump up against each other without thinking that we are upsetting the other person. Communication is everything. Once you have cleared the air by being honest with each person, you can still be in each other's space, and you can forgive a transgression. If you can't be assertive enough to tell those in your relationships the truth about how you feel, then boundaries are not the only pressing issue. Possibly for Jill, it was no accident that this person was in her face. She communicated to me that the person was getting way too personal. I, too, had become too personal by asking her to examine the huge charge it was evoking, so she ran away. When it's a Shadow projection, you will not be able to stand the sight of the other person and will "X" them out of your life completely. You will forget everything good about them or anything that you might have shared with them before.

Notice Extremes Between Yourself and Others

Another very clear way to see a Shadow quality in yourself is to notice extremes where you are polarizing — one person is doing one quality to an extreme, while you're doing the opposite extreme. Notice how often this happens. If it happens often enough, then chances are that you are lopsided in your character and need to learn how to do precisely what these people are doing to get your balance back — not to the opposite extreme, but halfway. This can be the answer to many of our relationship problems. We have to be willing to meet our partners halfway and see our part in whatever the situation is that is dividing us.

Sometimes there is Shadow projection going on between two people, and only one of them is willing to see their part in the situation. The other person is into blaming. It's impossible to work through situations like that because there is no meeting. Doing Shadow work requires that both partners are willing to come to the middle of the polarization. It requires honest and authentic communication. We have to meet the other person halfway, knowing it usually takes two to create an issue. It's never only one person. Here is where communication in long-term relationships is essential. We have to be willing to talk things out if we want the relationships in our life to last. Two people who trust each other enough to be vulnerable and who are committed to their relationship can work together to help each other in this process. The long-term benefit is that this kind of dialogue can bring about a more cohesive state of integrity within the self of each partner.

Both people are attracted or repelled, whatever the case may be, by an unconscious collusion. There is an order in the Universe

When a relationship is important to preserve and problems are only a matter of boundaries, you will talk to them.

Notes to Myself:

These people who irritate us and push our buttons are our mirrors. Especially take note of the experiences that start to repeat.

Notes to Myself:

_____

_____

_____

_____

_____

_____

_____

_____

_____

_____

_____

_____

_____

whether we can see it or not. The psyche is always striving for wholeness, and if we take our cues from nature, we will see that wholeness is balance. As Marian Woodman, a Jungian analyst, so aptly put it: "We have daytime and nighttime. Which one of us would want no nighttime?"[17]

These people who irritate us and push our buttons are our mirrors. Especially take note of the experiences that start to repeat. Repetition is your Shadow's way of saying "Pay attention. This is about you. You have a great opportunity here."

The following story beautifully illustrates this Shadow lesson. Randy was married to a woman who was aggressive, abusive and angry. Everything that happened was his fault, according to her. He couldn't do anything to please her. "How can this be about me?" he said. "I am even-tempered and try to be reasonable and logical." After talking with him for over an hour, it finally came out that this was his second marriage to an "angry woman." What's more, Randy's business partner also had the same exact character traits: he, too, would fly off the handle when provoked.

Now, it was easy for my friend to accuse all three of these partners of negative behavior, as it was obvious to everyone who knew them that they had short fuses, but what insights did this pattern have to offer my friend who saw himself as cool, calm and collected? The more he talked, the more he realized that he was angry with all these partners, past and present, and that he could not express his anger. He could not see himself as an angry person, because he would shove his real feelings down in the basement of his psyche. He could see anger only in *them*. Because the opposite extreme was in his unconscious, it was building up a powerful energy.

I explained this concept of the Shadow to him, and finally he had a brilliant thought and his eyes lit up. He said, "When I finally get angry, I explode! It is as if that part of me is all alone and has no help from the rest of me. So it comes out without the help of my logic, my kindness, my love for her or my willingness to be fair. All these other parts of me would help that angry part of me communicate effectively, if only I would let my authentic anger be a part of my daily interactions." This is the kind of "AHA" realization you can have when you are willing to do Shadow work. The awareness is enlightening.

In talking through his story with me, Randy recognized that he indeed was angry. Projecting anger onto his wife or business partner wasn't going to get rid of it. They would just have to carry a larger part of the load, as they had no problem expressing anger. Dealing with anger is a very common relationship dilemma.

Astrology describes anger in the birth chart as a strong or weak Mars function. We all have a Mars somewhere in our natal charts, so it has to be expressed one way or another. Some of us are aggressive, and some of us are passive-aggressive, but we all get angry. It's an instinct. No one is born without a Mars function. The sign, house and aspects to your Mars in your birth chart will tell you even more detail about how your particular buttons get pushed.

The inner wisdom and guidance inside us knows when something is amiss. What we deny and resist persists, but it's all alone. To become a whole person, we need to embrace the parts of ourselves that are angry or needy, are hurt or jealous or are afraid. When we make it OK to express these parts of ourselves, we won't keep drawing partners who have to be those parts of us so that we can see them. Our partners are our mirrors. They show us what we have yet to see about ourselves. Because my friend was so uncomfortable expressing anger, the Universe brought him first two marriages, then a business partner to show him what he badly needed to learn: how to express his anger in the moment with moderation so that it was related to what he was angry about and not so destructive to his relationships that he had to run away from them or explode and attack them.

The emotion of anger is difficult for everyone, so this dilemma comes up in my Shadow workshops a lot. It's usually our instincts — sexuality, anger, aggression, need, pride, etc. — that give us the most trouble and get delegated to our Shadow.

In one of my workshops, another man told us that when he got angry at emotional abuse, he just quit his job or left the relationship. That is a very common way to deal with this situation. A woman in the audience chimed in and said, "But I don't want to be angry and get out of control like my partner. How can that be healthy?" I answered them, "Is it unhealthy to stand up for yourself? Has this type of situation been repeating? Because if it is, you are being asked to learn to stand up for yourself. If you don't learn this, people will pick up that you are easy prey. Then, because it is unconscious, you can become a magnet for free-floating hostility in the environment. Your own unexpressed anger and resentment draw these situations to you to compensate for your unlived life. To paraphrase Jung, he said that if we ignore our instincts, we will be ambushed by them.

When you come from a position of strength and you have that quality on board as a part of your character, then other people will not challenge you. Strength becomes a part of our energy field, and people will sense it. There is so much that we sense and feel unconsciously about others.

Taking back projected anger is really tough for most people. We are taught from childhood that it is wrong to get angry, especially if you are a woman. What do people call a woman with a temper? A Bitch. This is how our Shadow develops in the first place. As children, we learn early on what will and won't get approval and acceptance. Since we all want acceptance, we learn to hide from others everything

Astrology describes anger in the birth chart as a strong or weak Mars function. We all have a Mars somewhere in our natal charts, so it has to be expressed one way or another.

Notes to Myself:

_____
_____
_____
_____
_____
_____
_____
_____
_____
_____
_____
_____
_____
_____
_____

If we don't express our real feelings, we are rejecting parts of ourselves and we will see this mirrored back in our relationships.

Notes to Myself:

that is so-called "negative" in our nature. We grow up afraid of the anger in ourselves and in everyone else. We may have grown up with a parent who was rageful, and we don't want to be anything like that parent. We also see violence on the news, and we don't want to end up like that, so we stuff our feelings or try to ignore our anger. Worse, however, is that we hide it from ourselves.

"Anger is like vegetables," I heard a teacher, Zardoz Magnadea, once say; "use it while it's fresh." The world would be better off if we could all learn to get angry in the moment when it is appropriate instead of pretending and being "nice" when we actually feel anger. We pat ourselves on the back and think to ourselves smugly that we are so spiritual because we didn't get angry. Then we'll go down to the post office or the drugstore and take it out on the clerk. They don't know us, so who will see this part of us? A good friend of mine told me she would take her anger out on her dog. She couldn't stand this one dog, so finally she just had to get rid of him. He was carrying her Shadow! Yes, a pet can carry our Shadow, as strange as that sounds.

There are many situations in which we may feel anger. If we can learn to express it — it may actually help us learn to be true to ourselves. If we don't express our real feelings, we are rejecting parts of ourselves, and we will see this mirrored back in our relationships. Who's rejecting whom when someone is angry? We reject ourselves when we don't stand up for what we believe or feel and speak our truth, and then we blame it on others. Yes, it makes us vulnerable to do the opposite and express our true feelings, but then we are really relating. The other person will know who we really are, not who we are pretending to be. Father Leo Booth, whom I've heard many times lecturing, says, "Screw nice; be real."

For example, what if you call and cancel plans with someone at the last minute after they have gone to a lot of trouble or expense? Wouldn't you expect them to feel angry or hurt when you suddenly change plans at the last minute, or worse than that, completely forget and not even call at all? Why does our society say to us that it is OK to feel hurt but that we shouldn't feel angry? Anger is an emotion. We don't have control or volition over our emotions. We don't choose to be emotional. We just are.

Take another example: What if you are with a date at a party or function and he or she leaves the event without telling you that he or she is leaving you there? This happened to a friend of mine. Without saying anything to her, the person she came with just up and left a wedding they had attended together. What if we are angry at that person and we say nothing to him or her? Where will all that energy go?

If we have the courage in situations like these or countless others to say honestly, "I felt hurt, and I also felt angry when you did such and such," we will usually find we get over our angry emotions a lot quicker as well as improve authentic communication and boundaries in our relationships. It's when we keep our anger inside because "nice people don't get angry" that it has nowhere to go, so it gets buried in the unconscious. Rather than going away, it builds up until it comes out in ways that hurt ourselves and others. Then sometimes, as Randy said, "We explode!" What could be healthy anger and appropriate boundaries becomes RAGE, which is an extreme. Extremes are what get us into trouble, not our authentic feelings. When people become violent, it is usually a sign that they have pushed themselves beyond their limits. Our prisons are full of people who have committed crimes of passionate emotion to the point that it became dangerous because they denied their Shadow until it demanded release, causing them to unleash their anger inappropriately.

We don't have to tolerate disrespect. We don't have to always be understanding of someone else's bad behavior. Sometimes just being willing to speak to them about our hurt, anger or confusion will open the door to communicating what's been left unsaid by both parties. If you aren't speaking, then how can you resolve anything? Unspoken resentment can build up between the two of you, and then you lose the relationship completely. Sadly, it's totally based on misinterpretation. It also does not allow for a person to apologize if they are

Rather than going away, it builds up until it comes out in ways that hurt ourselves and others.

And just as the cosmos is not a dissolving mass of particles, but rests in the unity of God's embrace, so man must not dissolve into a whirl of warring possibilities and tendencies imposed on him by the unconscious, but must become the unity that embraces them all.[18]

CARL GUSTAV JUNG

Go ahead and say what you have to say so you can both work through it. It's best to be vulnerable enough to be real.

Notes to Myself:

——————————
——————————
——————————
——————————
——————————
——————————
——————————
——————————
——————————
——————————
——————————
——————————
——————————
——————————
——————————
——————————
——————————
——————————
——————————

sincerely at fault and want to explain that they never intended to hurt the other person. How many times does this happen and a good friendship is ruined because no one is communicating? Go ahead and say what you have to say so you can both work through it. It's best to be vulnerable enough to be real. The love between you both will show up in the end if it's really there. Most of the time, it never left.

Healing can occur on a deep level, drawing both people even closer than they were before it happened. I have found the best relationships in our lives can handle friction, misunderstanding, anger, etc. When the relationship is solid, you can get past these situations as each person can acknowledge their own humanity and personality flaws since none of us is perfect.

Another Example of Projection

When I do Shadow workshops and explain projection, I tell this story from my own experience to demonstrate how completely unconscious a character trait can be and how the part that goes into the unconscious will look like it's only in the other person.

Before I did Shadow work, I was highly identified with how generous and extravagant I was. At the same time, I kept seeing people coming into my life in a repetitive fashion who all showed up with the same characteristic. Guess what that characteristic was? They were what I considered to be cheap!

I will never forget going out with a guy who took me to the racetrack. I brought $75 to spend, and by the end of the afternoon, I had spent it all. Afterward we went to a restaurant, and we sat talking for two hours at the table. When we finally got up to leave, I noticed he had tipped the waiter only $2 and I was aghast! If I hadn't spent all of my own money, I would've put more of a tip down on the table myself. I asked him, "Why are you tipping the waiter only $2?" He said, "Well, we only had salad and water, and the bill was $20." I said, "That is only 10%. I tip 20%." He said, "Well, I only tip 10%." I then said, "But we've been sitting here for two hours, and he was constantly bringing us water and asking us if we needed anything."

I was so repulsed by this man I could hardly speak to him all the way home. I made him feel so bad about it that he never asked me out again. This guy was not the first person I had seen acting out this behavior in an extreme form. It had happened over and over, and I could clearly see that their behavior was cheap, so it was easy to hang my Shadow "hook" on them to wear.

As life would have it, since this was an area where I was very out of balance, it was inevitable that I was going to attract to myself another scenario to show myself my own cheap side. Besides being an astrologer, I am also a graphic designer and a photographer. One day, I had an appointment to show my portfolio to a company that might need my services. I came into the office building's parking lot, took a machine-stamped ticket and noted that the lot entrance sign said one half hour cost $1. I looked at my watch and went into the building. When I came out to the parking lot, I gave the attendant a dollar.

She said, "It's two dollars, Ma'am." I said, "It is not. I was here only 28 minutes. I timed it."

She said, "I have nothing to do with this. The machine reads the ticket. I put it in and take it out, and it says you were here 32 minutes and you owe me another dollar."

I indignantly said to her, "I was not." I was livid. (Notice the disproportionate reaction when your Shadow is triggered.) I had to pay her another dollar because she was holding me prisoner in the parking lot. Yet, when I left the parking lot that day, I still hadn't gotten the lesson my Shadow was begging me to see. I was absolutely furious. I was arguing with her about a dollar! (But I'm not cheap, right? At least my ego thought not.)

I left there and went over to the Aquarian Age Bookshelf to exchange an astrology book. I have over 300 books on astrology, and I had accidentally bought the same book twice. When I told the girl at the front desk, she told me she would exchange it for me if I would pick out another book. After I found another one I wanted, I came back and handed it to her, saying, "I found a book I want, but it's two dollars less." I'll never forget what happened next. She said to me, "Well, we usually don't do this, but I will give you your two dollars." Then, without thinking, I said, "Plus tax." **Now we were talking about seventeen cents tax!** As soon as I realized what I'd said, I was so embarrassed. I walked out of there saying to myself, "Did you really say that?"

On this particular day, these two incidents happened so closely back-to-back that finally I got it. All those "cheap" people out there were me. Because I was so overly identified with the polar opposite of being generous and extravagant, my unconscious had constellated the extreme opposite in my Shadow, and it was operating behind my back. A Shadow quality that you cannot identify with can be operating completely out of your awareness, and all you know is that you keep seeing it in others. It's truly remarkable.

That day I took back a part of myself I badly needed. I needed to be less extravagant and overly generous (two extremes) and become more financially responsible and develop some temperance about how I was spending my money. This is as tough a lesson for me as expressing anger is a tough one for my friend Randy. It is one that constantly requires my attention and awareness. These repetitive situations drew to both of us people who could carry our "hooks" for anger or cheapness. Their behavior had allowed us to see our own rejected psychic content.

A Shadow quality that you cannot identify with can be operating completely out of your awareness, and all you know is that you keep seeing it in others. It's truly remarkable.

Notes to Myself:

Jung never tired of telling people that the Shadow needed to be made conscious.

You have to be patient with yourself when you discover these extremes in your nature. Being out of balance in this character trait has not changed for me overnight, but now at least I know about it and can work with it. Believe me, it takes time. I know that this is an area where I can get lopsided, so I need to watch myself and my spending habits. Similarly, my friend Randy will have to monitor when he actually does get angry, as his usual *modus operandi* is to remain calm and go into denial instead of feeling his angry feelings when he is provoked. That, too, is something so strong in his character that he will have to continually work on it.

This fact was obvious in his astrology as well. I was showing Randy his birth chart when we had this discussion, so I was able to point it out to him. If we consciously work at it, in time, we will have both depotentiated the lopsidedness that is inherent in us from birth. By this I mean it will not have the same affect it has had in the past. In this way, we each contribute to the healing and transformation of the planet by becoming more and more conscious, one person at a time, as we get to know ourselves and these opposites residing within us.

Jung never tired of telling people that the Shadow needed to be made conscious. He said it was the only way the ethically minded individual could stop projecting his or her hidden characters onto others and become a truly moral person. Otherwise, we would remain unconscious of vast portions of our own psyche, which can lead to illness, divorce, repetitive pain and suffering. On a global level, collective scale, it leads to prejudice, hate and war. If we project our Shadows, we can become that which we hate. Each of us as an individual makes up the collective, so this work is important.

Therefore, you can offer no excuse, O man,
whoever indulges in judging;
for by passing judgment on another
you condemn yourself, since you,
who are passing judgment practice the same things.

Romans 2:21

Notes to Myself:

_____
_____
_____
_____
_____
_____
_____
_____
_____
_____
_____
_____
_____
_____
_____

PRACTICE:
Write a list now of a few people who drive you nuts or you cannot stand the site of. Also write down a few people that you truly admire and wish you could be more like. As you study further, you will understand what they are in your life to show you and how to turn that around to your benefit. For now, it will help just to write down some names, characteristics and qualities. This will help you remember as you proceed further in this workbook.

Write the names of five people you rejected from your life because of their negative characteristics or qualities.

1. _____

2. _____

3. _____

4. _____

5. _____

Write the names of five people you admire and respect because of their positive characteristics or qualities.

1. _____

2. _____

3. _____

4. _____

5. _____

People We Make a Point of Avoiding

We have all met people we don't like. It may even be people we don't really know very well, but we will avoid them because something about them bothers us. We will go to a party or a function, and walk around the room so we don't have to be in their space. We may have met them only once or twice. They may have said or done something that irritated us. We will either avoid or vilify them. These people offer another way to see a Shadow quality we are rejecting.

This is a classic case of projection, when we get a charge about someone we don't even know. We are not really relating to them. We are only seeing a split-off part of ourselves. Isn't it interesting that we usually don't know exactly what we don't like about the person? It's probably an unconscious aspect of ourselves. It's a good idea to get to know this person and find out what it is that we are projecting. This isn't always possible, but sometimes the person you did not like upon first meeting can become one of your best friends once you get to know them. Then you find out who they actually are instead of what you were projecting onto them.

As I learned this information, I went back into my own memory banks. I remembered meeting a graphic artist I had to work with that I didn't like at all. She really irritated me. I was rude to her and basically ignored her. It didn't faze her in the least. She was as friendly as a puppy dog, chatting and generously giving of herself as we continued to work together. Fate arranged it so that I would get to know her over a period of time. This woman became one of my best friends.

We will go to a party or a function, and walk around the room so we don't have to be in their space.

Notes to Myself:

_____

_____

_____

_____

_____

_____

_____

_____

_____

_____

_____

_____

_____

_____

Jung says that the more our projections are thrust out into the environment, the more difficult it is to withdraw them.

Projection Can Be Felt in the Body.

Because the Shadow is everything about other people that drives us crazy, the hair will rise on our arms, and we will feel highly uncomfortable when we are around anyone carrying a part of our Shadow. Often there is a distinct physical aversion. Start to notice your body when you react to, or feel repulsed by, a person, an event or even a place. When the body reacts instinctively, this is a clear way to know that what you are reacting to is a part of you. You will usually find yourself making highly charged statements like "I can't stand so and so" or "I can't stomach this person." This intensity will confirm for you that it's definitely a projection. Jung says that the more our projections are thrust out into the environment, the more difficult it is to withdraw them. Shadow projections can even somatize in the body if we are not willing to see them.

There was a time in my own life where for over a year I had a rash from head to toe, and it would break out only periodically. My brother, who is a doctor, told me it was probably psychosomatic, as it would just come and go randomly. I started writing down in my journal what might be going on with me a day before it would come on. By doing this, I started to dialogue with my unconscious and ask for help. One day, one of my sisters said something to me about myself. All of a sudden, a man I was really angry with and had not spoken to in a year flashed before my mind's eyes. On the spot, it occurred to me just "who was under my skin." What she said made me realize I was just like him. The forgiveness was immediate. I felt it in my body. I never had that rash again, so a Shadow quality that we are projecting can even manifest in our bodies. In my studies, I had been told that the Shadow was projected only onto members of my own sex, but this experience told me our Shadow can be projected onto either sex. Ask yourself who makes your blood boil or your skin crawl? It might behoove you to do so.

Complexes

Jung defined the Shadow as a complex of energy, a split-off part of the psyche that is autonomous. He explained that a complex is formed when something happens to us in our childhood — an emotional trauma, an illness, physical abuse or abandonment which was an emotional shock to our system. This experience will have a lot of emotional energy formed around it because our ego cannot absorb it into consciousness. Therefore, our complexes behave like independent beings or splinter personalities. They will act as if they have a life of their own. Daryl Sharp in his book, *Digesting Jung, Food for the Journey,* says,

> It can upset digestion, breathing and the rate at which the heart
> beats. It behaves like a partial personality. When we want to say or

Notes to Myself:

do something and a complex interferes, we find ourselves saying or doing something quite different from what we intended. Our best intentions are upset, exactly as if we had been interfered with by another person.[19]

As long as we continue to deny our Shadow characters, they will remain in the unconscious, and therefore, will have a more distorted or primitive expression than if we were conscious of them. If we are doing something compulsively over and over and we don't even know we're doing it, we don't have any choice. The more we're able to learn about our Shadow, the more choices we have.

We all have several complexes. One of the ways of realizing we are caught in a Shadow complex is that it will show up in irrational outbursts of emotion that will bewilder us. "What came over me?" we've all said to ourselves at one time or another, probably even more often than we care to admit. If it's a characteristic that brings up shame for you, it can be a tough one to swallow. One evening I was having dinner with a friend and his wife. He was pretty irate about something he wanted to talk about. He told us he had volunteered to help with a project at the church they belonged to. A lady showed up, angry that they had moved the volunteers to another location, so now she had to carry a bunch of stuff she had brought with her. That irritated him, and he went off on her. He started criticizing her, telling her that they were at a church function and they should all be cheerful and Christianlike. It really made him mad that she was disrupting all the peacefulness he felt before she arrived. He was going on and on about her unchristian behavior. I suggested to him that maybe he could have been patient with her and offered to help her carry things in to calm her down. He could not go there. He could only see what she was doing wrong and couldn't see he was doing exactly what he was accusing her of doing.

This friend of mine has listened to my Shadow cassettes and knew of my classes, so I made the comment that a Shadow quality was poking its nose in the door. His wife, who was listening to this story, also said to him, "You have a tendency to want to put people in their place in a self-righteous manner." This, too, he could not take and kept defending his position, saying that sometimes people have to be told in a harsh way what they are doing wrong because otherwise they won't get it. He emphatically said to us, "Christians are the worst ones!" I decided to change the subject and let him think about what we said. It only took him about an hour. Suddenly he got it and started talking to us about how he could have handled things differently. Yes, maybe he, too, wasn't being very Christian-like in his behavior either. This was not easy to admit to himself or to us. It took a lot of courage and ego strength, but my friend stepped up to the plate and was willing to see his Shadow.

One of the ways of realizing we are caught in a Shadow complex is that it will show up in irrational outbursts of emotion that we will be bewildered by.

Notes to Myself:

It took a lot of courage and ego strength, but my friend stepped up to the plate and was willing to see his Shadow.

From the book *Meeting the Shadow, The Hidden Power of the Dark Side of Human Nature*, a compilation of essays on the Shadow edited by Jeremiah Abrams and Connie Zweig, a quote by Gilda Franz says, "Shame is the gristle we must chew on to integrate the Shadow complex."[20] We all want to be thought of as "good" Christians, Muslims, Jews, etc. Each religion in its own way is striving to give structure and rules of behavior that are positive. It's not easy to own it when we project something that is painful or brings up shame in us. To do so is indeed a humbling experience.

In the same book, Ken Wilber talks about how the best test of whether people are indeed a Shadow mirror is to ask yourself this question: Does this person *inform you* about who they are being at the moment or do they *affect you* emotionally?[21] If the quality they are showing you is indeed a part of you, the sheer strength of the obsessiveness will be the key. For days you won't be able to drop it. You have to talk about it incessantly to everyone. You will go on and on and on *ad nauseum*. We've all done this at some time or other if we are honest with ourselves. The challenge is to catch ourselves in the act and ask ourselves, "What is this about in me? Why is it bothering me so much?"

Edward C. Whitmont in his book, *The Symbolic Quest*, says,

> It is the emotional coloring that will tell us whether or not we are caught in a projection. Since a projection is always the visualization of a complex, it makes itself felt by a strong affect charge. In plain English, whenever a projection is involved, it "gets" us, it "gets under our skin." Our reaction is affect-determined and we are therefore unable to react adequately to a person or situation; we can neither accept nor modify nor leave that person or situation. This is one of the few basic laws of the psyche which is, without exception, one-hundred percent foolproof.
>
> As a rule of thumb, when such an uncomfortable situation occurs, when somebody really "gets under your skin" and you want to know what "gets" you in the other person. Say: "He is a dogmatic authoritarian (as aggressive as a bulldozer, or an opinionated old bat...) and I can't stand that!" Then take out the "He is" and put in an "I am" or "My complex is like" and you will have a description of the complex at work.[22]

If you are around someone behaving in an obnoxious manner and you tell yourself, "Well, he is a bit of a show-off" or "she is a name dropper," and the observation just slides by you, then you're probably safe in assuming that their behavior is just something you are seeing in them. However, if you get really angry and highly charged in your description of them and you cannot stand being around them, then they are probably mirroring for you something that you have not

Notes to Myself:

come to terms with in yourself. Your emotionally toned defensiveness will be intense. Pay attention. Maybe it is your own tendency to brag once in awhile or your own need to be the center of attention.

Our Voice Will Change Pitch

We can also sound as if we are possessed when describing someone who is carrying our Shadow for us. Our voice often changes pitch, and we tend to use highly charged adjectives to describe their behavior. We may see them as extremely obnoxious, rude, irresponsible, weak, needy, hypocritical, controlling, vain, selfish, dishonest, exhibitionists, crabby, cynical, pessimistic — whatever. When we start screaming at someone or someone starts shrieking at us, often this is a Shadow quality coming out. We will feel as if whoever they are is totally against our principles, moral values and ideals, so we'll feel justified in our reaction. The Shadow is again making its way into the forefront, trying to get our attention. To paraphrase Shakespeare, "Me thinks thou doth protest too much!"

Emphatic or vehement statements are yet another good way to see our Shadow. The sheer intensity of these emotion-packed statements will clue you in. Another friend of mine once was talking about an ex-office mate of his, when emphatically and with condemnation he said, "Did he tell you he emotionally abuses his girlfriend?" He was talking about himself. His voice changed pitch when he said it. I knew it because I knew of his own relationship dilemmas, but I didn't tell him because he wouldn't have heard it right at the moment. He was too charged by his officemate. I learned my lesson with Jill. It's best to save honesty for another time and place. Maybe you will never tell this person anything. If you always told the truth, you could lose your job and you wouldn't have very many friends. We certainly all have faults, so can you imagine if you pointed those out to everyone all the time? People would feel attacked. It all depends on the intimacy of the particular relationship. Can it take that kind of honesty? Each relationship we have is different. Some relationships are meant to be only social acquaintances, and we have no genuine intimacy with them. Our closest relationships, though, do require emotional honesty in order to be healthy.

Suffice it to say that emphatic statements are revealing, so notice your own emphatic statements or when your voice changes pitch. It's your own Shadow. Especially notice if you say something aloud twice with vehemence. That is a doubling. The unconscious is trying to get your attention! This is similar to having a dream repeat. The Shadow really wants you to know it's knocking on your door.

When We Dehumanize a Person

When somebody is carrying a part of our Shadow, we can even

When we start screaming at someone or someone starts shrieking at us, often this is a Shadow quality coming out.

Notes to Myself:

_____

_____

_____

_____

_____

_____

_____

_____

_____

_____

_____

_____

_____

_____

Doing Shadow work humanizes us. It allows us to no longer expect perfection from ourselves and others.

Notes to Myself:

_____

_____

_____

_____

_____

_____

_____

_____

_____

_____

_____

_____

_____

_____

_____

_____

completely dehumanize them. All of a sudden, we won't be able to see anything good about that person anymore. They become completely reprehensible and unacceptable to us.

We've all had a friendship where everything was going along just fine and then all of a sudden the friend will do something and we react. We say to ourselves, "Now I see their true colors." We forget everything good we ever saw in them, and the relationship becomes very divisive. If you find yourself dehumanizing someone, consider that you are possibly seeing your own Shadow. The more we can accept others' humanity, their less than noble sides and imperfections, the more we can accept our own. The more compassion we have for others' human failings and negative qualities, the more we will have for ourselves.

Doing Shadow work humanizes us. It allows us to no longer expect perfection from ourselves and others. All of a sudden a person that you dehumanized, that you didn't want to have anything to do with, will be normal again. You will start to see them as they are, and you will say to yourself, "How could I have missed that? How could I have stopped seeing all the good things about them?" When we are into our projections, we will be so angry or disgusted with them that we fail to see their light anymore, and we all have both dark and light. Our capacity for compassion grows stronger.

I am talking about learning to accept our own and others' weaknesses, the idiosyncrasies that we all have. I am talking about those characteristics that Robin Williams in the movie *Good Will Hunting* called "peccadilloes," such as not liking someone just because they talk a blue streak or laugh too loudly or brag a bit too much or whatever. We all see these character flaws in others, but we accept them if we want a real relationship to take place.

Do We Have to Like Everyone?

People have asked me, "Rebeca, do we have to like everyone?" No, we don't have to like everyone. We can't be in a relationship with everyone, and some temperaments have a harder time adjusting to each other. If you study astrology, psychological types and the qualities of introversion and extroversion, you will understand this further. Two individuals' Mars functions can be in hard aspect (opposition or square) to each other. This will show up in their birth charts. Their ways of asserting themselves are incompatible and will require adjustments if both people want to be in a relationship. Some people we just plain don't like or we have nothing in common with, and that is life. Others may have some really serious psychological problems and drain our energy when we are around them. We realize we can't help them with their problems, but we aren't charged with hatred for them. Some people won't like us. Often astrology will show you that simple dislike is all about the clashing of energy. When two people do not understand each other, there is often an elemental imbalance between them.

Furthermore, I am not talking about condoning unacceptable behavior, where one person subjects another to violence, cruelty or severe emotional abuse. There certainly are many situations that are socially unacceptable, and pathological behaviors require therapy for correction and resolution. But if we completely detest someone and blame another for the total problem in any experience, chances are that we are dealing with a projection of our unconscious Shadow.

I am also not talking about the less destructive but difficult situation where you feel out of balance with giving and taking. You feel you are being used, and you decide to end a relationship with a person who takes up time and energy that you are no longer willing to give. You will know when open and honest communication with that person has not produced a balance. You have spoken your truth, and they have made you wrong for feeling your feelings, or they are unwilling to reciprocate. That's a completely different experience. In that situation, you definitely have a boundary issue with that person. It takes two people who are willing to resolve the issue and meet each other halfway to have a healthy relationship. A person who cannot admit their part in a situation and consistently makes everyone else wrong has a strong need to always be the one in control. That person is barricaded and shut down. You can sometimes be beating a dead horse when you try and try and try to work things out with them. Trust your gut feelings and inner guidance on whether or not to work things out. Maybe you are just incompatible with that person.

Ever notice that you can be one way with one person and then another person will consistently bring out another part of you? For instance, my friend Terri and I really enjoy each others' company. We have deep conversations, but we also giggle and play around together too. It's a real pleasure to be in her space. A significant aspect of our relationship is that we do not take each other for granted or take advantage of each other. There is a beautiful balance of giving and receiving between us, and we've been friends now for over 20 years. It's not always completely harmonious with us, but when we get upset with each other, we deal with it right away. We talk things through, and make the effort to understand each other. We each express our anger or sadness. Sometimes we have to take into consideration what is going on in each others lives, as one or both of us may be going through some challenge that affects how we are relating. Then we forgive, and more important, we forget and we're back to square one. Grudges are not harbored, nor do I determine she is a totally difficult person. I accept her when she is disagreeable, and she accepts me the way I am. With someone else, I can hardly speak to

Furthermore, I am not talking about condoning unacceptable behavior, where one person subjects another to violence, cruelty or severe emotional abuse.

Notes to Myself:

Then we forgive, and more important, we forget and we're back to square one. Grudges are not harbored, nor do I determine she is a totally difficult person.

Notes to Myself:

_____

_____

_____

_____

_____

_____

_____

_____

_____

_____

_____

_____

_____

_____

_____

them when I get upset, as there is no meeting. This is energy, and as Jung said, "The meeting of two personalities is like the contact of two chemical substances: if there is any reaction, both are transformed."[24] When the meeting is really there between two people, you can work through anything through authentic communication. You create a history of genuine trust that is invaluable.

Destructive and Dangerous

The possibility of the dark side's taking over a person is more prevalent and common in those who do not take the time to question themselves and really evaluate their behavior in daily interactions with others. People who are overly identified with how "good" they are can be the most vulnerable because they are so lopsided. No one can be good all the time. It's humanly impossible. As Jung explains it, it's actually dangerous.

For example, we've all heard stories or read in the newspapers about a person who murdered a lot of people or committed some atrocious crime that was uncharacteristic of him or her. The people who knew this person say, "This was such a good person in the community! He or she was the valedictorian in high school or a very loving member of our church." No one who knew them in their daily life would have thought them capable of their unexplainable crime. What has happened is that this individual has repressed their dark side so much that the unconscious overwhelmed them. They do something out of the ordinary precisely because they have denied and suppressed their own dark side. So we're actually more vulnerable to our Shadow if we don't know about it. Our Shadow becomes hostile only when it is ignored or misunderstood.

This flipping from one extreme to its opposite is something Jung called *enantiodromia*.[23] He learned of this from the philosopher Heraclitis, who described it as "running contrariwise." In simple terms, what it means is that psychologically, when an individual goes too far in any one direction in their behavior or character, eventually of their own accord they will flip and become the exact opposite. A common and well-known example is the devout Christian who is prolife but flips to the other side and is charged with murdering a doctor they consider to be an abortionist. They have committed murder themselves, but they can't see that they have done the same thing they are fighting against. Another well known example is the powerful evangelist preacher Jimmy Swaggart, condemning sex from the pulpit, but is himself caught with a prostitute. Any area we are overly identified with is subject to an experience of *enantiodromia*. We are more in touch with our wholeness when we do not become lopsided in one extreme or another.

Jung also said that we do not always know what the unconscious is planning. Sometimes this "flipping" is a necessity to straighten a person out. A person will do one extreme, then flip and do the other extreme before they can balance out and come to the middle. In the end, the unconscious is striving for our wholeness and will bring it about in any way that it can. Sometimes, that can mean we will go through some kind of outer-world crisis such as an illness, an accident or a divorce, but it leads us to the inner world, which is the only place to resolve our problems and heal our splits.

If we are wise, we will recognize our own imbalances consciously so that we don't end up a news item like the infamous mother Andrea Yates in Texas who drowned all five of her children. Similarly, Mary Winkler, the minister's wife who shot her husband in the back in Tennessee, said in her trial, "My ugliness took over me."

In the case of Andrea Yates, a conservative Christian mother, here was someone selfless who was living only for and through her mothering role for a long period of time. When we understand that what was happening in her unconscious was the extreme opposite, we aren't surprised that she became a victim of her own capacity for evil and blamed her actions on the devil or voices inside her. It was her Shadow side that overtook her. When you understand the psychological law of *enantiodromia*, you will see how this "possession" could have been anticipated by those who knew her had they understood this principle of compensation that Jung described as the self-regulating activity of the psyche.

In the case of Mary Winkler, we can empathize with her difficult situation. Most ministers' wives are expected to be perfect, ideal women, always kind, always gracious and charming. God help one if she has an opinion of her own that goes against the grain of conformity or any expression that would resemble anger, selfishness or resentment. The pressure of always being watched is enormous. It is no wonder that ministers' wives cannot live up to this impossible standard 100 percent of the time. The loneliness of these two women must have been unbearable. When we hear stories like this, we can be horrified and repulsed or we can recognize that there is also a murderer in us quite capable of doing the same thing if we were to find ourselves in that person's shoes. It doesn't mean we condone it. It means we have to see the unexpressed Shadow working in the experience and come to terms with our own extremes and polarizations. We have to know what we are all capable of and not project it and see it only as them.

Someone who has lived their entire life with this kind of strong tendency to one-sidedness in their character has a greater chance of suffering from an *enantiodromia* in their psyche. The person who has lived their entire life as a hardworking, responsible person, obsessed with making money can all of a sudden become a lazy, irresponsible

In the end, the unconscious is striving for our wholeness and will bring it about in any way that it can.

Notes to Myself:

_____

_____

_____

_____

_____

_____

_____

_____

_____

_____

_____

_____

_____

_____

_____

When we are aware that we are getting lopsided anywhere, we are wise if we do some of the opposite for the sake of our own equilibrium.

wastrel and shock everyone. People will say, "We just don't know what got into him or her." The one-sidedness constellates the opposite. This is what Jung viewed as the great danger in the psyche of man — to become lopsided for too long. What we really all need is more balance in our lives, a little bit of this and a little bit of that.

We need to work hard, and we need to play and take vacations. We need to save money, and we need to spend money. We need to give and receive. The act of receiving is another hard one for a lot of people. When we are aware that we are getting lopsided anywhere, we are wise if we do some of the opposite for the sake of our own equilibrium.

It's Not about Getting Rid of Anything.

Shadow work is not about finding a characteristic or quality in someone else that you don't like in yourself and getting rid of it. It is about inclusion, not exclusion.

We've all heard the statement in the Bible, "Be ye therefore perfect, as also your heavenly father is perfect." [Matt 5:48] Jung explains in his book *AION*, that the word "perfect" was transcribed from the Greek word *teleios* which means "complete."[25] Jung's explanation is very different from what we usually understand as perfect. Perfect implies that you are flawless and have somehow achieved a level of mastery. Yet Jung stressed the impossibility of striving for perfection because this would split off our Shadow, and therefore without our knowing, constellate the opposite. He says, "The individual may strive after perfection but must suffer from the opposite of his intentions for the sake of his completeness."[26] We must be willing to suffer an acceptance of our own dark side in order to be a whole self and recognize that, try as we may, we will not once and for all be done with our faults and flaws. They are part of every living human being. Edward C. Whitmont put it very well. He said,

> The Shadow cannot be eliminated. It is the ever-present dark brother
> or sister. Whenever we fail to see where it stands, there is likely to
> be trouble afoot. For then it is certain to be standing behind us. The
> adequate question therefore never is: Have I a shadow problem?
> Have I a negative side? But rather: Where does it happen to be right
> now? When we cannot see it, it is time to beware! And it is helpful
> to remember Jung's formulation that a complex is not pathological
> *per se*. It becomes pathological only when we assume that we do
> not have it; because then IT HAS US![26]

Shadow work becomes especially important at midlife because the urgency to individuate (learn about our whole self — all the different parts conscious and unconscious) becomes much more pronounced.

Notes to Myself:

_____

_____

_____

_____

_____

_____

_____

_____

_____

_____

_____

_____

_____

_____

_____

_____

We become acutely aware that situations are repeating, and it is important for each of us to find out what they mean. As my teacher, Rev. J. Pittman McGehee, says, "What kept us alive in the first half of life will keep us from living in the second half of life." Our unlived life will be calling for us to see it and begin the process of taking it back. Taking back our projections at this stage of life is vitally necessary as the situations that repeat will become more intense. It's almost an irreverence and disrespect to the Universe when we ignore the feedback that it is giving us as to how we are doing. As the Taoists say, *"When one lacks a sense of awe, there will be disaster."* As our Shadow selves get further and further away from us, the darker and more destructive they get. We need the awareness that we are not perfect and no one else is either. Jung said,

> To strive for perfection is a high ideal. But I say: "Fulfil something you are able to fulfil rather than run after what you will never achieve." Nobody is perfect. Remember the saying: "None is good but God alone," [Luke 18:19] and nobody can be. It is an illusion. We can modestly strive to fulfil ourselves and to be as complete human beings as possible, and that will give us trouble enough.[27]

Making mountains out of molehills is another statement that comes to mind when we are projecting our Shadows. It seems that we react way out of proportion to whatever the person has done. We will blast them. Our ego gets too involved in what they said or what they did.

How our egos are formed and what happens to our Shadow during this process is explained by understanding what Jung called our personas.

Persona/Mask/Rising Sign

The persona, or the mask, is what we know about ourselves. This is our ego personality, but we are all so much more than what we know. This circle diagram represents our unconscious contents that Jung described as the structure of consciousness. In astrology, we call the persona the rising sign, as it is the sign on the horizon of our birth. The words "personal" and "personality" come from the term "persona" which comes

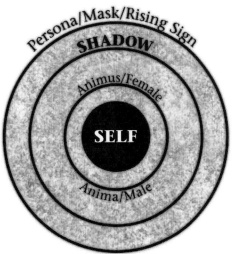

The Shadow is directly behind the Persona, so it's the first step into our unconscious.

Notes to Myself:

_____

_____

_____

_____

_____

_____

_____

_____

_____

_____

_____

_____

_____

When we learn about our Shadow, it becomes clear that we all are many more characters than we actually know.

from the Greek word *personare* and literally means mask. This is exactly what it was called in the days when actors wore masks in Greek dramas. They would speak through a mask; therefore the audience never saw the real face of the actor himself. This is how we experience each other when we first meet. We see each other's masks, while the real person is hidden. We all relate to each other through our personas. As a buffer between others and the vulnerable ego we are inside, our persona protects us as we go out into the world. This mask is a vital part of our identity because our personas give us the necessary distance from others and keep us safe.

Our persona is usually a highly idealized image of who we think we are. When we learn about our Shadow, it becomes clear that we all are many more characters than we actually know. The higher our ideals are, if we think we are a really good person, the darker we will be in the unconscious because of the compensatory factor going on within us. Descriptive of our personality or our ego, the persona constitutes everything we can tolerate in consciousness about ourselves. It includes both positive and negative characteristics and qualities. Our ego is the part of us that says, "This is who I am; this is what I want and what I know about myself." It's that "I" with which we identify.

Jung said of the persona that it is "designed on the one hand to make a definite impression upon others and, on the other, to conceal the true nature of the individual.[28] So we develop our persona in order to be accepted by the society we live in. When we're young, our parents and our culture will socialize us into having a persona in order to help us all get along with each other. We would all be pretty egocentric if we were not taught to be civilized, so developing a persona is a very important stage in everyone's psychological development.

Beginning in childhood, we learn early on what is acceptable to our society and what is not. Our ego thrives on acceptance, approval and recognition whether we want to admit it or not. We usually try to have as pleasing a personality as possible in order to belong and fit in. Depending on the family or culture we are born into, we can get different messages as we are growing up. As Robert A. Johnson says in his cassette, *Your Shadow, Friend or Foe,*[29] what is acceptable in one family or culture is not acceptable in another one. For example, in India or in Asian cultures, you do not go into a temple with your shoes on. In our Western culture, you are considered to be uncivilized if you do this, and you are not allowed to enter barefooted. Likewise, in one family, emotion and candid expression are completely acceptable and another family might value a much more stoic and reserved approach. We adapt our persona or mask to our particular family or culture and this can go 180 degrees against our true nature. During this part of our ego development, many useful qualities and characteristics will go into our unconscious and become a part of our Shadow complex. We all do this because we get the message loud and clear that it's not OK to be ourselves. If we can accept these Shadow parts, we become more authentically who we really are instead of hiding behind our masks.

Too Good to Be True

We've all met people who seem "too nice" and sickeningly sweet. We sense that they are somehow being fake when we are around them, and we also feel we never really know them. They are, as the saying goes, "too good to be true." These people are barricaded behind their masks or personas. They will deliberately avoid any negative reaction or emotion. They refuse to be real and suffer the acceptance of their own dark side. As we have seen, this can be dangerous. We are better off knowing about our dark side because whatever one does not live lives against one.

It takes a lot of energy to push down into the basement the parts we don't want anyone else to see. Society rewards those who are patient, calm, even-tempered and altruistic. It is quite natural to want to be thought of highly. We all, to some degree, have to put our best foot (our persona) forward to succeed in life. At the same time, it takes a lot of moral courage and ego strength to recognize we are not always like that. No one is. Identifying with our outward persona can be destructive to our relationships as well as to our health and well-being.

If we become accustomed to playing a role in life or acting out a part, then too much of our energy is unavailable to us. If we believe that our pleasing persona is who we really are, unconsciously, we are setting ourselves up with an unconscious opposite that will sooner or later come back at us from someone "out there" as the energy will build up until it has a release.

Sometimes the persona we show to others is the darker face and the Shadow is the light part. Some people are overly identified with how bad they are. They grew up being told this was all they were or ever would be, and they have come to identify with their darker side. They will disown their more humble, altruistic, nice and decent parts. It's as if they are embarrassed to be good. Most of us will have a mixture of positive and negative qualities in our unconscious Shadow, but there are some folks who would rather be thought of as "bad." Our prisons are filled to capacity with many people who need to be given the courage to look at their lighter, more positive sides. I heard someone describe it like this at one of my workshops: "They don't hide their ugliness!"

Slips of the Tongue

Slips of the tongue are another way to recognize a Shadow quality in

We are better off knowing about our dark side because, as we have seen, whatever one does not live, lives against one.

Notes to Myself:

_____

_____

_____

_____

_____

_____

_____

_____

_____

_____

_____

_____

_____

_____

_____

The Shadow side of us relates to life much more authentically.

Notes to Myself:

ourselves. How many times have you said something and then said, "I didn't mean it that way." Well, we did mean it that way, and our Shadow decided to have its say. The Shadow side of us relates to life much more authentically. What we mean will come out whether we like it or not.

I met a female plastic surgeon several years before I studied and started teaching classes on the Shadow, and I did not like her. Trish, my business partner at the time, didn't like her either. Although she needed some graphics done and was willing to hire us, we decided we would not work with this person, as she pushed both our buttons. Years passed before I ever saw her again, and I forgot about her.

One fall semester, there was a class at the Jung Center on the Shadow, and I decided to take it to see what else I could learn. One day right after class, I was having dinner with a friend at a restaurant and this surgeon that I had not liked walked in and came over to our table. As she was walking toward me, I said to my friend, "Here comes my Shadow." This woman was a cute and bubbly person, and she smiled this big, huge smile and said, "Rebeca, I want you to meet my new husband." She told him, "This is my good friend, Rebeca Eigen." I was aghast, as I was not her "good friend." I had met her only twice. I smiled, and they walked away. I turned to my friend, and I said, "Here I am in a city of four million people, I'm about to teach my class, and my Shadow walks into the restaurant." I explained to my friend what had transpired when Trish and I met this woman years before. Trish developed a headache after meeting her, and I had a stomachache on the second occasion we visited with her. Notice again the physical aversion and how our bodies speak to us.

After dinner, the surgeon, her husband and his daughter walked toward us as they were leaving, and I said to myself, "Now you be nice." They came over to our table, and she said goodbye to me and expressed how good it was to see me.

I said, "Congratulations on your marriage. You look like twins, and they say couples that look alike last longer."

She said, "Do we really look like twins?"

His young daughter who appeared to be about 12 years old said, "People tell you that all the time." Children are so much more honest than we are.

The surgeon turned her attention back to me and said, "This is his daughter, but we're going to have babies."

I said, "At your age?" Before I even knew that was out, I had said something totally awful.

She looked dismayed at my remark and said, "I'm only 31."

I said, "Oh, I thought you were older than that."

I did it again. I stuck my foot in my mouth twice. I had said to myself before she came over to the table to be nice. I was stunned at what came out of me, and so were they. They hurried to get away.

My friend had a hearty laugh. I couldn't believe it. The Shadow part of me had said those things to her. The fake persona that I wanted to talk for me was usurped by my Shadow. This is what I mean by "slips of the tongue." These can be embarrassing moments when the last thing you thought you would say has its say regardless of your good intentions. I was telling myself I was going to be nice. That was my conscious intent, but the Shadow knew I was being fake.

Another example of this happens when you know you've just said something that hurt someone. In order to save face or justify your statement, you protest by saying, "I was just joking" or "I am only kidding. Can't you take a joke?" You weren't joking or kidding. Or you might say, "I just wasn't myself. I don't know what came over me." Well, who were you, then? Another excuse is "the devil got into me." These are all statements that a part of you is foreign to you. The Shadow side of us is honest and will take over when it knows we are trying to weasel out of an experience. Our Shadow can really shock us, as in this example of a slip of the tongue.

When Alcohol Allows for the Shadow to Come Out

The Shadow can take over a person when they are drinking alcohol and their sense of self-control relaxes. An example of this is when a person has been overly accommodating and too "nice," putting everyone else's needs first. Then under the influence of alcohol when they can no longer put up their guard, all the resentment they hid from their partners comes out with full force. It's embarrassing when this happens, and I think at one time or another this has happened to everyone. It's important that we know we are better off expressing our hurts, our feelings, however negative, as the Shadow side will take over when we don't express ourselves. Jung says our Shadow contains infantile and primitive parts of us. When we are not good at expressing our real feelings, sometimes we can sound like a needy or angry, overly emotional child. Sober, we are self-contained and exhibit restraint. We make excuses for others' bad behavior and tell ourselves we are not petty and can rise above whatever the discomfort is. Well, it's not that simple. Our unconscious is building up an enormous amount of resentment and will have its say sooner or later. Our best bet is to be real even if it makes us vulnerable. Eventually with practice, and this does take practice, we will be able to express ourselves more easily to our partners, families, parents and friends, especially if they are willing to understand where we are coming from. If you do express yourself and they are not listening and make no effort to hear you and respect what you have said, then chances are they are not willing to be in the relationship. You will have to accept that and move on. Every situation is different. Just know the Shadow

The Shadow part of me had said those things to her. The fake persona that I wanted to talk for me was usurped by my Shadow.

Notes to Myself:

_____

_____

_____

_____

_____

_____

_____

_____

_____

_____

_____

_____

_____

_____

_____

*Just know, the Shadow
will come out between
you when you get
really close to anyone.
I see it as a great op-
portunity for more
self-knowledge.*

Notes to Myself:

_____

_____

_____

_____

_____

_____

_____

_____

_____

_____

_____

_____

_____

_____

_____

_____

will come out between you when you get really close to anyone. I see it as a great opportunity for more self-knowledge. Each person's Shadow has something to teach them through their relationship if they are both willing to be honest.

Jesus Knew We Have a Shadow.

In his extremely interesting book, *Evil the Shadow Side of Reality*, John A. Sanford has a wonderful chapter on Jesus and Saint Paul.[30] He describes how Jesus was accepting of human frailties, but was indignant when he encountered people identified only with their masks or personas. He knew this was psychologically dishonest and that this capacity for self-blindness more than anything else leads to "self-righteousness, lack of compassion and spiritual rigidity."[31]

According to Sanford, Jesus knew about our Shadow. He explains how many of his parables speak of retrieving this split in us that Christianity has encouraged through its emphasis that we develop and accept only our good side. Developing only good follows the teachings of St. Paul instead of the teachings of Jesus, which were more complex and psychologically healthy. St. Paul's teachings made it clear that we were to repress any of our negative emotions such as anger, revenge, greed and lust. Most of us try our best to do just that, but we will identify too strongly with only one side of us if we make the mistake of repressing and denying our Shadow self. Where will all of our natural and instinctive responses go? They will go directly into our Shadow, where they fester. Then, when we least expect it, they will jump out like a rattlesnake, ready to bite. The task, therefore, is not to deny and repress ourselves by being "holy," but to become conscious of this side of ourselves. We have to love even these parts.

*If you bring forth what is within you, what you
have will save you. If you do have that within you,
what you do not have within you [will] kill you.[31]*

JESUS IN THE GOSPEL OF ST. THOMAS

The story of the prodigal son coming home describes our Shadow coming home to us. Sanford does an exceptional job of describing several, so I won't go into them here. I highly encourage everyone to read his book for themselves, as it is one of the best books available on the Shadow.

A well-known quote by Jesus that is particularly helpful in doing your own Shadow work is "Before you take the splinter out of your brother's eye, why not take the log out of your own?" [Matthew 7:1-5] We would all do well to remember these words when we are condemning another, especially those others with idiosyncrasies and character flaws deluxe, such as:
- **people who lie, cheat or steal**
- **people who chew gum out loud, have bad manners**

- people who are too loud, obnoxious, rude, superficial or flaky
- people who come on strong, talk too much, are too friendly or get too close physically when they talk to you
- people who are aloof, cold or detached emotionally
- people who are name droppers and act as if everyone knows whom they are talking about
- people who are constantly telling you how much things cost them or who are braggarts
- people who are know-it-alls, egotistical or narcissistic
- people who run away from confrontation — the wimps of the world, superficial, people-pleasers
- people who use profanity and tell off-color jokes in public or are crass and unrefined
- people who are necking or groping each other excessively in public
- people who never return phone calls but will call you if they need something from you — the users
- people who are two-faced, smile at your face and talk behind your back in a negative fashion, hypocrites
- people who are greedy for excessive materiality
- people who are needy for emotional support and wear you out with their phone calls at all hours
- people who_____

_____

_____

_____

_____

Ever met anyone like these obnoxious folks? YES, they are US! Especially if you meet them repeatedly, and they give you an emotional charge. Say hello to your Shadow! It's so easy to say we want to know ourselves, but each of us has tremendous resistance to seeing that these parts of us are real. We begin to do our Shadow work by admitting to ourselves whenever we, too, are greedy, controlling, vain, stingy or hypocritical. If we can recognize these Shadow parts, then they don't get buried so deeply.

In *The Undiscovered Self,* Jung said, "Most people confuse 'self-knowledge' with knowledge of their conscious ego personalities. Anyone who has any ego-consciousness at all takes it for granted that he knows himself. But the ego knows only its own contents, not the unconscious and its contents. People measure their self-knowledge by what the average person in their social environment knows of himself, but not the real psychic facts which are for the most part hidden from them."[33]

Then, when we least expect it, they will jump out like a rattlesnake, ready to bite.

Notes to Myself:

We are all psychic to a degree, so we all sense when another person feels uncomfortable around us.

When Others Project Their Shadow onto You

Sometimes people who hardly even know you will project their Shadow onto you. You'll know it's a projection coming from them because they will constantly belittle you or be short with you when you are in their space. We are all psychic to a degree, so we all sense when another person feels uncomfortable around us. You may wonder what you did to these people to have them dislike you so intensely. You might even try to be nice and polite to them. If they still can't stand you, and show it in negative and hurtful ways, there is no need to stay in their space. Move on. No one needs this kind of psychological abuse. Maybe what you are doing is repulsive to them precisely because they need to learn from you, but they can't see you because they are only seeing a Shadow aspect of themselves. Often they will pick one thing you do that irritates them and determine that it is all of you. Again, this is a dehumanizing, exaggerated reaction on their part. Edward C. Whitmont says,

> Ask someone to give a description of the personality type which he finds most despicable, most unbearable and hateful, and most impossible to get along with, and he will produce a description of his own repressed characteristics — a self-description which is utterly unconscious and which therefore always and everywhere tortures him as he receives its effect from the *other* person. These very qualities are so unacceptable to him precisely because they represent his own repressed side; only that which we cannot accept within ourselves do we find impossible to live with in others. Negative qualities which do not bother us so excessively, which we find relatively easy to forgive if we have to forgive them at all — are not likely to pertain to our shadow.[34]

It is interesting to watch this process happen and recognize that unless a relationship develops in which you can get to know others and they can get to know you, their projection onto you isn't likely to go away. It's human feeling and relatedness that changes our rejection of others into a relationship of comrades or friends. This process is the same whether it goes on between individuals or countries, between ethnic groups or religious extremists and fundamentalists. After you accept a Shadow trait in yourself, it is very interesting how that characteristic completely stops bothering you. We have to experience this kind of turnaround in attitude in our lives to really appreciate Shadow work. Jung says one understands nothing psychological unless one has experienced it oneself. We have to change our own minds. This is healing to ourselves and to all the relationships in our lives.

Notes to Myself:

Self-Knowledge

Jung's major contribution to the field of psychology was that he was willing to go inside himself and explore his own unconscious, even though he was already a learned doctor of psychiatry. He had to humble himself to admit that there were other characters within himself that he had no control over. Being the true pioneer of a human being's need for self-knowledge, Jung's own self-analysis showed us a way to work with our unconscious to retrieve these hidden parts. In his autobiography, *Memories, Dreams, Reflections*, he begins with the following statement: "My life is a story of the self-realization of the unconscious. Everything in the unconscious seeks outward manifestation, and the personality, too, desires to evolve out of its unconscious conditions and to experience itself as a whole."[35]

Jung first observed in his mother the splitting of the psyche into two parts and then was able to see it in himself. We, too, must develop a strong enough ego to hold the awareness of our dark side in consciousness. We have to be able to contain the feelings of denigration that will accompany this kind of internal self-honesty and not let them engulf us. We need to be able to say, "Yes, I am like this. AND I am also like this." We have to remember we are always also the opposite of anything we uncover, and to the same degree, so that we don't overly identify with our Shadow negative or positive.

We each have to strive continually to be conscious, moral and ethical while at the same time seeing that we are all capable of the full range of human behavior. Every emotion, every reaction, every single affect is there in potential in every single one of us. We are all capable of doing everything. Some of these characteristics are dark indeed — greed, manipulation, hypocritical behavior, ruthlessness, cold detachment, lying, cheating, etc. My son, Kevin, and I were talking about the Shadow, and he reminded me of the saying, "It takes one to know one." Only a manipulator will recognize a manipulator. Only a user will recognize a user. When people tell me they know themselves, I just smile. I know they don't. No one knows their whole self. So much is in the unconscious. This is the task of an entire lifetime.

I remember when I first started doing this work how sad I felt. It was very painful, almost like a grieving process. It's definitely not easy to own your Shadow, and, as Jung says, it takes time. I felt as if a part of me was dying, the part of me that thought I knew who I was — which was my persona or my mask. I remember feeling a lot of guilt and asking myself what I could have done differently. I had a real dark; night-of-the-soul experience going into my unconscious for an entire week. I wondered if I would ever feel normal again. Gradually I came out of it. As painful as this work is, it's necessary to our wholeness. Our ego strength grows in proportion to seeing who we really

After you accept a Shadow trait in yourself, it is very interesting how that characteristic completely stops bothering you.

Notes to Myself:

_____

_____

_____

_____

_____

_____

_____

_____

_____

_____

_____

_____

Only a manipulator will recognize a manipulator. Only a user will recognize a user.

Notes to Myself:

_____

_____

_____

_____

_____

_____

_____

_____

_____

_____

_____

_____

_____

_____

_____

are and to holding the awareness of our destructive side consciously without acting it out. This in itself is the ever-present challenge: to hold the tension in the psyche of our opposites and not lean too much to either side. The Taoists called this the path of the middle way. As the Greeks said on the temple at Delphi, "Know thyself" and "Nothing in excess." These two very wise statements, made long ago, can help us today, but trust me, I am still working on this. It does not happen overnight. Just know that you are doing the work, and keep on keeping on when you fail or allow yourself to become one extreme or another. Pick yourself up and keep going. At least you will begin to know when you are out of balance. That in itself is pretty awesome.

Asking Our Higher Power to Help Us

I have a longstanding agreement with God, my higher power, the force, or whatever you want to call it. The agreement goes something like this: If I don't see something, and it's important for my well-being to see it, then I ask God please to show it to me three times, and I promise I will listen. That is a guiding philosophy of mine that has served me well over the years. A second life philosophy is that there are no accidents. I truly believe everything is showing us something we badly need to see.

If we can meet our partners halfway, then we will be doing Shadow work with them which will often bring both partners into balance. This is why I call this work a dance. It takes two. You need others to see yourself. As the Rev. J. Pittman McGehee, D.D. says in his lecture series *The Paradox of Relationships*, "I alone must become myself, but I cannot become myself alone."[36]

Some people think they can "go it alone," as it's just too hard to be in relationships. Jung would say to them that the unrelated human being lacks wholeness, for he can achieve wholeness only through the soul, and the soul cannot exist without its other side, which is always found in a "you."[37] We need others — our families, friends and partners. Our love for them, their love for us transforms and heals. We need them to show us our projections and help us take them back. Jung says, "Becoming whole is an intrapsychic process which depends essentially on the relation of one individual to another."[37] Without the mirror there is no recognition of our Shadow. Jung says:

> The meaning of 'whole' or 'wholeness' is to make holy or to heal. The descent into the depths will bring healing. It is the way to the total being, to the treasure which suffering mankind is forever seeking, which is hidden in the place guarded by terrible danger. This is the place of primordial unconsciousness and at the same time the place of healing and redemption, because it contains the

jewel of wholeness. It is the cave where the dragon of chaos lives and it is also the indestructible city, the magic circle or *temenos*, the sacred precinct where all the split-off parts of the personality are united.[38]

We need others — our families, friends and partners. Our love for them, their love for us transforms and heals.

SHADOW WORKSHOP EXAMPLES

The following examples below are from my workshops conducted from 1992 and to the present. My students have also been my teachers. The stories and life experiences they have shared while having open dialogues are presented here in their own words excerpted from tapes and videos. All names and identifying information have been changed to protect their privacy.

EXAMPLE 1: Extremes Show Us What We Need to Develop.

Audience: I noticed that the people that I really admire are very generous, very giving — you know, the people who will give their shirt off their back. As far as people I can't stand, well, there is this sales rep who comes to my company, and it's just like you were talking about. He makes my skin crawl, and I go to the opposite end of the office when he's there, and everybody makes a joke about it because I really do. He is the opposite of what I admire in people. He just walks into the company, and he's a man's man. His attitude is: "I don't have to do anything, and you all have to send me business. I know you're going to." So does that mean by what you're saying that he's bringing up something in my Shadow — obviously? But does that mean that I'm going to attract somebody who is very manipulative and the opposite of generous since that is what I admire in people?

Rebeca: (I nodded and smiled at him.)

Audience: Really? I give up.

Rebeca: Maybe there are qualities in him that you need to develop. Sometimes when we're seeing something in another person, they're doing it to an extreme. Notice extremes between yourself and other people. The unconscious is profound. You will see it, and you will project it onto that person. You do not identify with that quality or characteristic at all, but it's probably something you need to develop, not to the extreme that he's doing it, but somewhat. Maybe he's confident. Maybe you need to feel more confident about yourself. Whatever the quality or characteristic is, he is probably doing it to an extreme. If you can look at the value of that, then you can incorporate it into your being but in a more balanced way. The only reason you can't stand him is that he is a mirror for you; otherwise you wouldn't get an emotional charge when he walks in. Does that make sense?'

Audience: Yes. I can see it now.

Notes to Myself:

You do not identify with that quality or characteristic at all, but it's probably something you need to develop, not to the extreme that he's doing it, but somewhat.

Notes to Myself:

_____

_____

_____

_____

_____

_____

_____

_____

_____

_____

_____

_____

_____

_____

_____

_____

EXAMPLE 2: The "Never Angry" Individual

Rebeca: The never angry individual who is always totally in control of their emotions will attract their opposite because they prefer not to show you how they really feel. It appears that they never get angry. The key word here is *appears*. You can be screaming at them, and they will just stand there calmly drinking a cup of coffee and smiling at you. They will appear to be emotionless no matter what you say to them. You will find yourself getting madder and madder at them. The next thing you know, you are screaming at the top of your lungs, and then you will be shaking and incapable of thinking rationally, but they will still have that smile on their faces. Then they will condemn you for being out of control.

What has happened here between these two people is that one person is carrying all of the anger and the other person is carrying all of the self-control. It can get real uncomfortable, especially when it keeps repeating within a marriage or committed relationship. Eventually the relationship will break down because of the nature of the imbalance.

When you ask an overly passive person who never gets angry, "Do you constantly attract angry people to you?" they'll say, "Yes, but I never get angry. Why do people have to get so bent out of shape?" I ask, "What is it that they are expressing for you that you're not willing to express? What is it that you want? Where do you need to call the shots or be in charge?"

These people are so into denial that they ever get angry that they have to attract a whole lot of angry people into their lives so that they can see themselves. The truth is we all get angry, and sometimes getting angry is a healthy response to an intolerable situation. Not all of us can express our anger. Some of us just stuff it. Those who cannot express it at all will continually attract anger in the mirror of others and then conveniently project that out. It is always the other person who is unreasonable and angry.

If you are around one of these overly passive people, you will unconsciously start to pick on them because you are trying to get them to be real. You are trying to get them to have an authentic response. If you're constantly being mean to someone and they're being nice, it drives you crazy after a while. I'm not saying we do this consciously. We don't. We're so unconscious most of the time, it's amazing.

What is really interesting is that if you are a person who easily expresses anger (and you can see this in the birth chart for a person with Mars prominent), then you will attract the opposite. This will continually happen so that you can come into balance with yourself. Your lesson is to learn to fight with someone in a more productive way, because when you are out there angry and spilling your anger out everywhere willy-nilly, you won't get the results you really want. Again, it will behoove you to pay attention to these opposites. Learn to cultivate a little bit of what they are doing and make a conscious choice to do so.

Audience: What came to mind while you were talking was my ex-husband. Thank goodness he's my ex-husband. People say to me, "I'm so sorry that he's your ex-husband," and I say, "No, it's a very good thing; otherwise I wouldn't have divorced him." He was several things. He was real, real, real jealous, and I would never let myself be jealous like that. I would think something was wrong with you if you acted like that. So maybe that's one of the reasons I picked him, because he could express jealousy. He would express anger a lot, and when he would get mad at me, he would harangue me for 20, 30, 40 minutes. I would sit on the couch with my fingers in my ears when he would go on and on and on. I never ever do that that I know of, but maybe that's something I needed? The jealousy thing was real obvious. I know that there have been times when I wished I could act like that, but I would never, for my own self-esteem, let myself act like that. So when you were talking, I could certainly see that. And yes, I do have a lot of trouble expressing anger. I don't think it's productive to scream for 30 minutes.

Rebeca: Well, that's an extreme. You see that's a clear example of an extreme.

Audience: Yes, you're right. The more I would put my fingers in my ears, the more he would go on and on and on.

Rebeca: Absolutely.

Audience: So that is what you're talking about. But I don't see how... when you are polarized, how do you figure out what it is that you're polarized about? I don't see how you come to the middle.

Rebeca: Well, take this example that you just gave us. You would have to be more willing to express your own anger sometimes. We all get angry. Getting angry is human. It's normal. A lot of times what can happen to us is that one of our parents or somebody who influenced us was so out of control that we decided we were never going to be like them. Someone who impacted us made us feel that getting angry was wrong. Well, getting angry, when appropriate, can be very healthy. There were probably times when you probably had every right to get angry at him. Chances are that if you had gone ahead and spoken your real feelings, then he would have had to back off. Whatever you need to learn, you are going to draw it to yourself. If you need to learn to stand up for yourself — *voila*, you draw an angry partner who is always in your face! It's so amazing. I love the way this works all the time.

Audience: Well, one time I threw a bowl of eggs and liver across the yard at him.

Your lesson is to learn to fight with someone in a more productive way, because when you are out there angry and spilling your anger out everywhere willy-nilly, you won't get the results you really want.

Notes to Myself:

_____

_____

_____

_____

_____

_____

_____

_____

_____

_____

_____

_____

Sometimes people get angry because you are ignoring them or you've done something to hurt them.

Rebeca: Well, that's not expressing feelings. It's being willing to say out loud what it is you are angry about. Yes, sometimes you might even have to say it loudly. At least you would get the point across in the moment in a decisive way. That's what I mean.

If you're not used to getting angry in the moment, then you need to practice on little things so when the bigger things come up, you're ready. For instance, say something irritates you. You can just say out loud, "I don't like it when you do that," "Don't go there," or "That attitude doesn't work for me. Can you please explain to me what's irritating you?" Sometimes people get angry because you are ignoring them or you've done something to hurt them. Sometimes they are just in a bad mood. So if you communicate when someone snaps at you the first time, then you are practicing being assertive yourself. This can depotentiate a lot of disagreements. It's being willing to communicate on the spot. It takes practice. First you have to admit to yourself, yes, this is an area where I need to learn something from my partner, instead of looking at him like he is a jerk and thinking, "I am out of here." If it's something in you that is lopsided, then it will just repeat. Does that make sense?

Audience: Yes, thanks.

EXAMPLE 3: When We Continually Attract "Overtakers"

Audience: Why do I always attract guys who end up living off of me? Then I get fed up with them, and then I have to kick them out, and it's a real long process.

Rebeca: And you have done this over and over and over?

Audience: Over and over again. They'll have money before we get together. Then when they are living with me, they are suddenly stone broke. They don't have any money, and they're having to rely on me. Then after they move, they have money again. Why does this continue to happen to me?

Rebeca: Probably because you are too "overgiving."

Audience: That is what is really frustrating me. I don't stand on the side of the street with a sign saying, "Please come home with me."

Rebeca: I know. Jung says that there is so much about ourselves that is unconscious. It's almost automatic. We will unconsciously attract our opposites to us.

One of my friends is like you. One guy she dated ripped her off for a thousand dollars. The second guy took one of her credit cards and bought a car. They were going to get married, so he wasn't just a guy she was dating. He put four thousand dollars on her credit card, and then he just up and disappeared. Then she had to pay that credit card off herself. I promise you she was not a happy camper. Now she is in a new relationship. She says to me, "Rebeca, I have to close my purse

Notes to Myself:

_____

_____

_____

_____

_____

_____

_____

_____

_____

_____

_____

_____

_____

_____

_____

and let him pay. I have to force myself not to overgive." This relationship has lasted a long time for her, and they are looking at getting married. He is not taking advantage of her financially, but she doesn't allow it.

It's usually about ourselves. It's about our own behavior. When it keeps repeating as you said, then some part of you is split off and totally unconscious, and you need to see it. You will continually have this situation in your life so that you can see it. This can be puzzling, but it can also be very, very freeing. If you were to say to me, "That person is incapable of treating me with respect," I would want you to say to yourself, "I am incapable of treating myself with respect." It's all within. We are doing it to ourselves. It will just keep repeating until we get it.

Audience: Could it just be a situation where she's the nurturing type, and, therefore, others are drawn to her for that?

Rebeca: Yes, but we all need to be in balance regardless, even if we are the nurturing type. I'm the nurturing type, too. I'm overly generous, so I have to hold back. I don't do it as much anymore, but when I was younger, I would do it a lot and then I would resent people. The dance is: I'm so giving and you're not. I would go around resenting everybody. Well, that doesn't work either.

Audience: You should be giving because you want to give, not because of what you will get in return.

Rebeca: Exactly. Now I am trying to be as real as I possibly can with all my relationships, even if it's going to make others mad at me. If that person is really your friend, they're not going to leave you. You'll find out who your real friends are when you express your real feelings and they stick around after an unpleasant event takes place between you.

EXAMPLE 4: The Always Strong, Capable Individual

Audience: I keep attracting weak, needy people. Am I supposed to be a weak, needy person? I don't want to be anything like that.

Rebeca: How about looking at that a little differently? How about looking at it like that person is more flexible, that person is willing to bend? There's always another way to look at those qualities or characteristics that we've decided are negative. Everything is both. Everything in the Universe is energy. Up/down, black/white, yin/yang — everything has its opposite, so there's always another way to look at that quality. Instead of identifying with one extreme or the other extreme, stand in the middle and see the value of both. Robert A. Johnson, who wrote the book *Owning Your Own Shadow,* says that only then will you understand the paradox of life. He says being spiritually mature is to be able to see this paradox. Then we can look at everything in a different light. The opposite quality that before was so repulsive to us, if we can make the effort to own it, can be

You will continually have this situation in your life so that you can see it. This can be puzzling, but it can also be very, very freeing.

Notes to Myself:

_____

_____

_____

_____

_____

_____

_____

_____

_____

_____

_____

_____

Instead of identifying with one extreme or the other extreme, stand in the middle and see the value of both.

made more productive. Otherwise it will just have a life of its own and live against you. Don't you get tired of having no one to lean on or always being in charge?

Audience: Yes, I guess I am too independent at times.

Rebeca: Well, then you have to be willing to be vulnerable enough to show that you, too, sometimes need others. That's probably hard for you, so maybe you can do it slowly. But you will have to make a conscious effort to practice needing others' help occasionally so that you can be a whole person instead of always being the strong, capable person. It leaves you exhausted, doesn't it?

Audience: Yes, it does. I feel I always have to do everything myself.

EXAMPLE 5: When We Completely Reject a Part of Us

Audience: For many years I hung out at bars, playing the singles scene, and being what I thought was independent, sexy, confident and self-assured. Well, that led to a lot of heartaches and troubles —broken/ failed relationships, intimacy issues, a lower self-worth based on bad choices. It wasn't working for me anymore, so I actively pursued changing my behavior and habits for the "better," settled down into a stable relationship, didn't go to bars alone, etc.

One night out with my boyfriend, we ran into a mutual friend. She was drunk, loud, with cleavage on parade for all to see. My body stiffened and clinched. I made sure we didn't spend too much time around her, but for DAYS afterward, I would bring her name up in conversation and ridicule her attire and attitude. I see now that the reason she bothered me so much is that that part of my life and attitude went into my Shadow. It wasn't gone, although my overall lifestyle has changed. I will work on embracing the fun, sexy side in balance with the responsible girlfriend side of me now that I know this information. So thank you!

EXAMPLE 6: When You Don't See It, but Someone Else Points It Out

Audience: What if it's something that you don't see that somebody else tells you you have? You said that it was in the unconscious. For instance, I'm a boss at my job, so I am bossy at home, I think. I don't know. My husband says that I'm just like I am at my job. Well, at my job, I am the boss, so there I am real bossy. I come home and still tell everybody what to do, and I just think, well, that is what I am supposed to do. He says that I'm real bossy, but I don't see it that way, but that's what you're talking about, the unconscious things about yourself you don't see. So then what do I do? Admit to myself I am being too bossy and it might be better to be less bossy and come more to the middle with that? So even listening to what people

Notes to Myself:

tell you can be very helpful?

Rebeca: Yes, it's very helpful.

EXAMPLE 7: People Who Speak Their Mind

Audience: I identify myself as being openhearted, able to recognize people's gifts, but I still get really pissed at people who are domineering and really right — just express their opinions at any cost. I just go off on that! Inside, I mean. I don't do it on the outside. I just can't believe they do that. So, this is really interesting.

Rebeca: So, can you see that you, too, are doing that without knowing it, maybe? (She smiles and nods her head in the affirmative.)

Practicing the Process

Now that I've given you some examples, let's get started on Shadow work. The six processes on the following pages were written to help you get started. Each of them will help you ask yourself questions and dialogue with your own unconscious. Your commitment in making a daily habit of using Shadow work processes will be invaluable in facilitating greater self-awareness. Your intention and choice to make this work a part of your everyday life will invite your unconscious to work with you for amazing results.

He says that I'm real bossy, but I don't see it that way but that's what you're talking about, the unconscious things about yourself you don't see.

Notes to Myself:

_____

_____

_____

_____

_____

_____

_____

_____

_____

_____

_____

_____

_____

_____

_____

_____

Characteristics and qualities about myself I am highly identified with can be both positive and negative.

The opposite extremes will be in our unconscious to the same degree as what we see represented by our conscious ego.

Describe five very fundamental characteristics about yourself.	What would be the exact opposite characteristics?	How might it benefit you to develop some of these opposite qualities?
1.		
2.		
3.		
4.		
5.		

What do I deny, ignore or hold back?

Write about three times when you felt angry, hurt or sad but didn't say anything about it to the other person. Holding back our negative reactions can reveal important clues about what we are denying.

Do you remember a time when you said to yourself, "I don't like what I am feeling; therefore I will ignore it." Ask yourself what you were feeling at the time. Later you may have thought to yourself, "I wish I had said this or that." You may even have forgotten about it when some time had passed. You will find many helpful clues for doing Shadow work by exploring what you ignore, hold back or deny.

1. I was really angry, hurt or sad when…

_____

_____

_____

_____

_____

_____

_____

2. I don't like it when I feel… or I'm sure glad I never feel…

_____

_____

_____

_____

_____

_____

_____

3. I wish I had said something the last time…

_____

_____

_____

_____

_____

_____

_____

Blame is one way that we discharge our negative experiences onto others, but blaming others can give us only a short reprieve.

We've all had challenging experiences with others that are purposeful and a part of our ongoing evolutionary unfoldment. Instead of blaming, try reflecting.

Write about three situations or events in which you found yourself feeling victimized. Maybe you've made comments to yourself such as "Why did he or she do that to me?" or "Why does this always happen to me?" Does this help you remember?

Describe three scenarios and what you were feeling:

1.

_____

_____

_____

_____

_____

_____

2.

_____

_____

_____

_____

_____

_____

3.

_____

_____

_____

_____

_____

_____

Negative or embarrassing experiences in our lives can help us see our Shadow.

Write about three of your most embarrassing moments. Looking back, you probably still nag yourself about these events. Do you remember a time in your life when you said to yourself, "Why did I act that way?" or "How could I have said that?"

Over the years, these parts of ourselves grow bigger and bigger until they break free in ways that surprise us — often with embarrassing results. When we refuse to look at the Shadow quality in us that is sabotaging us in this way, it just keeps repeating. Ask yourself what you've done that you wish you could do over. This is one aspect of your Shadow.

1. I embarrassed myself when I... _____

_____

_____

_____

_____

_____

2. The last time I remember that "I just wasn't myself" was when...

_____

_____

_____

_____

_____

3. I'll never forget the time I shocked myself by... _____

_____

_____

_____

_____

_____

_____

_____

Our friends know us. They see things about us we haven't seen yet.

No one likes to hear unpleasant truths about themselves, but the honesty of a true friend is a real gift. We can't change anything we don't know about. The more we know about these parts of us, the more choices we have about our own behavior. Has a friend told you something about yourself that left you feeling misunderstood or judged? Do you still resent them?

Has it happened before? Have two or more people pointed this out to you? You will know it's about you by the sheer fact that it will repeat. Do you find that this particular characteristic or quality is highly repulsive when you encounter it in another person?

When I was told this about myself I really overreacted:

1._____

2._____

3._____

I am repulsed when I see this characteristic or quality in others:

1._____

2._____

3._____

This person pushed my buttons. What was it they did or said that I reacted to? Do I recall having done this myself?

1._____

2._____

3._____

Here are more ways to see our Shadow.

There are people I hardly know and yet I find myself avoiding. If I were to write a description of what I am judging in them, it would say... _____

_____

_____

_____

_____

_____

There are times when I noticed my voice or someone else's voice changed pitch. One time was... _____

_____

_____

_____

_____

_____

There are ethnic or religious differences in people I am repulsed by. Some of these are... _____

_____

_____

_____

_____

_____

Occasionally a person leaves me extremely irritable and I go on and on and on about them to others. One example of this was... _____

_____

_____

_____

_____

_____

NOTES PART ONE:

CW - The Collected Works of C.G. Jung (hereafter denoted as CW)

1) C.G. Jung, CW 9 - Pt. 2 - *AION, Research into the Phenomenology of the Self,* Princeton University Press, Bollingen, 1959, par 126, pg 71

2) C.G. Jung, CW 9 - Pt. 1 - *The Archetypes and the Collective Unconscious, The Concept of the Collective Unconscious,* Princeton University Press, Bollingen, 1959, par 99, pg 48

3) C.G. Jung, *Memories, Dreams, Reflections,* (MDR) New York Pantheon, 1961, pg 161

4) C.G. Jung, CW 11 - *Psychology and Religion: West and East,* Princeton University Press, Bollingen, 1958, par 146, pg 89

5) Liz Greene & Howard Sasportas, *Dynamics of the Unconscious,* Samuel Weiser, Inc., 1988, pg 260

6) C.G. Jung, CW 18 - The Symbolic Life, Moser: *Spuk: Irrglaube Oder Wahrglaube?* Princeton University Press, Bollingen, 1950, par 759, pg 318

7) Edited by Joseph Campbell, *The Portable Jung, Marriage as a Psychological Relationship,* Penguin Books, 1971, pg 167

8) Robert A. Johnson, *Owning Your Own Shadow,* Harper San Fransisco, 1991, pg 90

9) Hermes Trismegistus, *The Emerald Tablet,* an alchemical treastise

10) C.G. Jung, CW 16 - *The Practice of Psychotherapy, The Psychology of the Transference,* Princeton University Press, Bollingen, 1946, par 499, pg 289

11) C.G. Jung, CW 9 - Pt. 2 - *AION, Research into the Phenomenology of the Self,* Princeton University Press, Bollingen, 1959, par 17, pg 9

12) C.G. Jung, CW 9 - Pt. 2 - *AION, Research into the Phenomenology of the Self,* Princeton University Press; Bollingen, 1959, par 15, pg 8

13) Liz Greene & Howard Sasportas, *Dynamics of the Unconscious,* Samuel Weiser, Inc., 1988, pg 267

14) C.G. Jung, CW 9 - Pt. 2 - *AION, Research into the Phenomenology of the Self,* Princeton University Press, Bollingen, 1959, par 14, pg 8

15) C.G. Jung, CW 10 - *Civilization in Transition, The Undiscovered Self (Present and Future),* Princeton University Press, Bollingen, 1960, par 572, pg 296

16) C.G. Jung, CW 9 - Pt. 1 - *The Archetypes and the Collective Unconscious, Conscious, Unconscious and Individuation,* Princeton University Press; Bollingen, 1959, par 513, pg 284

17) Marion Woodman, Cassette tape recorded live, *Holding the Tension Between the Opposites,* Sounds True, 1991

18) C.G. Jung, CW 16 - *The Practice of Psychotherapy,The Psychology of the Transference,* Princeton University Press, Bollingen, 1946, par 397, pg 196

19) Daryl Sharp, *Digesting Jung, Food for the Journey,* Inner City Books, Toronto, Ontario, Canada, 2001, pg 11

20) Edited by Connie Zwieg and Jeremiah Abrams, *Meeting the Shadow, The Hidden Power of the Dark Side of Human Nature,* Jeremy P. Tarcher, Inc., 1991, pg 272

21) Edited by Connie Zwieg and Jeremiah Abrams, *Meeting the Shadow, The Hidden Power of the Dark Side of Human Nature,* Ken Wilber, *Taking Responsibility for Your Shadow,* Jeremy P. Tarcher, Inc., 1991, pg 274

22) Edward C. Whitmont, *The Symbolic Quest,* Princeton University Press, NJ, 1991, pg 60

23) C.G. Jung, *Two Essays in Analytical Psychology,* Meridian Books, NY, 1953, pg 82

24) C.G. Jung, CW 9 - Pt. 2 - *AION, Research into the Phenomenology of the Self,* Princeton University Press; Bollingen, 1959, par 124, pg 69

25) C.G. Jung, CW 9 - Pt. 2 - *AION, Research into the Phenomenology of the Self,* Princeton University Press; Bollingen, 1959, par 123, pg 69

26) Edward C. Whitmont, *The Symbolic Quest,* Princeton University Press, Princeton, NJ, 91, pg 168

27) C.G. Jung, CW 18 - *The Symbolic Life, Analytical Psychology: Its Theory and Practice, The Tavistock Lectures,* Princeton University Press, Bollingen, 1935, par 298, pg 133

28) C.G. Jung, *Two Essays in Analytical Psychology,* Meridian Books, NY, 1953, par 309, pg 193

29) Robert A. Johnson, cassettte, *Your Shadow, Friend or Foe,* Sounds True, Louisville, CO, 1992

30) John A. Sanford, *Evil, the Shadow Side of Reality,* Chapter 6, Crossroad Publishing Company, NY 1982, pg 67-84

31) John A. Sanford, *Evil, the Shadow Side of Reality,* Chapter 6, Crossroad Publishing Company, NY 1982, pg 69

32) Interpretation by Harold Bloom, *The Gospel of Thomas, The Hidden Sayings of Jesus,* Harper, San Fransisco, 1992, no. 70, pg 53

33) C.G. Jung, CW 10 - *Civilization in Transition, The Undiscovered Self (Present and Future),* Princeton University Press, Bollingen, 1957, par 491, pg 249

34) Edward C. Whitmont, *The Symbolic Quest,* Princeton University Press, Princeton, NJ, 1991, pg 162

35) C.G. Jung, *Memories, Dreams, Reflections,* (MDR) New York Pantheon, 1961, pg 3

36) Rev. J. Pittman McGehee, cassette, *The Paradox of Relationships,* Broadacres Center, Houston, TX, 1999

37) C.G. Jung, CW 16 - *The Practice of Psychotherapy, The Psychology of the Transference,* 1946, Princeton University Press, Bollingen, 1954, par 454, pg 243

38) C.G. Jung, CW 18 - The Symbolic Life, *Analytical Psychology: Its Theory and Practice, The Tavistock Lectures,* Princeton University Press, Bollingen, 1935, par 270, pg 123

Our Parents, Our Partners and Our 7th House

Planetary aspects also can have as much to do with the Shadow as the
sort of people that fascinate you among the opposite sex. Points in the chart
such as the descendant [the 7th House] and the IC [the nadir or bottom point]
also have a great deal to do with what falls into Shadow in the personality.[1]

LIZ GREENE

This is how it all starts. Our parents have affected us deeply. They
are in us and will give us clues as to what parts got delegated to the
Shadow. Usually, we make a statement to ourselves that goes like
this — "I will never be like them."

Our Parents

The parent we couldn't stand the most is the one who's more dominant in the unconscious. The other parent will be more acceptable because we can identify with them, but
even parts of that parent will go into the unconscious as well. In order to explain this
fully, I have to tell you my own story and those of a few others who have shared their
stories with me.

In most families one parent will take "the good one" role and the other parent will
be "the bad one." What happens (and this is very common in marriages and even in
some of our close friendships) is that there is an unconscious collusion between the two
people. Both parties enter into an unconscious agreement that goes something like this:
"I'll be your good side if you'll be my bad side. I'll be the strong one if you'll be the weak
one. I'll be the responsible partner, if you'll carry all the carefree and playful parts so
I can see you as irresponsible, etc." Partners polarize and take either opposite of any
extreme. A nursery rhyme expresses this idea really well:

Jack Sprat could eat no fat. His wife could eat no lean.

It's truly amazing how unconscious this is. This unconscious collusion gets set up at the
very beginning and usually comes down the pike from one generation to the next. We
inherit this dance from our parents just as they inherited it from theirs.

My Parents' Dance

When I was growing up, it was easy to see that my dad was the bad one and my mom
was the good one. My dad, being a Leo, was very Leonine. He was very self-centered and
egotistical, domineering and bossy. At the same time, he was all the positive Leo traits as
well. He was entertaining, magnanimous and idealistic. My mom is a Scorpio. She was
his polar opposite, very quiet, kind and gentle. She would give the shirt off her back to

Notes to Myself:

_____

_____

_____

_____

_____

_____

_____

_____

_____

_____

_____

_____

_____

_____

anyone, but she was very much a martyr and complainer. She would acquiesce to whatever it was that my dad wanted. Still, she was the good one as far as I was concerned, and he was the bad one.

Until I studied astrology, I was unable to recognize my mom's dark side. By reading about Scorpios, I was able to see how sometimes she would manipulate my dad into being the bad one. She would do things covertly to irritate him so that he would get really angry with her. For instance, he would say, "Don't do this or that." Then, she would do whatever it was that irritated him anyway and often. Finally, he would just start screaming at her and be totally out of control. Then she could say to us, "See how he is?" and we would all agree. Yes, he is so awful. True to her Scorpio nature, she was also very secretive and very emotional. Her feelings would get deeply hurt by his domineering, brusque behavior, so she would do these things to get even with him.

My mom was also very identified with how good she was. Much later as an adult, I realized they were both very much the same in many ways. They appeared to be very different from each other because they were so polarized. I was lucky that they both knew their time of birth and I was able to do a chart on both of them. That told me a lot about how they had split up the energy. I'll explain more about their astrology later when I explain planets in the 7th house.

Shared Unconscious Collusion

If only my mom could have seen that she, too, was self-centered, that she, too, was domineering. She just wasn't doing it overtly; she was doing it covertly. If she could have seen this and been willing to live some of this energy out openly, then my dad would have had to back off. They wouldn't have been so polarized into two huge extremes. Vice versa, if my dad had been more into his loving and kind nature and less self-centered, then the same is also true. To be fair to my mom, my dad was hell on wheels and she lived in a time when women of our culture, as I am Mexican-American, did not assert themselves as easily. Confronting him would have been a very difficult thing for my mom to do. All she knew was to submit to his domination because she was dependent. She had six children she had to take into consideration and was unwilling, I later found out, to grow up and fend for herself. I was raised Catholic. I remember my dad telling us, "I'm the devil and your mom's an angel, and I don't know how she puts up with me. I just hope God takes me to heaven." He was very identified with being the darker half.

It was very interesting for me to see that when I got married, I repeated this in my own marriage. One of us took "the good one role" and one of us took "the bad one role." We were so totally unconscious that we were repeating their contract, their unconscious collusion. We marry our parents, and our unfinished business with our parents gets projected onto our partners. They have to live out the parts of us that we cannot own in ourselves that gave us a huge charge with our parents. Our partners reactivate these old wounds.

Jung says it is not the conscious mind that falls in love; it is the unconscious that makes this decision. You know it's highly unconscious because it just randomly happens to us. We don't choose to fall in love. Until we get older and wiser, we will only be attracted to and fascinated by people who can fulfill this task with us. We will disregard anyone who does not meet our unconscious needs. It's truly remarkable how this happens to everyone over and over. It's energy.

This is the dance of opposites I call a Shadow dance. As Jung says, these opposites are forever seeking each other out. Most people aren't aware of this psychological dynamic that gets activated unconsciously. They need each other to do this dance; otherwise they would have to be BOTH the light and the dark sides. Then there would be no one to blame. Keep in mind when I say "dark," I mean what is hidden from awareness in our personal unconscious. This is not to be confused with archetypal evil, which is not the subject of this book. It is almost impossible to do this process alone. We need a partner and a partner of the opposite sex, or at least a very close friend to dance with to see our opposite side and begin this process of taking back our projections. Like most of us, my parents were not aware that the opposite existed within them.

After I learned this information, and as I learned more and more about astrology, I stopped taking sides in their relationship quarrels and informed my sisters and brother of what I was observing in my parents' behavior. I could also see that I was a lot like my dad. Although his faults were obvious, I still admired him for his strengths and could identify with many parts of his character. All five of my siblings exhibit character traits of our parents. Some favor Mom more or Dad more, but we all have both of them in us. Our astrology has a common thread of the signs of Leo and Scorpio prominent in all of our charts as well as other dominant signs, as no one is just one particular archetype. Several signs will be a factor in seeing a person's character. Your astrology is not limited to your particular sun sign.

Every sign of the zodiac has its positive and negative qualities. My dad was also popular, humorous and loved to tell us jokes and make us laugh. He was a typical outgoing, larger-than-life Leo character. Sometimes he was outspoken in the community and would write letters to whomever he had an issue with. You never knew

Jung says it is not the conscious mind that falls in love, it is the the unconscious that makes this decision.

Notes to Myself:

_____

_____

_____

_____

_____

_____

_____

_____

_____

_____

_____

_____

_____

_____

Notes to Myself:

_____

_____

_____

_____

_____

_____

_____

_____

_____

_____

_____

_____

_____

_____

when he might be on television expressing his views about problems with the city streets or whatever he was unhappy about. Leos have strong ideals, and politics is a strong part of their forte. We all admired his courage to fight for what he believed in. I am also truly grateful that, before my father passed away, I was able to see a really kind and compassionate side of him. When I was growing up, all I saw in my parents' relationship to each other was how horrible my dad was because of the intense polarization going on. So many people see only the opposites in their parents, not realizing both are actually a lot alike. The opposite dynamics of either may also closely resemble our own marriages or business partnerships. Jung says, "So long as a positive or negative resemblance to the parents is the deciding factor in a love choice, the release from the parental imago, and hence from childhood, is not complete."[2] Of course, we don't consciously know that this is what is happening to us, but it is. We marry our parents and their issues.

In my early thirties, I took a two-weekend course called "Life Training." In this seminar, the realization became clear to me that my ex-husband and I had repeated my parents' marriage. I literally wanted to throw up. I physically felt a revulsion in my body. I almost didn't go back to the second weekend of the course, as it was so hard to face this fact, but my best friend talked me into continuing. As painful as it was, it was worth it. When we feel something emotionally and physically, we have truly become conscious of it. Otherwise it will not affect us. Jung says, "In psychology one possesses nothing unless one has experienced it in reality."[3]

As the Bible says, the sins of the father are passed on to the children up to seven generations. What is conscious in one parent will be unconscious in the other and vice versa. They are two people carrying the same complex. If these complexes are not passed down to the conscious part of the psyche, then they will be in the unconscious. Often a child's Shadow is formed from these split-off parental parts. Jung says that children are highly susceptible to picking up and living their parents' unlived lives, their opposites. In fact, he says we will be driven by their unlived lives. Looking at our parents and their relationship to each other, and to us, is the first step in getting clear on our relationship patterns.

A Natural Cross

Diagram 1 shows the houses of an astrological birth chart. Notice the relationship involved between Self and Other/Marriage Partner and Mother and Father. It's a natural cross that we all have to experience as part of being alive. Our relationship to our parents and to our marriage partner is a veritable cross, a crucifixion. This cross creates a tension in our psyches as we are striving to know ourselves,

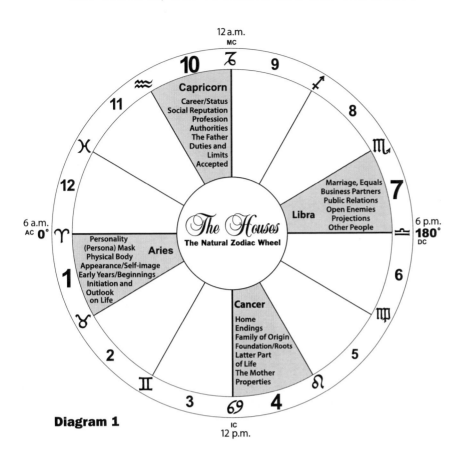

Diagram 1

*Our partners inevitably
are unconsciously
chosen in order to
show us our missing
parts.*

Notes to Myself:

and knowing ourselves is each individual's responsibility. Our partners inevitably are unconsciously chosen in order to show us our missing parts. Becoming conscious of each aspect of this cross within ourselves gives us clues as to what parts of us are being projected onto our partners.

When I first learned this information, I was immediately impressed by its accuracy. Not only did my marriage and business partners have the energy described by my marriage house, but every person I had a lasting relationship with after that also contained energies of the sign on my 7th-house cusp.

Inside Us or Outside of Us, It Is All the Same — a Reflection *Par Excellence.*

This is where I would like to introduce the meaning of the astrological 7th house. It is considered to be the marriage house, and it is also called the house of open enemies, i.e., the Shadow in us all. It is directly opposite the 1st-house, which is our persona or our mask. We also call this 1st-house cusp the rising sign, as that is the sign at 6:00 a.m. of our birth when the sun was rising. The 7th-house cusp is exactly 180° opposite at 6:00 p.m.

The 7th-house shows us who we are and what we can expect when we are in relationships. It also shows us what the character traits are of people who so fascinate us when we meet them that we

Our partners become our enemies when we don't see and own our Shadow.

fall in love with them. Whatever planets and signs fall in the 7th house, or the ruler of this house, will be ripe for projection. This is the house of the "Other," and therefore the most foreign to us. This "Other" is our own contrasexual side. It will also describe the nature of business partners, because any legal contract for partnership comes under its domain.

The symbols in the 7th house will clearly show us what we are required in this lifetime to integrate *in ourselves* if we want to be in a healthy, committed relationship. Here is where the trouble begins, because it is a very misunderstood house (area) within the psyches of all of us. Most of us are used to finding our partners "out there somewhere" instead of looking inside ourselves. Our partners become our enemies when we don't see and own our Shadow.

Now, I don't expect you to follow the next few paragraphs completely if you are not well versed in astrology, but bear with me as I explain it to those who are. You will see that you can read the rest of this workbook and still benefit whether you know astrology or not. It offers such a good description of how people split up energy that I have to include it here at the beginning of this chapter. Later you can see exactly how this plays out for you and your significant other and how you can also do this for yourself when you have your own chart and your partner's chart in front of you.

My mother, although a double Scorpio (Sun and Moon), had two planets, Jupiter and Neptune, in Leo in the 7th house. In their synastry (which is an astrological term that describes putting two peoples' planets together), my father's Leo Sun was tenanted in mom's marriage house. My dad had Scorpio rising, so her Sun and Moon closely conjuncted his rising sign, which is directly opposite his 7th-house cusp. These are very common conjunctions or oppositions for those who get married. In his book called *Synchronicity,* Jung uses as an example a study of the astrology of marriage partners. Astrologically this shows up as conjunctions and oppositions to their Sun, Moon and Venus or Ascendant (1st house - rising sign), or the Descendant (7th house) axis. A conjunction which is 0° means that the two planets or angles are united within an eight- to 10-degree orb of each other. An opposition is 180°.

This symbolically shows how we project ourselves onto our partners. As I described them earlier, my mom had Leo energy in her own archetypal structure in her 7th house, and my dad was chosen unconsciously from the very beginning to carry this archetype of Leo for both of them. We are all the most disassociated from our 7th-house energies. He had Scorpio energy in him, and she was carrying this mysterious, secretive, manipulative part of him. The truth was they were a lot alike, although they split up the energy between them as most couples do. You can see this happening over and over

Notes to Myself:

when you look at the charts of those who are married. One person is one part of their energy, and the other one carries the opposite pole. This is precisely why I am writing this book, to help the general public understand how valuable this information is. If you can talk about this information openly with your partner, then you can help each other do Shadow work together.

My parents also had Neptune as a symbol of relationship, with mom having Neptune in the 7th house. My dad had a close conjunction of Venus and Neptune in Cancer that synastrically was situated in Mom's marriage house as well. Out of six children, five of us have Neptune aspects to the Moon and Venus. There we are fated to continue the patterns that have come before us. In Part 3 this will become more concrete and applicable to your own chart where I describe each planet in the 7th or in aspect to Venus. For now, I want to continue describing what this all means. Our astrology will show us that these predisposed archetypal contents come down the pike like our genetic structure, only it's our psychological predisposed patterns and archetypes we have inherited.

The Story Repeats

Patricia (Trish) was a very good friend of mine as well as one of my best clients. We had worked together on creative advertising projects for six years. We worked extremely well together, and I was really excited when she left her company and came to join me in my graphic design business. Then something amazing started to happen. Within six months after she joined me, my experience of her was that she was exactly like my ex-husband! We quickly found out that there is a real difference between just being friends with somebody, or even client and customer, and actually working with them day in and day out. Having a business partner is a lot like being married. What started happening was the same exact thing that had happened with my ex-husband, but this time it was more conscious, so we were able to see it and talk about it.

Trish was passive and introverted, and I was aggressive and extroverted. Our opposites were activated by our partnership. I had owned my own business since I was 24, and I wasn't used to compromising with anyone. I was bossy and dominating like my dad, and I knew exactly how I wanted things done. She would get angry with me and not be able to express her anger, so she would get even with me. She would do the same things my ex-husband would do, the same things my mom would do that would irritate my dad. It was remarkable. The big difference was that she had been studying Jungian psychology and astrology right along with me, so she was open to looking at us and our behavior. One day I sat her down at the table, as it was becoming more and more obvious to me what

Then something amazing started to happen. Within six months after she joined me, my experience of her was that she was exactly like my ex-husband!

Notes to Myself:

_____

_____

_____

_____

_____

_____

_____

_____

_____

_____

_____

_____

_____

_____

So we made a commitment, which is the essential container that is needed to do this kind of Shadow work.

Notes to Myself:

we were doing. I said to her, "We're polarizing here, and I don't want to do this. I want this to work. I want you to express your views. I want your input and your creativity. Otherwise, we're not going to do anything different here. I am committed to our partnership. I really believe we work well together. I need and welcome your input. If you're angry with me, or you don't agree with me about something and you can't say it, then please write it down. I am willing to listen. I am willing to negotiate whatever we're doing that you don't like, but if you don't communicate with me, then how will I know what is upsetting you?"

I created a safe space for her to open up and share her thoughts and needs. In time, Trish stopped being passive-aggressive. She started to be more assertive. I also told her, "You're stuck with me. I am committed to this working. I don't care what side of you comes out. I am not going to walk away." She agreed and said she felt the same way. So we made a commitment, which is the essential container that is needed to do this kind of Shadow work.

All of her childhood, Trish was not allowed to get angry or express her true feelings. Her mother was a Leo — believe it or not — just like my dad, ***born on the same day, the same year!*** When we found that out, we marveled at the Universe and the synchronicity of how we came into each other's space. Synchronicity is another of Jung's concepts that explain events that are not cause and effect. Astrology is a synchronistic model that clearly explains how life situations that are similar in meaning will be attracted or will correspond to one another. The way Trish internalized that dominant Leo mom was to tell herself, "I will just be real quiet and do whatever I want to do, but I'm not going to say anything." With Aquarius rising and Venus in Pisces in the 1st house, her outer persona or mask was by nature gentle and soft-spoken, therefore more introverted. With Leo rising, I was more identified with my Sun-in-Leo father. As the Leo archetype was strong in my own character, I was the opposite. Trish and I actually had the same unconscious collusion going on with us, the exact same energy pattern that our parents did.

Jung explains that the parental imagos will demand integration. They are in us: BOTH PARENTS. Because we refused to be anything like our parents (in my case my mom, and in her case her mom), we came into each other's energy fields. Through our relationship, we constellated what Jung would call a mother complex. The universe that we live in is amazing. Even quantum physics is beginning to see the correspondences that are synchronistic in their occurrence. Astrology is a language of synchronicity like no other. The astrological birth chart shows us that what is inside us shows up in our outer-world experience. Whatever sign is on the descendent or

7th-house cusp, whatever planets reside therein are a detailed picture of what we will develop in this lifetime **with or without our intention or consent.** So we might as well learn about this part of us and make a decision to develop it. Then we can experience the more productive aspects of that particular energy.

I hear people with Mars (planet of action, male principle, directedness) in the 7th or ruler of the 7th telling me over and over again how violent their ex-husbands were, how they have constantly attracted aggressive or angry partners. People with the Moon there tell me how needy and engulfing their partners are, how dependent. Uranus … how unpredictable, detached and aloof. Saturn … how cold, unresponsive, limiting and critical. Jupiter … how opinionated, inflated, self-indulgent. These are brief, simplistic descriptions of projection. Again, Part 3 will provide a more detailed picture of these archetypes.

Knowing your 7th-house planets, the aspects to your Venus, and the ruler will give you a very clear understanding of what your own needs are in relationships. These can be different from everyone else's. We are all unique. Don't feel something is wrong with you if you throw out the cultural model of the white picket fence and the two-car garage. That may not be what your soul is requiring in this lifetime. Stop feeling guilty if you aren't creating it. What you have is what you wanted on a soul level. As Glenn Perry, Ph.D., puts it, "Who you're with is where you're at." Know that, and then you can make it livable.

Coming to the Middle

I have Aquarius as the sign ruling my 7th-house cusp. Trish is an Aquarian. My ex-husband had the Moon in Aquarius at the exact degree of my marriage-house cusp. Trish had Leo ruling her 7th, and my South Node-Pluto in Leo conjunction closely conjuncted her 7th-house cusp. The symbols were very telling. What ended up happening between Trish and I was that, in time, we actually became more like each other. We consciously worked together to create a very loving and happy relationship. She learned to express herself more assertively and take charge as she became more and more like me. I also became more and more like her. I needed to learn to be more receptive and let others help me by contributing their views instead of taking over all the time. We were both able to come to the middle and be a little bit more like each other instead of two huge, polarized extremes. We talked about our relationship, and **we helped each other with love, not with criticism.** We had a lot in common, and we liked each other, so we were compatible in many ways. We were willing to communicate about everything. Both partners have to be willing to come to the middle,

Knowing your 7th house planets, the aspects to your Venus, and the ruler will give you a very clear understanding of what your own needs are in relationships.

Notes to Myself:

_____

_____

_____

_____

_____

_____

_____

_____

_____

_____

_____

_____

_____

Chances are this is where we are lopsided in our character, and we need to learn how to do precisely what they are doing if we want to grow. Come halfway.

and no one can be doing an extreme anymore. Shadow dancing with our partners requires honest, authentic communication, trust and a commitment to the relationship.

Whatever it is that a person in our life is doing that we do not like, we need to learn to welcome the part of ourself that they are showing us. Chances are this is where we are lopsided in our character, and we need to learn how to do precisely what they are doing if we want to grow. Come halfway. The unconscious has brought this perfect person to us to irritate us into our own wholeness. Unless we are willing to see it, it will repeat. If we don't want to see it, it gets stronger and stronger, more and more painful.

To demonstrate this, let me tell a part of our story. There were many times when Trish and I were involved in a business situation where things were going wrong, and we were not being dealt with fairly. I would be very brusque and demanding as my Dad would be. Then we would get our way or a resolution to the problem. At that time, it was the only way I knew to be. She taught me that you could still assert yourself and be more tactful. She taught me that I didn't have to cut people's heads off. I taught her that she didn't have to passively sit by when someone was taking advantage of her. She learned to stand up for herself instead of ignoring things until they got huge so that she'd either leave or explode in rage. This is a lifelong challenge for both of us because our natural energy is to do the opposite. It takes work and consciousness to realize these things and then make the effort to change. More than anything else, it takes really vulnerable communication. That can only happen when two people have established trust and commitment to the process. They both know and acknowledge why they are together.

The more I came to the middle with Trish, the more she was able to come to the middle with me. Being around her helped me to work on developing that side of me. I needed her so that I could be more of myself. We needed each other as most couples do, if they can see the valuable mystery behind their meeting.

After five years, Trish left our business partnership. She found out about her own courage and independence — which she at first saw only in me — and started a dog kennel, her lifelong dream. During some of the build-out process of her kennel, she had to assert herself forcefully. She would say to me, "You wouldn't believe these people. They say they are going to do something, and they don't do it until I get really upset and yell at them." She watched me do that — sometimes.

Now we laugh about it when we share what is going on with us. I tell her, "Trish, you're beginning to behave just like me." When we started the process of taking back what each other was carrying, we stopped polarizing. We got along beautifully because we were making an effort to stay in balance. No one was a huge extreme anymore, which is so divisive. Our energy fit really well together as we had many similar values, likes and dislikes. We are both air signs, her being Aquarius, myself Libra, so communication was essential to our natural way of being. The Air signs in the zodiac are mental in their orientation toward life. We would talk everything over and really enjoy this about each other. Our relationship could have ended in disaster. My relationship with her taught me that this material of Jung's was powerful.

We've all been in a situation with a partner where we look at the other person and feel "I don't want to be around you anymore." This is called marriage and divorce and marriage and divorce again. Trish and I could have walked away had we not been willing to work consciously together. It definitely takes two to make or break a relationship. One person cannot do all the work. How many times have we walked out of people's lives because we don't want to be anything like them? We cut them out of our life, and we condemn them as inappropriate. We judge them and their way of being. In many situations, we are just like them in the unconscious; we just don't know it, or else they are what we actually need to be. They are having to carry our unlived life. Precisely because we are unaware of how badly we need that part of us, *we can provoke them into the behavior we are also repelled by.* There is always an unconscious collusion going on between partners.

Trish and I continued to have situations we didn't agree on. It wasn't always easy between us, but in time we learned to accept our differences and compromise. We learned to accept the unacceptable, and we became tolerant of each other's idiosyncrasies.

Until Trish joined me, I realized that I had never loved anyone. I only loved people if they did what I wanted them to do, when I wanted them to do it, the way I wanted them to do it. If they didn't do it that way, my way, I didn't love them. What I found out from being around her and having to accept another person who had a totally different view and a different way of doing things was that I could love someone completely. I was learning what it is really about to relate — to truly accept another and really love. There were so many things we had in common that it really was wonderful, but there were a lot of things we didn't. I just came to accept her, and she accepted me. We were both committed to our friendship. I remember that when we started this process, I felt a huge aversion to some of the things she would do, but I was determined that I would accept her. So whenever she did anything I didn't particularly like, I would say to myself, "And she is this and this and this also." I would focus on the good about her. No doubt, she had to do the same about me.

In many situations, we are just like them in the unconscious; we just don't know it, or else they are what we actually need to be.

Notes to Myself:

79

*The people we are ex-
tremely attracted to are
the parts of ourselves
that we are missing. The
curious thing is that we
can be repulsed by and
attracted to the very
same person.*

I cannot overemphasize the strong bond that can occur when you are with somebody you are totally committed to. If you can find just one other person that you can be committed to and allow all of yourself to be there, not just put on your good side, a healing takes place in both people. If you can be accepted for all of yourself and accept them completely, you will heal a lot of the emotional baggage we all carry from our early parental complexes.

Projection and Differentiation

A couple came to me for an astrological reading. They wanted to know "Is this the person for me? What is our compatibility?" These two people were in their mid- to late 30s, and had both been married before. I asked them each this question: "Are you the person for you?" Yes, I know it sounded strange, but this is the real question at the bottom of relationship struggles that we need to ask ourselves.

The people we are extremely attracted to are the parts of ourselves that we are missing. The curious thing is that we can be repulsed by and attracted to the very same person. When we have a feeling that we are "in love," when we have that kind of fascination or compulsion toward an individual (and this applies whether we are gay, straight or whatever), it's a real clue that it is a projection of our own unconscious contents. There will be an almost erotic, magnetic feeling within us when we meet someone who can carry the projection of our Shadow, our "Anima" or "Animus," as described in Jung's analytical psychology.

Eventually, (and this has to occur for our own psychological growth), all couples will begin to polarize and find fault with each other, and a crisis (which is also a turning point in the relationship) will occur. The relationship will start to deteriorate so that they can differentiate. At first, it is quite compelling. We are compulsive about the person and obsessed when we are in this state, which Lévi Bruhl called *participation mystique*. No amount of logical reasoning can talk us out of it. Edward Edinger explains,

> To the extent that the opposites remain unconscious and unseparated, one lives in a state of participation mystique, which means that one identifies with one side of a pair of opposites and projects its contrary as enemy. Space for consciousness to exist appears between the opposites, which means one becomes conscious as one is able to contain and endure the opposites within.[4]

Jung says,

> To put it briefly, it means a state of identity in mutual unconsciousness. Perhaps I should explain this further. If the same unconscious complex is constellated in two

Notes to Myself:

people at the same time, it produces a remarkable emotional effect, a projection, which causes either a mutual attraction or a mutual repulsion.[5]

The Shadow Is In Us All.

This is why the ancients believed the 7th house was also the house of open enemies, because the partner becomes the enemy we polarize with. At first, all is wonderful. You feel you have met your true "soul mate." You think, "I have known you forever." Well, yes, because you are projecting aspects of yourself onto the other person. That's why at first they seem to be so familiar to you.

We will generally not be able to see and accept our Shadow until we actively dislike something in another person, one or both of our parents, our siblings or when we fall in love — which is another very strong case of projection, *or transference,* as it is called in psychological counseling. This transference can also occur between teacher and student or doctor and patient. Because it can wake us up and help us see many things differently, what we call "falling in love" can also be a very transformative and wonderful experience. Let us now talk about the phenomenon of falling in love from a Jungian perspective.

Falling in Love = *Participation Mystique*

There is something very magical about the experience of falling in love. Psychologically it is their feeling function (the Water element) that gets activated when two lovers first meet. Emotions burst forth, and sparks fly that ignite a passion and an unmistakable bliss. When you are with the beloved, you are "in heaven," so to speak. When you are away from them, you are longing for the next encounter and there is a poignant angst that replaces ordinary consciousness. As the song says, "Suddenly life has new meaning to me," and they are transported into the realms of the Gods (the archetypes). In Western culture, our movies provide us plenty of examples of this experience — so much so that we all yearn for it.

We mistakenly call this love, and many find themselves searching for their other half, their "soul mate." We believe that this is what will complete us and that this magic is what we feel we must have in order for us to truly value another person. As you will see when you understand the nature of the Anima and Animus, this is only the beginning of an encounter with our unconscious. It's interesting that the word "soul" also means psyche. Jung explains this phenomenon of projecting our Anima and Animus (the contrasexual soul images in our unconscious) onto each other. The psyche seeks wholeness, and a union of our inner opposites is what Jung

As you will see when you understand the nature of the Anima and Animus, this is only the beginning of an encounter with our unconscious.

Notes to Myself:

_____

_____

_____

_____

_____

_____

_____

_____

_____

_____

_____

_____

_____

Logically the opposite of love is hate, and of Eros, Phobos, (fear); but psychologically it is the will to power. Where love reigns, there is no will to power; and where the will to power is paramount, love is lacking. The one is but the shadow of the other.[6]

CARL GUSTAV JUNG

Notes to Myself:

called the process of individuation. The Anima desires eros, and the Animus desires reflection.

The Alchemists called this the archetype of the *coniunctio*. The Greeks called it a *hierosgamos*, the inner marriage taking place within each person, whether we know it or not. When projection occurs, this alchemical process has begun, as these contrasexual images within us are now out in the open. We will learn a lot about ourselves through the people we either extremely love or hate.

> *The factors which come together*
> *in the coniunctio are conceived as opposites,*
> *either confronting one another in enmity*
> *or attracting one another in love.*[7]

CARL GUSTAV JUNG

At the beginning of any relationship between lovers there is a lot of projection going on. We all see mainly what we want to see. There is a kind of veil of illusion that places itself between us and the person carrying our projection. Many times we fall in love and get involved in some very unsuitable, destructive and soul-destroying relationships, but these, too, are showing us aspects of our Shadow or undeveloped "eros" function. The word *eros* means the capacity to relate, to connect or create.

In order to grow and be a whole person, we need to become aware of what is really happening to us. When someone is "into us" (as one relationship book on the market calls it), we need to ask ourselves, is it love or is it just projection? Two people won't really know until a period of time has given them a chance to see who each other actually is. This requires self-honesty and self-disclosure. There is no other way to see these parts of us. It's inevitable that they will be projected. The intoxication and the intensity of the experience are clues that we are into a projection. Ordinary human beings do not evoke the instant passion that "love at first sight" evokes.

The Anima and Animus

A woman carries an archetypal image of her male counterpart made up largely of her history with her father, as he is the first male in her life. The image is also shaped by brothers and any early experiences with men. This inner masculine, the Animus, helps her to achieve her goals, gives her greater intellectual clarity, helps her have clearer boundaries and becomes a mediator between her ego and her unconscious. This unconscious inner male is her God (soul) image that gets projected onto a man in the outer world. As inner and outer create a mirroring effect, she will know a lot about what shape her inner partner is in by the person upon whom the projection lands. This can be a real eye-opener if the woman is willing or ready to see her own Shadow or Animus.

The clue to knowing a projection has occurred is the peculiar feeling of intense fascination or obsession with a man whom she will feel is her ideal mate. He, of course, unless he has a huge ego and enjoys the power that he now has over her, will feel as if something sticky and uncomfortable is smothering him. He will make comments to her like "You don't know me. You put me on a pedestal, and I'm not like that." His perception is a correct and valid one. Because of the veil or illusion that is placed on the man when there is a projection, at first she doesn't know him at all until they spend more time together. What she is seeing at first is only a reflection of her Shadow or her Animus — as the two can become contaminated with each other.

According to Jung, a man faces a similar dilemma. When a man projects his perfect God (soul) image onto a woman, she becomes the carrier of his Anima. She is seen as desirable and as the prize he must conquer and win. The woman he is fascinated with is in reality mirroring qualities to him that he is unaware of in himself. This can distort his perception of the real woman in his life.

Two people won't really know until a period of time has given them a chance to see who each other actually is. This requires self-honesty and self-disclosure.

Notes to Myself:

83

Woman stands just where the man's shadow falls, so that he is only too liable to confuse the two. Then, when he tries to repair this misunderstanding, he overvalues her and believes her the most desirable thing in the world.[8]

This is why the initial attraction is usually accompanied by strong erotic fantasy that will not leave him alone. It's this woman inside of him that is choosing who his partners will be. He has no choice in the matter because it is compulsive.

A man's Anima is comprised of his relationship to his mother, sisters, daughters, lovers and companions as well as the archetype of woman. In her proper place as part of his relationship to his inner feminine, his Anima will give him emotional sincerity and depth. Once he realizes this woman that he really needs is actually the feminine side of himself, he can consciously strive to know her by withdrawing his projections from the actual women in his life. He can get in touch with his feelings as they come up for him in his relationships. He will become more heart-centered. He can learn to express himself and acknowledge that he, too, has feelings. Then his Anima acts as a muse to bridge the gap between his inner and outer worlds. She animates him from within. She will show him his own need for soul growth, his spirituality and his ability to be creative.

When projection happens to both people at the same time, we call this "falling in love." They definitely fall. They fall into their own unconscious image as each projects part of himself or herself onto the other person (same sex or opposite sex), evoking a feeling of fantasy and Eros. The erotic and sexual nature of the encounter is psychologically quite symbolic. It is each one wanting to merge with or penetrate into themselves. In reality, this is an unconscious, narcissistic impulse and a distortion of reality. If either of them remains stuck in this kind of projection or *participation mystique* for too long, it can even be a deterrent to any real or authentic, long-term, loving relationship. Its primary importance for both people is that it generates movement toward the process of individuation. Our partners lead us to our own souls.

This is the real challenge for both males and females, recognizing our projections and what they actually want from us when they get activated. They may merely want us to get our life going again if we are stuck in a stagnant place in consciousness.

In the film called *Shall We Dance?* Richard Gere meets Jennifer Lopez, a beautiful dance instructor who has caught his Anima. In time — and time is of the essence to see what is going on — he is able to see that the reason his inner feminine has been projected is that he is bored and unhappy with himself. Instead of blaming his wife, Susan Sarandon, for this unhappiness, he takes dancing lessons which help him feel alive again. The Anima and Animus ani-

It's this woman inside of him that is choosing who his partners will be. He has no choice in the matter because it is compulsive.

Notes to Myself:

84

mate us and give us the energy to live our lives. Because they are archetypes, we can never really directly experience them, so we project them onto a suitable lover whom we then begin to idealize. Sometimes the beloved can become the devil personified when the relationship doesn't work out. We can then project our worse Shadow traits onto them. They can be demonized and devalued to the same degree that they were once worshiped. The degree that we "fall" for anyone will be the same degree to which we will feel let down once we begin to see them as a real person in need of a real human relationship. It's a difficult situation in this day and age of romantic illusion. We are brought up with Cinderella and Sleeping Beauty stories. The belief "someday my prince or princess will come" is part of the collective psyche. Movies like *Romeo and Juliet* and *Titanic* are examples of the modern myth in our culture that says this magical numinosity is what we should be experiencing. These fantasies in the collective get projected out every time we are fascinated by a potential partner. I say fascinated because "attracted" isn't the word for it. The fascination is what holds us like glue, where simple physical attraction is more subtle and not quite as intense. Jung says that in order for a fascination to take place, both people are involved. He says:

> A fascination of this kind is never exercised by one person upon another; it is always a phenomenon of relationships, which requires two people in so far as the person fascinated necessarily has a corresponding disposition. But the disposition must be unconscious or no fascination will take place. The fascination is a compulsive phenomenon in the sense that it lacks a conscious motive; it is not a process of will, but something that rises up from the unconscious and forcibly obtrudes itself upon the conscious mind.[9]

Just as with the Shadow, this fascination can also be experienced as repulsion. We can be simultaneously attracted and repulsed by the very same person if all of a sudden they say or do something we don't like. They can annoy us, and it's usually out of proportion to what they actually did, because they are carrying a projected Shadow part of us. Notice also that in both of these movies, *Titanic* and *Romeo and Juliet,* there is a death that occurs. This, too, is symbolic, as we have to go through the death or removal of our projections onto the "Other."

Withdrawing Our Projections Is Vitally Necessary.

As time goes on, it is inevitable that these projections are going to fall off. This can take two weeks or two years, but eventually it will happen. They have to so that we can see who the other person

The fascination is what holds us like glue, where simple physical attraction is more subtle and not quite as intense.

Notes to Myself:

Our Parents, Our Partners and Our 7th House

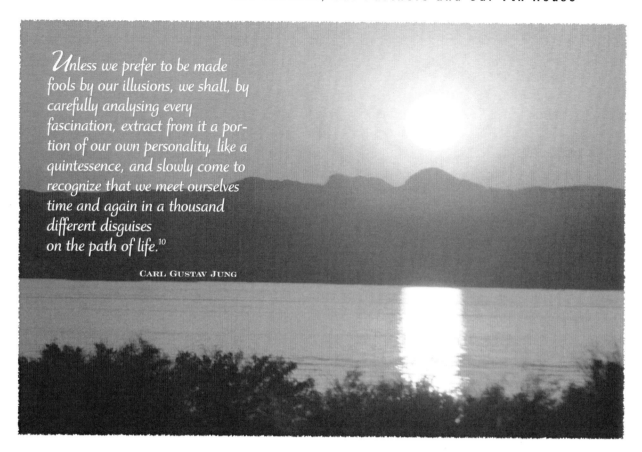

Unless we prefer to be made fools by our illusions, we shall, by carefully analysing every fascination, extract from it a portion of our own personality, like a quintessence, and slowly come to recognize that we meet ourselves time and again in a thousand different disguises on the path of life.[10]

CARL GUSTAV JUNG

actually is and start relating to a real person instead of a God or a Goddess (a symbiotic extension of oneself). Many times when a relationship reaches that stage of familiarity, people who are addicted to this kind of **high** start looking around outside their primary marriage or partnership if their maturity level is still in the *puella* or *puer aeternus* stage of consciousness. This is the archetype of Peter Pan, an adolescent eternal child who wants to be mirrored instead of related to the people in his life. Many relationships end at this stage and the alchemical process *(the coniunctio)* begins all over again with someone else. Yet, some go on to marry the person with whom they feel they are in love, and become disillusioned when they realize that they have married a person who is not who they thought they were. You will hear couples talk about how the "magic" is now gone from their relationship. They will make statements like "She's not the girl I married; she became someone else" or "He has changed." The truth is most people are unconscious of what has happened to them because they don't understand projection.

A commandment in the Bible says, "Thou shalt have no other Gods before me." When we "fall in love," we do exactly that. We place the person on a pedestal and worship them as if they are an extraordinary creature, God incarnate. We give all our power away and transfer to them our own God image. If we are with them long enough, we become disillusioned. We need to understand why. In Episcopalian priest and Jungian analyst John Sanford's book, *The Kingdom Within*, he says,

> The John and Mary who fall madly in love, which means they project on each other their own idealized images and feel the enormous pull of the opposites to unite, characteristically fall violently out of love again in a short time. This is no accident. In order for a conscious development to take place in such people, rather than their simply being immersed in the sea of unconscious love, it will be necessary that they recognize both their own individuality and the individuality of the other person. To do this, each must be driven apart from the other to facilitate this separation. Since the disappointment in each other now becomes very great, the earlier love easily turns to hate and disillusionment. Only if John and Mary can come to see the inner meaning of their relationship, and so bring it to a higher level of consciousness, can it hope to last.[11]

By inner meaning, he is talking about the withdrawal of projections and the assimilation of previously unconscious contents within the psyches of each person. Whenever we get close to anyone and really intimately spend quality time with them, we are going to see more of who they are. Sometime or another they will do something selfish, pushy, secretive, inconsiderate, sneaky, manipulative, coercive, bossy, whatever. Since these are all human characteristics and we are all human, we exhibit our humanity much more when we relax our guard by spending enough time around someone. Then we can reject them or they can reject us.

"You are not perfect" is the message we give and we get as it's never just one way. We do it to our mates or our potential mates, and they do it to us. Since none of us is perfect, we can't expect perfection in anyone else, either. Doing Shadow work allows both people to butt up against their rough edges and empathize. Putting ourself in their shoes when they do something that irritates or repulses us is the Libran way to get to the love. As my teacher Rev. McGehee says in his tape series called *On Becoming Married*,[12] what we really want most of all is to know someone and be known for who we really are, keeping in mind that at any given moment we are only seeing one part of their character and not the whole person.

Many people refuse to give up romantic delusions and do the work of making a relationship conscious. Even after they've married for the second or third time, they still think maybe the next one will be the perfect person for me. Others use their grievances against

Notes to Myself:

_____

_____

_____

_____

_____

_____

_____

_____

_____

_____

_____

_____

_____

The relationship will have to have a stronger foundation than chemistry for it to have a chance to make it. We have to like the person we love and enjoy them as a human being.

Notes to Myself:

_____

_____

_____

_____

_____

_____

_____

_____

_____

_____

_____

_____

_____

_____

_____

_____

each other to flee the tension they feel within themselves. They run away, believing they are leaving a set of circumstances in hopes of creating a better relationship elsewhere. It is only when we stop blaming our partners and look carefully at the mirror they represent, no matter how bleak, that we can change our patterns. This requires seeing our Shadow and their Shadow. Usually they will dovetail. We will have similar or complimentary opposites. Let's say, for example, they will be extroverted and outgoing and we will be introverted and a homebody who refuses to socialize. Another common example is one person is open, honest and vulnerable and the other is very shut down about sharing their feelings. Each person needs what the other has to become balanced.

Yet the romantic in us all dreams of a day when we will meet someone and it will be just like in the movies. They will be our Romeo or our Juliet. Initially, when we have this euphoric feeling of falling in love, there is a very strong erotic and lustful sexual attraction. We begin to have sexual fantasies about being with the person who evokes what we call chemistry. The unconscious pull toward a person can feel so intense that it's like a magnet. We desperately want to merge. It's compelling, fascinating, captivating and enchanting to meet someone who evokes our God image. The passion is unbelievable. These are the scenes of grasping and groping at one another sexually that we see in movies. We are frantically pulling the other person's clothes off. The real motivation behind this, or should I say underneath all of this, is the urge to unite with ourselves. When we go through it with another human being, we experience this as blissful and heavenly, but it is not the basis for a conscious relationship. It's only a short-term phenomenon. The relationship will have to have a stronger foundation than chemistry for it to have a chance to make it. We have to like the person we love and enjoy them as a human being. We have to have things in common we can share with each other. We'd stay their friend even if we couldn't be married to them. This is the kind of relationship that can last. Too many of those blissful, quick, instant marriages end in divorce.

I recently attended a wedding. I didn't know anyone at the reception except the bride's mother, so I stood alone. As everyone stood up to watch this young couple dance their first dance, I could almost feel the energy of sadness and hear the mind talk going on in the room. Why don't we have that kind of love for each other anymore? When will this kind of love happen to me? How lucky they are to have found each other. This is what I could silently hear and feel all around me. I thought that I was the only person in the room who probably thought the way I do. I went to the table I was assigned to and sat down. No one else who was supposed to be seated at that particular table came to the wedding. I thought this was rather symbolic. I got up to go get a glass of wine, and the young priest who had married the couple came over to speak to me. He asked me how I knew the couple, and at first we made some of the usual small talk as one does with strangers. Then I told him I thought that a wedding is only the beginning until the couple sees each other's Shadow. He said to me, "Wow! Are you into Jung? I've been reading a lot of his work lately, and I totally agree with you." I told him I was an astrologer and that I specialize in the marriage house, which is where most of us put our Shadow. I told him about my Web site, and he asked me for a business card. This young priest had begun to question life and was learning about the unconscious. It was no accident that we met, as we were energetically and psychologically *simpatico*. The majority of people will be especially wistful when they see romantic love happening to someone else or when watching a romantic movie. They think something is missing in their relationships because their relationship is not this dramatic and extraordinary. Either they are married and it was like that at the beginning but has since dissipated, or they long for the day this will happen to them if they are single. People keep going from one relationship to another, searching for that romantic ecstasy and bliss.

Why Is Love So Scary?

Just as quickly as a relationship begins, it can end. The original love can turn to hate. When relationships end that violently, you know that neither partner was able to get past his or her own unconscious projections. No one was communicating authentically. Power plays were probably more in effect than love. Power plays say I will get you for me so that I can own you, not, "I will cherish you for who you are and encourage you to be your best self." Unless they are both willing to do some inner work and recognize what is really going on between them, they will just go on to find other partners. The pattern will repeat over and over and over again as victim consciousness continues.

As Paul McCartney sings in a song that he and John Lennon wrote:

> *I'm looking through you.*
> *What did I know?*
> *I thought I knew you.*
> *What did I know?*
> *You don't look different, but you have changed.*
> *I'm looking through you.*
> *You're not the same.*

People keep going from one relationship to another searching for that romantic ecstasy and bliss.

Notes to Myself:

_____

_____

_____

_____

_____

_____

_____

_____

_____

_____

_____

_____

_____

_____

_____

CHORUS
Why, tell me why, did you not treat me right?
Love has a nasty habit of disappearing overnight.

I'm Looking Through You, by the Beatles, 1965 on Rubber Soul

The reason this happens to everyone and is so archetypal is that the Shadow side and the contrasexual aspects of us, the Anima and Animus, are so hidden from our consciousness. What's really interesting is that everyone else can see our Shadow and we can't. We then become our own worst enemy, because anything unknown is not under our conscious observation or direction. As Jung said,

> I should like to emphasize that the integration of the shadow, or the realization of the personal unconscious, marks the first stage in the analytic process, and that without it a recognition of the anima and animus is impossible. The shadow can be realized only through a relation to a partner, and the anima and animus only through a partner of the opposite sex, because only in such a relation do their projections become operative.[13]

I'll tell one of my stories about falling in love as an example of when we project our inner male (Animus) or Shadow onto a person. As I said earlier, I am also a graphic designer. A printing salesman I will call Craig called me one day and said, "I've kept your card for seven years and just moved to a new company and want to see if you will work with me again." I did not remember even meeting this guy. We made an appointment for him to come meet Trish and me. He came to our office at my home. The moment he walked into the house it was, as they say, "love at first sight." This had not happened to me in a very long time. The feelings were euphoric and intense. We started to get to know each other, and I could tell he was also smitten by me. It didn't take long before I found out that he was a very secretive person and had a double life. As I got to know him, he told me that he didn't like people at all and preferred his solitude. He even told me he would never go to a restaurant like Benihana as he wouldn't want to sit with strangers. He was extremely cautious and didn't trust anyone. He had several planets in Scorpio in his chart although he was a Capricorn Sun. I didn't know it at the time, but another part of my mother complex was being activated by this man. My mother has Capricorn rising besides being a Scorpio Sun and Moon. Craig was extremely sexual and earthy. Dark hair, penetrating eyes, I would describe him as a Greek god. At this time, I was very closed off and repressed. He woke up the sexual being inside me that had been slumbering for several years. He was exactly the opposite of me in every way. So many parts of me had been shoved into the unconscious that I needed this experience to find and relate to huge parts of myself. The relationship was the most painful and destructive relationship that I ever had in my life, but I remembered that at the very beginning, the very first night we were together sexually he asked me a very important question. He said, "Rebeca, do you take care of yourself?" I unconsciously said, "Yes, I do. Do you?" He said, "I don't think so."

Well, I absolutely did not take care of myself in regard to him. We went round and round for several years, and eventually it had to end. He was also involved with another woman and moved in with her.

One day he came over to my office. Even though we were not seeing each other romantically, we were still working together. I was sitting at my computer, and he said to me, "I have to leave. A tiger never loses its stripes." He was being sexually aroused by being near me so he left, as I was no longer willing to be in a sexual relationship with him. I was still awake thinking about him at 3:00 a.m., and I decided to write him a letter. I got out of bed and looked for my favorite quote in the Bible from Timothy to put in this letter. It says, "For God has not given us a spirit of timidity, but of power and of love and of a sound mind." I wrote "God gave us the ability to think and therefore to choose. I choose to love and forgive and move on."

The next morning I went into my son's room. He was only about 11 or 12 at the time. He had been in the habit of taking everything apart, as little boys do. There on his dresser was one of those tiny stuffed tigers they sell that clings to one rose. Someone had given me a rose, and that little tiger was on it. I forgot all about that little tiger. Apparently my son found it and took it to his room. He had scalped it with my x-acto knife (a knife graphic designers, artists and hobbyists use). The stripes and tail were sitting there on the dresser, and the little plastic tiger was naked. I stood there staring at it and smiled inside my heart.

Craig came over to bring me a press proof that morning, and I gave him the letter I wrote in the middle of the night. He read it. I said to him, "Now come in here, as I want to show you God's sense of humor." I showed him the little tiger my son had scalped. He looked at me incredulously and said, "Did he know?" I said, "No, of course not, but these synchronistic things happen to me all the time." These experiences are numinous and give me a direct experience of the divine.

A tiger can loose its stripes. I had become way too holy when I got into metaphysics, and I had cut off my sexuality. Craig and I were so polarized. I was carrying all the spiritual aspects of this man's nature. He told me that he saw me as lyrical and angelic and

These experiences are numinous and give me a direct experience of the divine.

Notes to Myself:

_____

_____

_____

_____

_____

_____

_____

_____

_____

_____

_____

_____

_____

When I met Craig, I felt the intense urge to connect to that part of me, and I made him into a God.

he thought of himself as evil. He actually said that to me one day. We were so unconscious as to what was happening between us. I even had a dream during this time that all of the lingerie I was saving in my drawer for marriage was black. My sexuality was in mourning, as I had killed that part of me. Of course, it was much later as I continued to study analytical psychology before I understood this or what the unconscious was trying to tell me through the dream.

What I was looking for and seeking through Craig was within me all the time, only I was like everyone else. I was looking for myself out there in a person instead of inside me. I wanted to find a real-life direct experience of the transcendent in him.

The minute I heard my first love story, I started
looking for you, not knowing how blind that was.
Lovers don't finally meet somewhere.
They're in each other all along.[14]

JELALUDDIN RUMI

Notes to Myself:

_____

_____

_____

_____

_____

_____

_____

_____

_____

_____

_____

_____

_____

_____

_____

_____

_____

Experiences show up in the outer world that have meaning for us and evoke a feeling that cannot be replaced or ever forgotten. If we can see the higher meaning of our experiences and not fall into cynicism and despair, we are headed toward the possibility of a *coniunctio,* the sacred marriage between the masculine and the feminine within that is taking place in all of us. These people are carrying the Anima or Animus which the alchemists called the royal road to our wholeness. We all want to know ourselves, and the only way to do so is to project our opposites outside us.

By the law of opposites, an intense awareness of one side
constellates its contrary. Out of darkness is born light.
In contrast, dreams that emphasize blackness usually occur when
the conscious ego is one-sidedly identified with the light.[15]

EDWARD F. EDINGER

When I met Craig, I felt the intense urge to connect to that part of me, and I made him into a god. The Taurean earthiness (Taurus rising) in him just oozed sexuality. He was the living embodiment of all of my lost sexuality I had repressed for years among other parts I was missing, like caution in moderation, reservation about communicating with strangers and especially my capacity to take care of me. Unfortunately, when we project ourselves into the "Other," we do not really see them as a real human being. They are now divine. That's precisely why things become so compelling and compulsive. ***Anything compulsive is activated by unconscious*** *forces.* Our unconscious is constantly striving for this union of opposites whether we know it or not. Jung says,

> Both of them are unconscious powers, "gods" in fact, as the ancient world quite rightly conceived them to be. To call them by this name is to give them that central position in the scale of psychological values which has always been theirs whether consciously or unconsciously acknowledged or not, for their power grows in proportion to the degree that they remain unconscious. Those who do not see them are in their hands, just as a typhus epidemic flourishes best when its source is undiscovered.[16]

If we don't see these people as a part of us, then, yes, we are going to suffer at their hands because we don't realize we've projected our own divinity onto them. They represent our Anima or Animus/Shadow. To the degree we are unable to see exactly what part of us they represent, that is how painful it will be when we try to distance or separate from them because we need that part. We'll feel like a part of us died when they leave us. The emotional pain is agonizing.

As I was writing this book, I remembered the extreme hate that I felt emotionally when this relationship ended. I actually burned up one night with a fever. The alchemists would call this a *calcinatio*, an alchemical process where the object of our desire frustrates us and our will is thwarted. I started praying and asked God to help me send Craig love instead. I could not sleep, so in the middle of the night, I got up and went to my bar area where I kept many cassette tapes of classes I have taken at the Jung Center. I found the original tapes from my very first class with Rev. McGehee. These were from the Basic Concepts of Analytical Psychology class I took in 1990. I started listening, and his words soothed me. They helped me analyze my experience. By morning, the fever broke and I was at peace. I was able to go on, determined to see what Craig represented to me and the meaning of our experience. Often, when a person rejects us and the projected content cannot reach consciousness, this anger is really powerful. We want to hurt them. We hate them with the same intensity we once loved them. Unconsciousness is what will set us about to destroy that person, yet we mistakenly have called this love.

Divine Love

What we are feeling in their presence is love, but it is divine love, or what the alchemists called this process — the mystical marriage, or seeking the transcendence in a human being. We actually call this chemistry when we feel the pull of the opposites within us as we are desiring to unite with the beloved. This is a very long

Alchemists called this process the mystical marriage or seeking the transcendence in a human being.

Notes to Myself:

_____

_____

_____

_____

_____

_____

_____

_____

_____

_____

_____

_____

_____

Our unconscious is moving us toward wholeness and seeing our whole self.

process that happens inside us over and over as we meet ourselves in the mirrors of our passionate relationships where there is indeed a "spark." Jung says,

> Seen from the one-sided view of the conscious attitude, the shadow is an inferior component of the personality and is frequently repressed through intensive resistance. But the repressed content must be made conscious so as to produce a tension of opposites, without which no forward movement is possible. The conscious mind is on top, the shadow underneath, and just as high always longs for low and hot for cold, so all consciousness, perhaps without being aware of it, seeks its unconscious opposite, lacking which it is doomed to stagnation, congestion, and ossification. Life is born only of the spark of opposites.[17]

This would account for the passionate attractions we feel to others. Our unconscious is moving us toward wholeness and seeing our

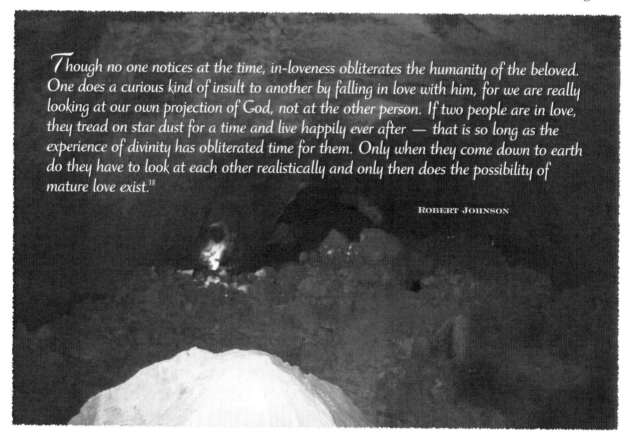

Though no one notices at the time, in-loveness obliterates the humanity of the beloved. One does a curious kind of insult to another by falling in love with him, for we are really looking at our own projection of God, not at the other person. If two people are in love, they tread on star dust for a time and live happily ever after — that is so long as the experience of divinity has obliterated time for them. Only when they come down to earth do they have to look at each other realistically and only then does the possibility of mature love exist.[18]

ROBERT JOHNSON

whole self. The problem is, in order for us to become whole, we have to differentiate from the person that we love. We have to have what alchemists called a *seperatio* (a separation) where we can objectify and see our differences. Because there is no longer a state of oneness or symbiosis, we are separate human beings and that blissful state of unity is gone. But if we value friendship, then we will not be so disappointed. We don't expect our friends to be exactly like us, so why do we expect this from partners? The feeling of being in love will go away, but the love that replaces that unconscious unity is much more satisfying because it's based on who each person actually is as a unique human being. There is more tolerance and acceptance of a person we truly love as opposed to a person we think we are "in love" with.

Again, we need to return to seeing our Shadow, as that is going to be the starting point. We can't get there any other way. Skipping this part of the process will short-circuit us. Then we will have to start all over again with another person.

Our Dreams Can Also Provide Help.

Much of Jung's work included using dreams to reveal what is going on in our unconscious. Our dreams can also show us attitudes that are the exact opposite of what we identify with. Jung stressed that dreams were often compensatory. They are striving to regulate our splits and father and mother complexes and bring about a balance in this way. Here's another story that will make this more clear.

A woman I will call Jennifer had a successful import/export business. She had several employees who were actively involved in sales for her company. She had hired one girl in particular whom I will call Susan, whom, after a while, she could not stand the sight of. Jennifer described this employee as a person who exaggerated her importance and talked incessantly about "who" she knew —the mayor of the city, the richest people in the area, etc. She bragged constantly about her sales ability and generally repulsed Jennifer. It started to drive her nuts, so much so that, although this girl was doing her job and doing it well, Jennifer wanted to fire her. She couldn't stand Susan anymore and told me so. I had come to visit her and stayed with her and her family for a couple of months as I was working on this book. During the time I was there visiting, I noticed Jennifer doing the exact things she was accusing Susan of doing. Her teenage daughter, Amy, and I talked about it, as it became very obvious to both of us, and together we told her. At first she hotly denied it, but because she was an introspective woman, she said she would think about it.

Things got worse before they got better. Jennifer resented me for pointing it out, but because I was a guest in her home, she couldn't exactly get rid of me. Then one night during all this, Jennifer had a dream. She dreamed that Susan, her employee, was walking toward her with a cigarette in her hand. Susan took the cigarette and swallowed it. Jennifer took this to mean that her dream was showing her that Susan was obnoxious. "She's even swallowing cigarettes," she said to me — which would be a very literal interpretation. The unconscious gave her this dream to show her this figure was inside her, that she was blowing a lot of hot air and she needed

Skipping this part of the process will short-circuit us. Then we will have to start all over again with another person.

Notes to Myself:

_____
_____
_____
_____
_____
_____
_____
_____
_____
_____
_____
_____
_____
_____

to swallow it. In other words, she needed to own it. It was a great example of a compensatory dream and how the unconscious will make a statement to correct the denial of our conscious mind. From studying Jung's theory of dreams, I knew that dream figures often represent your Shadow, especially when they are a person you can't stand.

It became a touchy subject with Jennifer, so I didn't tell her what I thought the dream really meant. I let it alone and allowed her to process the information in her own way. Life itself helped her get clear. One night we were all at dinner with a new prospective client. It was Jennifer's daughter, Amy, myself, her husband and this couple that she was entertaining. Jennifer started doing exactly what she had accused her employee Susan of doing, and her daughter and I looked at each other and smiled. She saw us, and she got it. In that instant, she saw it herself and she stopped.

Susan did exhibit some traits of braggadocio, but it was obnoxious only to Jennifer and no one else at the company. Jennifer would zero in on just that aspect of Susan because it was part of her own Shadow.

The next day the three of us went to lunch, and Jennifer admitted to Amy and I that she got it that Susan was a Shadow figure inside of her. She also now knew what it meant and why she drew this situation to her. Her mother had often belittled her and made her feel she wasn't important. Unconsciously, she was compensating for this complex she had been carrying around her entire life. She told us it didn't matter how successful she became. She knew she could never live up to her mother's exaggerated expectations. She couldn't believe it when it got clear. This is another example of how our Shadow is bringing us important information that can help us heal our parental imagos. Though her mother had already died, that mother complex lived on inside of her until she could relate to it. Edward C. Whitmont says,

> A dream represents the dreamer's situation as it is, externally or
> internally or both; and it compensates the one-sidedness of the
> conscious view, that is, it relates a message which is unknown
> to the dreamer but is potentially vital and in need of being known.[19]

Another dream that also activated a parental complex was one told to me by a good friend of mine. She said, "In my dream, my dad came to visit me. It was after his death, and I was awakened by his kiss on my cheek. As I came to consciousness, I saw him standing there beside my bed wearing a houndstooth, small-plaid shirt. He startled me in this apparition state, and I swatted the bed covers at him, which dissipated the image. Three nights later, my boyfriend came in wearing the same shirt my dad was wearing in my dream!

Unconsciously, she was compensating for this complex she had been carrying around her entire life.

Notes to Myself:

It told me they were cut from the same cloth!" This is another example of synchronicity and how the unconscious will help us if we pay attention to our dreams. The man she was dating was bringing up for her unfinished issues with her Dad. Paying attention to our dreams, writing them down, and making an effort to remember them is the best way to start a relationship with our unconscious. Your unconscious will help you if you start asking questions.

When we cannot forgive our parents, we are destined to repeat many of their fears and failures. Our parents were human beings who had a light and dark side. We will actually gain from knowing that we are everything we wish they weren't. In that self awareness, you can make an effort to change the patterns that you've inherited or resolve the hurt that you experienced through your relationship with them. Most important, you can begin to accept this aspect of yourself. Otherwise, you will continually project it out onto your partners or you will go through several marriages if that's what it takes to become conscious. Jung says,

> So long as the patient can think that somebody else (his father or mother) is responsible for his difficulties, he can save some semblance of unity. But once he realizes that he himself has a shadow, that his enemy is in his own heart, then the conflict begins and one becomes two.[20]

Anima as a Projection of Maya and Illusion

A man came to me for an astrology session and told me he was getting a divorce. He was very bitter and depressed as he told me his story. He had been married a year and a half to a woman he fell "in love" with. She had actually come on to him and pursued him like gangbusters until he fell for her. She was very beautiful, had a professional career and was very intelligent. She loved antiques and rock collecting, and he found her very fascinating. At the beginning, she was very sweet, good natured and crazy about him. He fell madly in love, and he married her after knowing her a short period of time. She was perfect for him, or so he thought.

They decided to go to London for their honeymoon at a later date, so the weekend that they were actually married they decided to stay home. It just so happened that he had car trouble one night of that weekend. He needed to replace a fan belt in his car in order to avoid missing work the next week, so they went and bought the part he needed. She was disappointed that instead of spending this time with her, doing what she wanted to do, they had to repair his car. That totally turned off his new bride. Later, when the two of them were in counseling after the marriage started falling apart, she told their therapist that she knew it would never work after that night. That she had to help him for 20 or 30 minutes by holding a

When we cannot forgive our parents, we are destined to repeat many of their fears and failures. Our parents were human beings who had a light and dark side.

Notes to Myself:

_____
_____
_____
_____
_____
_____
_____
_____
_____
_____
_____
_____
_____
_____
_____

Robert says that more best friends should marry each other because they actually care about each other as real persons, not how they feel when they are in each others' presence.

Notes to Myself:

_____

_____

_____

_____

_____

_____

_____

_____

_____

_____

_____

_____

_____

_____

_____

_____

_____

flashlight for him in the dark while he repaired his car was too much for her fantasy of who she needed him to be. She expected him to go get it fixed and not bother her with it. Most of us would be embarrassed to admit that we couldn't help our partner like this, but this didn't occur to her.

He told me that she was estranged from her immediate family. She had no friends that he knew of unless she needed something from them. He caught her lying to him and to her own daughter several times. She refused to communicate, was constantly depressed and couldn't get out of bed on weekends. All of this took place after they got married. He was in complete shock. What on earth had happened?

I listened to his story and explained the concept of the Anima to him. In this particular case, the femme fatal was the seductive, mermaid or siren-type woman that he "fell in love" with. I told him that in truth he was in love with and married a person he didn't really know. It didn't matter what I said or explained to him. He couldn't relate, and he was very much still in the grief of the ending of his illusion of who he had thought she was and what the marriage was about. I sent him away with the book by Robert A. Johnson called *We, Understanding the Psychology of Romantic Love.*[21] I always keep several copies of Johnson's book handy for people who come to me, and loan it out whenever I meet someone in that state because it's so well written. Robert uses the myth of Tristan and Iseult to explain the narcissism inherent in romantic love. He explains how different our culture is from, say, that of India, where people don't marry because they are "in love," so they don't have to worry that they'll fall out of love. He explains the peacefulness of giving our devotion to God and living out our spiritual life with God as our beloved. In romantic love, we are placing that energy on each other instead of seeking this divinity inside us, where it truly belongs. Then we act like fools, being severely disappointed and disillusioned when that "in love" phase is over. Robert says that more best friends should marry each other because they actually care about each other as real persons, not how they feel when they are in each other's presence. The emphasis is not how that person makes you feel but more on getting to know, love and respect another human being. He talks about a new paradigm in relating where the emphasis is on giving of yourself and caring about the well-being of someone other than yourself. This book changed me completely, so I suggested my client read it.

He read the book and called me two weeks later, as he wanted to return it to me. He said that he actually started getting clear that night he talked to me, and it hit him that he was in love with an illusion. He realized I was right; he never really knew his wife before he married her. It was the death of a dream. We began to dialogue openly now, and here is what he said: "It made me very sad that I was so unconscious."

"She didn't know you and you didn't know her, so you married a stranger, basically."

He said, "Yes. She even wrote a poem about me when she was into the passion of being 'in love' with me, and when I heard it, I told her, 'That's not who I really am.' I guess when I told her that, among other things that happened, she began withdrawing from me. Then there was nothing I could do right anymore."

He said, "I, on the other hand got zapped right between the eyes! I took this leap of faith when I married her. Even her children warned me. They told me to live with her instead of marry her. She had been married several times, so her kids knew the possible outcome if I married her. They had already gone through it with her previous marriages. I've learned a lot from the pain now that it's all over with, just like it says in the book. The sad part is there are two people inside me. One part of me understands that it was an illusion. This part of me feels sad, guilty, embarrassed and ashamed that I was so unconscious. I ask myself, 'Where was I?' The other part of me is like a monkey with his hand stuck in the jar — who won't let go of the banana! I miss her. I want to lie in bed next to her and touch her. Can you believe it?"

I said, "Yes, it's hard to let that kind of fantasy go. It took me many years to let it sink into my own consciousness that those people that I couldn't have, who couldn't love me back, were not completely real. I didn't really know them. What you see at first is only what you want to see. You ignore signs that are actually there from the very beginning. In retrospect, you know that there was no compatibility or even similar values shared with this person, but you are like a bug attracted to the light. Like you said, you got zapped!"

Projection brings to mind that song by the Righteous Brothers: "You've lost that loving feeling, oh, that loving feeling. You've lost that loving feeling, now it's gone, gone, gone and I can't go on." Then they grovel. "Baby, baby, I'd get down on my knees for you. If you would only love me like you used to do. We had a love, a love, a love you don't find every day. So don't, don't, please don't let it slip away... etc." It seems incredible that we would still want a person who treats us badly, one whom we do not even like very much, yet many of us, when we get caught in this kind of situation, can't leave it. It's compulsive; therefore it's mostly unconscious. When the pain is bad enough, though, we do leave, or if we're lucky, we don't have to make that decision as they will have left us.

My client went on with his story. He said, "On our honeymoon

What you see at first is only what you want to see. You ignore signs that are actually there from the very beginning.

Notes to Myself:

You've Lost That Loving Feeling, sung by the Righteous Brothers, Philles label, 1965, produced by Phil Spector

Basically, analytical psychology would say the projections have fallen off.

Notes to Myself:

_____

_____

_____

_____

_____

_____

_____

_____

_____

_____

_____

_____

_____

_____

_____

in London, we didn't even make love. She didn't want to. I wanted to take her to see the museums and to Big Ben. She didn't want to go to the museums. I wanted to share the experience with her, and all she wanted to do was sunbathe at the hotel, read books in our room and basically be by herself. She wasn't there with me. I was on my honeymoon by myself. Within two weeks of being in this marriage, I knew I was in trouble. She became very critical of who I was. She thought I should go to the doctor because I was forgetting things. She was cruel and unkind. She told me she didn't want to end up like my mother, who takes care of my dad, who is an invalid now in his old age. I could do nothing right. Before, when she was so fascinated by me and into the relationship, I was exactly what she wanted."

I said, "I know. It's so common that there's a phrase for it we've all heard. They call it 'when the honeymoon is over.' Sounds like you didn't even make it through the honeymoon. Basically, analytical psychology would say the projections have fallen off. Sometimes that takes a year or two but it sounds like for her it happened relatively quickly after you married her." The song continues, "And girl you're starting to criticize little things I do."

He said, "Yes, and I thought I was making a conscious choice when I married her. I remember I was so confident. I thought I knew what I was doing. I had never made a commitment before. It was my first marriage, and I thought she was so perfect."

"You were in what Jung calls an inflation," I said. "You were inflated with the archetype of the God Eros. It was not your conscious mind who chose her. You know that because you were compulsively drawn into the situation even when others saw it and told you. Others warned you. 'This person does not have your best interest at heart. They are using you until something better comes along.' Your friends will tell you what they see, but you don't want to believe it. You keep going, thinking you can somehow change the outcome. Like a runaway train, you are not in charge of the destination until it comes to a dead halt. Then you are forced to acknowledge the truth. Pain gets you off the train. Enough pain, and you will stop eventually."

He said, "Well, I am angry. When I was smack in the middle of it, I thought to myself, 'Who is this person acting like this? This is not the one I thought I was marrying.' Women have a label they put on you after you are married and become a husband. When you are a boyfriend, it's OK for you to fix your own car, but when you are a husband, now you're supposed take care of everything by hiring someone else. A husband cannot make any mistakes. He now has to make more money and be a big success. If he isn't, then he's a failure. If he's a failure, then she is, too, because she married you.

She wanted me to be extravagant when it came to her, but whenever it was her spending money on something, she'd do it the cheap way. I noticed that about her when we were dating, and I actually admired her for it. I thought to myself, 'This person is frugal.' After I married her, she had a different set of rules for how a husband should be with money. To her, money was very important. She grew up without money, so it became a big issue and everything was about money for her. Although she worked in a social field, she didn't really like to be around people. To me, people are more important."

I responded, "Well, here's the old Shadow dilemma again. If you get lopsided with that view, you will pull to yourself the opposite. People are important, and having money is important also — both in balance. Neither can become too important or you get out of balance. We are all striving for this balance — a little of this and a little of that. If you're doing too much and you're doing all the giving, there is no balance. You have to communicate with each other like I did with my business partner, Trish. 'Hey, we are getting out of balance. This is what I am doing. This is what you are doing.'"

"She wouldn't communicate with me. She refused to communicate. Then what?" he asked.

I said, "It definitely takes two to experience a real relationship. We cannot force the other person to communicate, especially if they have already made up their mind to leave. The most difficult people to be around are those who believe they have it all together and who are unwilling to communicate. No one has it all together. I don't care how old they are, what their social position is or how many degrees they have. We are all in process, and we are all perfectly imperfect. A more mature person strives to become a team player. Yes, they would understand your needing to get your car fixed before work. If you needed them to run to the store to buy another part for you, they would do so. A team player even gets out there and helps you wash your car. They make soup for you when you're sick and go get your medicine. They do not feel they are put out when you are in need of their help. They are your partner in life, and they like you and love you as a person. You are not just their fantasy or their projection, because although there will inevitably be some elements of that in every relationship, you are also real."

I know how hard it is, but when you are finally grateful for what they represented and what you needed to learn, you can even forgive the whole situation, especially yourself, for being unconscious. A good question to ask ourselves now is "What do I want?" Children rush headlong into blind emotion, but women and men who have some experience can wait and bide their time.

Neither can become too important or you get out of balance. We are all striving for this balance — a little of this and a little of that.

Notes to Myself:

Men can very easily put their projections onto this type of woman because there is a fragile and soft elusiveness about them. They attract guys easily.

Anima Types

There are some women who are what Jung called Anima women. Marilyn Monroe comes to mind. An entire nation projected the sex goddess onto her, but even ordinary women that are not movie stars can be what he's describing as Anima women. They are usually very beautiful, kind of vague, not real defined and seem to be helpless. Men can very easily put their projections onto this type of woman because there is a fragile and soft elusiveness about them. They attract guys easily. "Men are lining up at the door," as one of my friends put it in describing a woman he had known since childhood. This woman had been carrying his Anima since he was a 12-year-old, an adolescent. Jung says,

> There are certain types of women who seem to be made by nature to attract anima projections; indeed one could almost speak of a definite "anima type." The so-called "Sphinx-like" character is an indispensable part of their equipment, also an equivocalness, an intriguing illusiveness — not an indefinite blur that offers nothing, but an indefiniteness that seems full of promises, like the speaking silence of a Mona Lisa. A woman of this kind is both old and young, mother and daughter, of more than doubtful chastity, childlike, and yet endowed with a naive cunning that is extremely disarming to men.[22]

Elsewhere he says,

> Since this image is unconscious, it is always unconsciously projected upon the person of the beloved and one of the chief reasons for passionate attraction or aversion.[23]

This man's experience is archetypal. Many of us fall in love with people we don't really know. Nor do they know us. This is the difficulty inherent in the projection of these inner figures. It behooves us to learn more about them, how we may come to understand more of what they mean in our relationships and how they function in our everyday lives.

A very good movie that describes this kind of projection onto an "Anima-type woman" is the romantic comedy *Alex and Emma,* with Kate Hudson and Luke Wilson.

Luke Wilson, a writer, is madly in love with a very conniving and self-centered woman. As she is a personification of his own internal Anima/Shadow, he doesn't see her underhandedness, her narcissism or her dishonesty. He is caught in a projection. Watch this movie and you will see that you've gone through this very same scenario. Most of us have fallen in love with someone like this. It's an archetypal possession, but we think we are "in love."

Notes to Myself:

Lothario Men — the Equivalent

Men, too, can personify a lothario, a Casanova or a Don Juan so this kind of disillusionment doesn't happen just to men. The dictionary describes a lothario as a man who behaves selfishly and irresponsibly in his sexual relationships with women. I know a woman who fell in love with one of these characters. He was a charming, smooth-talking, flattering and flighty male. He was from out of town, and they met in an airplane on one of her business trips. He went to the trouble of hiring a white limousine and wearing a white suit and came to town to wine her and dine her. Then he invited her to an all-expenses-paid weekend in New York City. This went on and on. Meanwhile she was being swept off her feet. When she insisted on getting closer by going to where he lived, she found out what he was hiding. It turned out this man was engaged to a woman in Florida! It's not just women who can be the illusion in this kind of projection or fantasy.

Taking care of ourselves is very important in this day and age, and being cautious and **not trusting every Tom, Dick and Jane** is a requirement. People can say whatever they want to say to you and not mean one word of it. If you're falling madly in love with someone, be mindful; there's still a lot of projection going on. This person can turn out to be an extreme version of our worst Shadow traits as I found out with Craig.

Will They Approve of Us?

The dark side of romantic love happens when we are placing someone on a pedestal as Luke Wilson does in this movie. We stop being true to ourselves because we want them to love us. John A. Sanford, says, "The person who carries a projected psychic image from another person does have power over that person, for as long as a part of our psyche is perceived in someone else, that other person has power over us."[24] We become afraid to lose that person. We now want them so badly that unconsciously they become the parent figure instead of the partner/lover. We become like a child seeking his or her parents' unconditional love. Unconsciously we go back to a place and time when our very survival was dependent on acceptance from our parents. Jung says you can actually see the projection of the parental imagos by the way lovers will caress each other's hair and face, talk baby talk to each other and swoon in each other's presence. They are back to wanting the safety of their mother's womb. Brugh Joy says,

> My informal impression at this time is that in most, if not all, first marriages, both partners, at unconscious levels, have transferred the necessary incestuous bondings between the infant/child and

Taking care of ourselves is very important in this day and age, and being cautious and not trusting every Tom, Dick and Jane is a requirement.

Notes to Myself:

the countergender parent to the marital partner. There may be other reasons for a relationship between two particular individuals, but if the initial aspects of the relationship included anything closely resembling "falling in love," the incestuous parent/child aspects are surely present.[25]

When we are afraid of loss, we stop being authentic and real with our "beloved." We begin to act. We lose them eventually because a relationship can exist only between two adults who are being real. We've already left ourselves. We might as well get ready, because they will leave us too sooner or later. As within, so without. If we are honest with ourselves and we reflect on past failed relationships, we even know the turning point, when the relationship started to end. At that point, we had already left ourselves. We become paranoid and afraid of loss. We think it's them we're losing, but it's really us that we're losing. This is the sad thing about not being willing to be real and vulnerable in relationships, and expecting a perfection in each other which does not exist.

Ideals and preferences we are looking for in a partner are usually what we projected onto them in the beginning. No one is perfect, and only a child expects perfection from a human being. Eric Butterworth put it like this: "Forgive me for expecting in the human what can only be found in the divine."[26]

When you stop communicating authentically, the sexual passion goes out of the relationship relatively quickly. After a time, your body won't even respond when unconsciously you are projecting your parents onto this person. That is one of the reasons you hear about couples' no longer desiring each other sexually. It's not much fun to have sex with your father or your mother. When something like this particular example happens — and it happens to both sexes — it is a real defeat for our ego to realize that we projected our parental imagos onto each other. We never loved each other as real human beings in the first place. We were caught by our own unconscious contrasexual images and/or our Shadows. In effect, we were strangers.

A song written by Bobby Braddock and sung by Martina McBride, *Strangers*, goes like this:

> Two strangers passing in the hallway
> Barely touch each other's heart
> Now they're pretending
> Two shadows blending
> But they're a million miles apart
> Soon she'll be packing up her suitcase
> They'll be dividing all the blame
> They know how they started

Now empty hearted
They don't have a clue how they became
Strangers, strangers
The world's greatest lovers
And now they are strangers
The world's greatest lovers
Have turned into strangers

When we are projecting our 7th-house planets and signs onto the beloved, he or she will bring up emotion and feeling, great highs and lows, physical sensation and intense passion. We will act as if we are possessed. All logic, values, rational behavior, etc. can go out the door as we feel compelled to follow a person who has triggered this unconscious, archetypal possession. My teacher, Rev. McGehee, once said to us in class, "If you want the projections to fall off, just marry the person." We all laughed because many of us in the room were over 40, had been married at least once, and we knew that what he was saying was true.

Giving Up Blame

Some people will say to me, "But he's incapable of treating me with respect," or, "she is untrustworthy." I say repeat after me: "I am incapable of treating myself with respect" or "I am untrustworthy." We always need to own it ourselves. Nobody does anything to us. We do it to ourselves. We collude with the person. We choose to be in the situation. If someone is treating us badly and we don't get angry and put our foot down and stop it, then they are not doing it to us. We're doing it to us. We have chosen to be in this situation; then we blame them. We all do this. Nobody is excluded from playing the victim in relationships. We all do it sometimes. We have to be willing to say to ourselves, "I am responsible for my world, and I am responsible for my own feelings." The more we can change ourselves in any situation, the more we can set our own boundaries. If we don't like something that is going on, then we need to say so. We have to learn to take care of ourselves if we want it mirrored back. As soon as we take care of ourselves, others change toward us, not because they changed, but because we did. We communicate that we will no longer put up with whatever we feel we don't like. We have to mean it and be willing to take a stand if we have to.

Sometimes people will run late and they won't call you to tell you they are running late, or they don't return phone calls. Good manners says to call someone if you are running late and to return phone calls. This sounds like common sense, but it's amazing how many people don't do this and don't think anything of it. You would do that for your friends or clients, right? Well, what if you don't say anything to them? You just stuff it. Next time they'll do

Every long-term relationship will have tests that require both partners to come into balance. No one can have it all their way.

Notes to Myself:

it again because they know you are going to put up with it. This is where the balance of respect and common courtesy goes out the door. It doesn't mean you don't ever run late; we all do. At least say something about it when you walk in. "Hey, I'm sorry I am late." That's just being considerate. These things, no matter how uncomfortable, have to be discussed openly with our partners from the very beginning; otherwise they get out of control. Every long-term relationship will have tests that require both partners to come into balance. No one can have it all their way.

This is the dynamic aspect of relating. A relationship has to continually be open to modification and change or it will become static. Since no two people are exactly alike, it's inevitable they will not always agree on everything. Differences will come up between them, but passion is kept alive by being willing to be real. We have to discuss issues that upset us, ask for what we want and not stuff our feelings — or worse — let the other person get away with never doing anything that we've asked them to do! Richard Idemon in his excellent book *Through the Looking Glass,* says honesty is erotic.[27] He says that static relationships occur where an unspoken rule is never really let the other person know what you are thinking or feeling. When partners hide intense emotions, especially anger, neither person really knows the other. There is nothing more unbearable than a fake harmony.

Some people cannot do this. They will go their whole life blaming others for their problems and never looking at how they set life up to have it turn out exactly the way it did. So life will accommodate them and just bring another teacher until they can see that they do indeed need to change. Some of us are stubborn about our lessons. We'll keep doing something over and over and over and think we're going to get a different result, but we won't until we acknowledge these ingrained patterns. Like Charlie Brown continually believing that Lucy is not going to pull away the football when he attempts to kick it, we, too, continually expect our partners to change so that we can have what we want. The truth is we BOTH need to change. We are both colluding to have exactly what we have.

If you are being too nice and generous, then your partner will happily oblige you and keep taking and ignoring your needs. If you're handling all the money, responsibility and chores and they barely help you at all and don't contribute financially, then who are you — the Mommy or the Daddy? Why should they change if you have never expressed your dissatisfaction and you just put up with it? But it's like standing on a board in the water — if we go toward one side or the other, eventually we're going to fall off. We have to learn to get in the middle.

We can't blame the opposite sex for what happens in our lives. We can't say all women are like this or all men are like that. When we understand Jung's theory of opposites, we realize we all have both masculine and feminine functions. We have to become both our masculine and our feminine sides. We have to look at our part in the relationships we've created. The only person we have to trust is ourselves, because when you trust yourself to take care of you, you'll see it outside. If we are willing to be honest with ourselves and with our partners, we can change our relationships.

Quality Time Is the Key.

You also have to take time to know people in all kinds of situations to learn to adjust and dance with them before you decide they are "the one." You have to get to know a person by spending quality time with them — slowly. You have to get to know each other as people, especially if you are madly "in love." That should tell us something right from the get go — that we are into a projection, not a real relationship. It doesn't mean it can't become one. It can. But initially that is not what it is. As Jung says in the Houston films,

> The archetype is a force. It has an autonomy and it can suddenly seize you. It is like a seizure. Falling in love at first sight is something like that. You see, you have a certain image in yourself without knowing it, of woman, of the woman. Then you see that girl, or at least a good imitation of your type, and instantly you get a seizure and you are gone. And afterwards you may discover that it was a hell of a mistake. A man is quite able, he is intelligent enough, to see that the woman of his "choice" as one says, was not a choice, he has been caught! He sees that she is not good at all, that she is a hell of a business, and he tells me so. He says, "For God's sake, doctor, help me get rid of that woman!" He can't though. He is like clay in her fingers. That is the archetype of the Anima. And he thinks it is all his soul, you know![28]

When We Receive a Projection from Another

We may experience being the object of someone else's fascination or ideal. Certainly, when this happens to us, it is very flattering. One guy I knew put it this way. He couldn't resist that this girl he met was seducing him and paying extra attention to him. He was already in a long-term relationship with a woman he loved and re-spected, but he was uncommitted to their relationship, so his libido was still leaking out all over the place. You can tell when someone's libido is leaking, as they flirt with everyone and anyone. They love to be the center of attention, and they need a lot of it. He was one of these people. Now this other woman appeared in his path. The

We can't blame the opposite sex for what happens in our lives. We can't say all women are like this or all men are like that.

Notes to Myself:

We can also become bored if we have nothing in common — something we paid no heed to when we were "in love."

Notes to Myself:

_____

_____

_____

_____

_____

_____

_____

_____

_____

_____

_____

_____

_____

_____

_____

_____

woman he was with was no longer enough to satisfy that deep longing to find someone out there who would be "the one I've always dreamed of." That illusive fantasy our culture has come to idealize and accept as authentic love. Unfortunately, he'll end up with some big surprises if being "in love" is his main criterion for choosing a life partner.

Many married men or women have an extramarital affair as projections land on a secretary or a coworker. The magic now appears elsewhere, especially when it's forbidden love. Of course, when they don't live with this person day in and day out, they can continue to be a magical, mysterious being. Once you live with someone for a long period of time, you are going to see them in a different light. You will see their humanity. You will see their Shadow. When they are not on their best behavior, then the projections have worn off. The cute secretary who idealizes you doesn't see your dirty socks or odd habits like refusing to brush your teeth at night, or even worse, refusal to take a bath for five days! She doesn't know you are always running late and never call home to say so or that you think expressing these common courtesies and consideration of others impinges on your freedom.

We can also become bored if we have nothing in common — something we paid no heed to when we were "in love." Now with familiarity, it becomes glaringly obvious that we are not even friends with this person and wouldn't be if we had to choose them for a friend. That is the sad part. We don't even enjoy this person's companionship. This is all too common in many marriages today.

In our culture, we still have a huge task ahead of us. The strong desire to be what is called "madly in love" or to find our "soul mate" drives many people long past adolescence to seek out a romantic ideal in a human being. Puppy love — what that kind of intoxication is called in teenagers — is still motivating many adults. We want someone who will "knock us off our feet." When this occurs in our relationships, the question to ask ourselves is "Yes, but for how long? What happens when the new wears off? Will you even like this person? Will they like you, or will they reject you and go on to someone else? Will you do that to them? Do you really want to land on the floor?"

As the Dixie Chicks say in the song *"Tonight the Heartache's on Me."*

> *I wonder if he told her*
> *She's the best he's ever known*
> *The way he told me ev'ry night*
> *When we were all alone*
> *She'll find out when the new wears off*

He'll find somebody new
She'll learn what heartache's all about
And what I'm going through

Tonight the heartache's on me, on me, Yeah!
Let's drink a toast to the fool who couldn't see
Bartender pour the wine, 'cause the hurtin's all mine
Tonight the heartache's on me

Our songs and movies begin to change as we are changing and recognizing these archetypes that affect our lives in such fateful ways

If we listen to our songs, we will recognize that this information is slowly coming into the awareness of the collective. Our songs and movies begin to change as we are changing and recognizing these archetypes that affect our lives in such fateful ways. The pain that comes with a new birth is what is required, as most of us don't grow unless we are in pain. When we are caught by an archetypal possession, we cannot see what is happening unless we have the detachment to get out of the muck and the willingness to understand Jung's theories as valid and real.

To the degree we are unconscious, we will experience the dark side of this kind of romantic love, but if enough of us begin to accept that there is no "magic other," as Jungian analyst, James Hollis, put it in the book, *The Eden Project: In Search of the Magical Other,*[29] then we will be moving into the Aquarian Age with our eyes open. Detachment, objectivity, freedom and intelligence are key words for the sign of Aquarius. Aquarius is not a Water sign as most people who know nothing about astrology believe. It is an Air sign. Air signs require authentic communication. This is what will be required of us collectively to move into a new way of relating. "Friendship" is also a key word for Aquarius. We will extend true friendship to our partner and not expect him or her to be what we want them to be. We will want them to be themselves, and they cannot be themselves if they are prematurely invested. By that I mean if you have sex too soon. If we have sex, we become possessive. Now you are mine and I am yours. We don't even know each other, but now we are committed — superficially —but committed. Why? From the man's point of view, because I want to have sex with you again, I will do whatever you want me to do. I may even tell you whatever you want to hear. From the woman's perspective, I will be what you want me to be so that we can have a relationship because to the woman it's the relationship itself that counts, not just the sex. So now we have two people having a relationship with a false intimacy because they had sex way before they got to know each other. This is a big mistake. WAIT. Wait at least three to six months minimum and one year if you possibly can. Then you will get to know a real person and find out if you are truly compatible with them. You'll know if they genuinely care about you and you

Notes to Myself:

Trust does not happen overnight. It never has, and it never will.

Notes to Myself:

them. When sex is too freely given, we are no longer free to be ourselves. If we are ever going to learn how to be in real relationships, then we have to be friends first for a long period of time. There is no substitute for time. That is why Saturn, the planet that rules time, is exalted in the sign of Libra. Saturn means we have to be patient. We have to take our time to get to know each other and learn what it means to trust someone. Trust does not happen overnight. It never has, and it never will. Trust is built one day at a time by helping each other out when needed, by doing what we say we will do (keeping our word to each other), remembering what the other has asked us for because they are important to us, by being forgiving when they do something dumb and by telling each other the truth, even if it hurts to do so. Trust is earned, not had as a gift. A good friend gave me a plaque with that on it. I appreciate it now that I am older.

The truth is we are all vulnerable to loss, grief and sadness. Life is a series of these ups and downs in difficult relationships. We suffer in order to learn to love, but we can grow from down times. The alchemists believed that these were processes going on in the human psyche that were refining us and completing us.

Real relating is accepting somebody for who they really are, not who we thought they were or who we want them to be. We begin relationships accepting the person and wanting their acceptance. Then we try to change the other person. Often we begin to criticize our partner instead of just asking for what we want. Then we wonder where all the tenderness and affection that was there at the beginning went. Unnecessary criticism begins to destroy the relationship. Shakespeare put it well when he said, "Love is not love that alters what it finds." Jung put it like this:

> Recognition of the shadow, on the other hand, leads to the modesty we need in order to acknowledge imperfection. And it is just this conscious recognition and consideration that are needed whenever a human relationship is to be established. A human relationship is not based on differentiation and perfection, for these only emphasize the differences or call forth the exact opposite; it is based, rather on imperfection, on what is weak, helpless and in need of support — the very ground and motive for dependence. The perfect have no need of others, but weakness has, for it seeks support and does not confront its partner with anything that might force him into an inferior position and even humiliate him. This humiliation may happen only too easily when high idealism plays too prominent a role.[30]

Listening to Our Partners

Relationships work better if we learn to listen. Make the effort consciously to hear what your partner is saying to you or what he or she desires. We have a tendency to want others to fulfill our fantasies of who they are. We need to spend equal time getting to know them as real people. What do they dream? What do they need? What do they want? Ask them and listen. We need to do all of this long before we have sex with or marry anyone.

Especially when it comes to sex, it's truly important to listen. If your mate tells you, "I get turned on when you kiss my neck" or "I would like you to go slower," pay attention and remember what they've asked for. It's hard to be so vulnerable and ask your partner for what you need sexually, as you don't want to offend them or imply they are not a good lover, but we all have preferences if we know our own bodies. If we ask for what we need and they do it right then, and then they forget the next time we are intimate, what's the point in asking for anything? They don't listen. We want our preferences heard by our partner. It takes a certain amount of maturity not to take offense if our partners have sexual requests. If you know yourself and ask for your needs to be met, then you are free to love. If you don't take care of yourself, you will probably give up a part of yourself to do so. Partnerships can happen only between equals. Mothers, fathers and bosses don't make good lovers. In the Aquarian Age, best friends make great lovers.

Loving Our Imperfect Selves

It's also extremely important that we love ourselves especially when we've made a mistake. That is probably a lifelong task. Whenever we feel insecure we can easily revert back to the nerdy 8th grader we once were. Loving ourselves means we accept who we are even if that means being vulnerable, wrong, awful, needy or obnoxious. When two people are best friends, they can help each other learn to love themselves just the way they are since we are not going to change anyone. Paradoxically, we will grow and change in a loving, caring relationship.

After I had apologized for doing or saying something I felt bad about, my ex-boyfriend, who is still my friend, would say to me, "Oh, come on Rebeca, don't beat yourself up. You are also a truly kind and wonderful person. That's only one part of you." This kindness and generosity of spirit that he exemplified is real different from the partner or person who shames you, and even after you've apologized, will still put you down and tell you just how awful you are. His loving acceptance made me want to be a better person. We can't love people in their imperfection until we can love ourselves in our own. When we can see their humanity and how they also

If you know yourself and ask for your needs to be met, then you are free to love. If you don't take care of yourself, you will probably give up a part of yourself to do so.

Notes to Myself:

_____
_____
_____
_____
_____
_____
_____
_____
_____
_____
_____
_____
_____
_____
_____

His loving acceptance made me want to be a better person. We can't love people in their imperfection until we can love ourselves in our own.

represent Shadow sides of ourselves, we can truly love them. As my nephew said to me recently, there is no positive without negative. Vulnerability is intimacy (in-to-me-see). We also want to know who that person really is, not who they're pretending to be, for their sake as well as ours. If we don't get this in our first marriage, the subsequent ones get worse. Swallow your pride. Tell the truth about what is going on with you.

Invisible Partners and Inner Work

There is no better book on describing in detail what Jung meant by the Anima and Animus than the book by John A. Sanford called *Invisible Partners*.[32] In this book, the author describes how the Anima

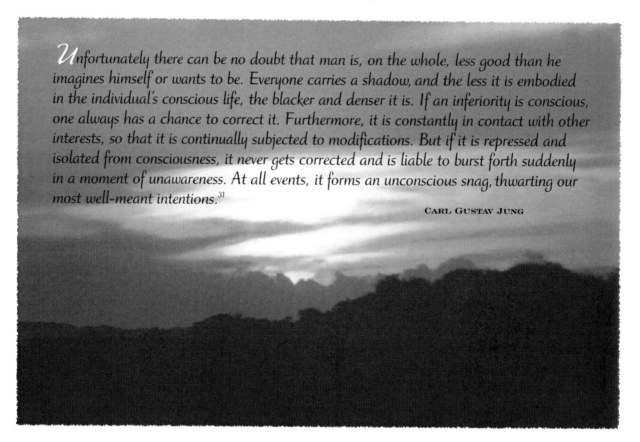

Unfortunately there can be no doubt that man is, on the whole, less good than he imagines himself or wants to be. Everyone carries a shadow, and the less it is embodied in the individual's conscious life, the blacker and denser it is. If an inferiority is conscious, one always has a chance to correct it. Furthermore, it is constantly in contact with other interests, so that it is continually subjected to modifications. But if it is repressed and isolated from consciousness, it never gets corrected and is liable to burst forth suddenly in a moment of unawareness. At all events, it forms an unconscious snag, thwarting our most well-meant intentions.[31]

CARL GUSTAV JUNG

and Animus are projected, how they relate to each other, and many other important aspects of their effect on us. Jung's books can be very complicated if you don't know a lot of theory, so I highly recommend anything by John A. Sanford.

When I read this book, I took it very seriously. Sanford said that we have to have a relationship with that inner part of us because they will be inferior to the degree we don't know about them. What this looks like in real life when the Anima is taking over a man's expressions is he will become very moody, sulky, a constant complainer and overly sensitive. For a woman, she will be highly opinionated and argumentative, and she will use innuendos and words that are not her own. She will make pronouncements instead of expressing her feelings. She will sound brusque or harsh like an inferior male, and he will sound carping and waspish like an inferior female. They are inferior because they are primitive and unrelated. Being in our unconscious, we don't know them.

I did realize after reading that book that many times my Animus would take over and embarrass me. For myself, it was the beginning of being able to recognize that there was someone inside of me I didn't know. I would make the wrong remark, or in a lecture, I would interrupt the speaker inappropriately. I might say something that was sort of related to what the speaker was talking about, but it really wasn't. Before I even spoke up, I started to notice that I felt a tension in my body or a pounding in my heart. I would feel a distinct physical sensation before my Animus would speak. He would then erupt forcefully. I hadn't even thought through what he would say. This was difficult because it left me feeling exasperated with myself. I had no idea that there was someone inside me who was speaking for me that had his own agenda. After I read Sanford's book, I began dialoguing with my inner male. At first, you could say it was my imagination that there was a male inside of me, and I would make an effort to talk to him. I would tell him out loud to listen to me. "We are going into a business meeting. If you have something to say, then you ask me before you say it." I got into the habit of communicating with my inner male. If I wanted to say something and my heart would start pounding, I would tell him to be quiet. I would tell him, "We can talk about this later when we have time to think about what it is you want to say to me." Jung called this active imagination, and Sanford explains active imagination on page 119 in the Appendix of his book. Robert A. Johnson also has a great book on how to do this called *Inner Work*.[33] I highly recommend both of these books so you can do this work, too. Let me describe how this eventually helped me in my own relationships.

After I stopped seeing Craig, I decided to do some online dating as a few of my friends were dating men they had met online. I thought, "Why not? I'll try it." One guy I started dialoguing with asked me for an astrology reading, and the first time we met he came to my house. He had counseled with a therapist that I knew of, so I wasn't afraid to let him come over. His office was only five miles away. We marveled at how close to each other we were, and I fantasized that he could be "the one." Now, this guy was very physically attractive, and he also found me attractive, so that spark was there for both of us the minute he walked in the door. The physical magnetism was intense.

Whenever I do an astrology reading, by looking at their birth

At first, you could say it was my imagination that there was a male inside of me and I would make an effort to talk to him. I would tell him out loud to listen to me.

Notes to Myself:

_____

_____

_____

_____

_____

_____

_____

_____

_____

_____

_____

_____

_____

_____

Sanford says when a woman's Animus speaks for her, it is a real defeat for her ego.

Notes to Myself:

chart, it creates an intimacy because I am telling people things about them no one knows but them. They will be amazed at how accurate it is, and that in itself evokes what psychology calls the transference or the projection of these invisible partners. Right away he started asking me to go out with him. We had gone out only twice when one day he invited me to lunch. He was telling me his dream that he wanted to buy a candle shop and expand it into a franchise. He was also an architect and wanted to build his own house in the country but still be close enough to the city. Many of his dreams were similar to my own. It was only our third date and this guy and I started to merge. A romantic euphoria had entered the situation very rapidly. On the way back from this lunch date, we were in his SUV and he reached over to hold my hand and I put his hand in my lap and a bit too close to my chest. He was telling me that his dream was to build a two-story house, and he was describing this house as we got to my driveway. He came to my side of the car and held the door open for me. As I was getting out of the car, I said out loud in a strange voice, "Well, we can't live together. I have to live in a one-story house." It just came out. I shocked myself and him. We walked into the house, and he was totally turned off by my remark. He hung out for a brief while and then said he needed to get back to work. He was visibly uncomfortable, and so was I. I didn't understand why I even made the remark. He never called me again. I had totally turned him off.

I was sad and confused by what had happened. Sanford says when a woman's Animus speaks for her, it is a real defeat for her ego. She will feel terrible afterward, and she'll know something came out of her that she didn't choose to say.

After that, I was invited by two couples to go to the Woodlands to hear the Moody Blues in concert. I invited my dear friend Andrew to go with me. Andrew and I are like brother and sister and had been good friends for years. That night, sitting there on the hill at the Moody Blues concert with two married couples, I felt a sense of despair and sadness inside of me. There was a full moon that night, and it was so beautiful. Andrew dropped me off after the concert, and I went into my house and sat down on the love seat in my bedroom. I asked myself, "Why? Why when I meet someone I am so attracted to like that architect do I open my mouth and say something to them to turn them off? Why do I do that? I wish I could understand." The voice inside my head said out loud, "Because if you don't protect yourself, I will." I heard this voice clear as a bell. My inner male spoke to me inside my head. Keep in mind I had been actively trying to have a relationship with him, and as Jung says, if you work with the unconscious, the unconscious will work with you. Well, this is really true.

Now notice that what was blurted out to that guy was only sort of related to what we were talking about. That is how the Animus in a negative fashion will blurt things out and embarrass you. Now I knew why. He was also trying to protect me. I was in awe as this realization became crystal clear to me. That night I went to my bathroom cupboard. I wrote in magic marker "TAKE CARE OF YOURSELF FIRST. AND GIVE THANKS AGAIN AND AGAIN AND AGAIN." Every day after that I would open my bathroom cupboard to take out my toiletries and I would see this affirmation I had written to remind me of that night.

I continue to dialogue with my inner male. My inner male was the one I knew started the process of consciously taking care of me. I was able to trust myself and him more and more. I knew that I

Now notice that what was blurted out to that guy was only sort of related to what we were talking about.

If attention is directed to the unconscious, the unconscious will yield up its contents, and these in turn will fructify the conscious like a fountain of living water. For consciousness is just as arid as the unconscious if the two halves of our psychic life are separated.[34]

CARL GUSTAV JUNG

could drink wine, and I would not jump into bed with anyone prematurely. I could easily say no and protect me. I knew that if I wanted to be loved, I had to love me first and take care of me.

Even the painful, destructive relationship with Craig was a blessing. He was so important to me that I wrote down in my journals every single thing we said to each other. I had a lot of dreams about him, as the unconscious was trying to help me see he was a representation of my Shadow. Looking back at those journals with these

*Go back into your
own past, and you
will see that each one
of these relationships
has been important
to your growth.
They represented
a part of you.*

Notes to Myself:

_____

_____

_____

_____

_____

_____

_____

_____

_____

_____

_____

_____

_____

_____

new Jungian realizations, I learned so much more about the pain of all those difficult relationships and what they actually meant. Go back into your own past, and you will see that each one of these relationships has been important to your growth. They represented a part of you.

Pain and tears will guide us to our souls, to our Self and to the best parts of us in our unconscious if we understand this information that Jung taught. I realized I had always exhibited traits of what Jungians called "Animus possessed." I remember thinking how unfair that was. I was born with eight out of 10 planets in masculine signs — which are the Air and Fire signs — so it was my fate. I also realized I could choose to integrate more and more of my feminine side if I made this part of me (my Animus) my friend instead of my foe, as Robert Johnson says in his cassette tape *Your Shadow, Friend or Foe*.[35] Letting him be there for me became a boon instead of the constant embarrassment, shame and despair that I had felt in the past. In *Knowing Woman,* Irene DeCastillejo explains that the Animus shines a light on what's important to a woman.[36] She also explains that it's important for a woman to cry and that when a woman cries, she spontaneously expresses her thoughts and her real feelings come through.[37]

Being afraid to be thought of as weak, many women refuse to cry and show their emotions, especially those of us born with so much masculine energy in our charts. This is confusing and painful as we try to adjust ourselves to society. We are not male. We are still female, but we have to work harder at accepting this though our natural way of being is not typical of what is considered to be the ideal feminine. We are more inclined to think that we want to be successful. We can make our way in a man's world. We have courage and spunk and can be independent. This causes us untold pain when it comes to relating to men, as they aren't used to us. I had to teach myself to show my feelings and to cry in front of a man. Fortunately, it gets easier as we age. I feel for young women born with so much masculine energy as they start to try to relate to men. I would encourage them to embrace their softer qualities earlier than I did. With so many divorces, a lot of women are having to support themselves and their children. It's important to know that your Animus can be your guide into your unconscious as you work with your dreams and your experiences that repeat.

Being patient with yourself as you are growing and living with some of these ideas is important. I found out recently that if I don't learn to express my hurt feelings, my Animus might still blurt out something inappropriate but at least now I know he's trying to get my attention. I am still learning to express all of my feelings even when they are negative in order to be real.

I also no longer look at rejection as any more than an opportunity to love myself more. Thank God others rejected you. Take back your projections and see them for who they are instead of what you wanted them to be. If you express your hurt to a man and he rejects you, or worse, he starts screaming at you, he is in the grips of his Anima. Unbeknownst to him, her intention is usually to sever the relationship. This doesn't just happen to women. Men can get caught up in a dark mood and become vicious, critical and carping themselves. Jung says when the Anima and Animus are in this kind of a dialogue, a woman can express like an inferior male and a man will express himself as an inferior female. Animosity between them is the result. Instead of letting these two inner figures express for us, we have to learn to communicate. I also noticed that when a man starts acting out his Anima, it's also a defeat for his ego. He will usually apologize sometimes right away or at least the next day. Women are much more forgiving of this kind of thing happening than men are. Men are more apt to want to run away when the Animus attacks them, or else they leave the house and condemn the woman as inappropriate. Now she is seen only in a negative light, whereas before she carried all the positive projections. If you live with someone long enough or you get closer to them, these inner partners will assert themselves. They actually are the determining

If you express your hurt to a man and he rejects you, or worse he starts screaming at you, he is in the grips of his Anima. Unbeknownst to him, her intention is usually to sever the relationship.

Both have a dark and destructive side, and when they come close together it is more like two loving people where the more the love increases, the more doubts and distrust increase too; one is very often afraid, since if one opens one's heart, the other can do so much harm. If, for instance, a man shows his love for a woman, then he is exposed to her animus. If he does not love her, he just says it is her damned animus, but if he does, then he minds when she makes the horrible animus remarks. The same thing holds good for the woman, for if she acknowledges her love for a man, the poison of his anima may hit her. Therefore there is always that trembling fear in approaching each other in the human love situation, mirrored symbolically in the process of sun and moon becoming one.[38]

MARIE LOUISE VON-FRANZ

They actually are the determining factors of whether a relationship will take place or not, although our egos think we are the ones who made the decision.

Notes to Myself:

———————————
———————————
———————————
———————————
———————————
———————————
———————————
———————————
———————————
———————————
———————————
———————————
———————————
———————————
———————————
———————————

factors of whether a relationship will take place or not, although our egos think we are the ones who made the decision. This really is remarkable information when you become aware, and Jung came closer than anyone in explaining this phenomenon between men and women.

Men have a very similar dilemma when they are born with a preponderance of feminine energy. Feminine energy includes the Earth and Water signs. These men know that they have preferences, thoughts and desires that are considered to be feminine, so they work hard to suppress themselves in order to conform or fit in with what they deem to be the right way for a man to be in the world. Just like women who are strongly masculine and don't want to be thought of as weak, these men don't want to be thought of as weak either. Yet they are gentle, receptive and much more sensitive to their environment. Not to be so would be to deny who they inherently are. This is another area where astrology can really help a person understand who they are and not what everyone in society thinks they should be. It's not natural for them to be aggressive, logical or anything else considered to be typically male. It's not that they are never logical, because both females and males are all logical sometimes. These men just exemplify more intuitive, emotional and nurturing tendencies and are usually extraordinarily kind. It appears to be the feminine energy in both sexes in our culture that is going through major transformation. We women with a preponderance of Air and Fire need to embrace our feminine sides as much as men with a preponderance of Earth and Water also need to not be ashamed of their natural inclination to be gentle and nurturing.

A man such as this needs to learn to stand up to a woman when she is getting overly emotional and giving him hell. Sometimes women will hold things in until they explode. It's a horrible way to deal with their emotions, but women can get caught up in dazes and moods and need a man's help to snap out of it. A man has to say, "STOP IT!" He can grab her face, look into her eyes and be more aggressive, which is what is needed to get her back to herself — not aggressive in a sexual way, but in a caring way. He can then say to her, "What is going on with you? Tell me about it. I want to know." By his expressing his masculine strength, this will immediately help her to shift back into her feeling nature, and then she can express herself without the Animus's barbed tongue. The Animus was constellated because she did not express her hurt. Similarly, a man must learn to express his own feelings or remain inwardly a child afraid of his mother. Sanford says,

> A man who always avoids emotionally toned encounters with other
> people is contained within the Mother. One way for him to get out

of his Mother complex is to express himself in relationship. If he fails to do so he remains emotionally a little boy who is afraid of women, who resents them if they don't keep him happy, and who is out of touch with his own masculine strength.[39]

In *Civilization in Transition* Jung says,

> Into this territory, a man must venture if he wishes to meet woman half way. Circumstances have forced her to acquire a number of masculine traits, so that she shall not remain caught in an antiquated, purely instinctual femininity, lost and alone in the world of men. So, too, man will be forced to develop his feminine side, to open his eyes to the psyche and to Eros. It is a task he cannot avoid, unless he prefers to go trailing after woman in a hopelessly boyish fashion, worshipping from afar but always in danger of being stowed away in her pocket.[40]

Finding Shadow Work Partners You Can Trust

We should also not admit our demons to just anyone. To do our Shadow work, we need close, intimate partners and friends to dance with who genuinely love us and know us as they have history with us. Therefore, they do not see just the bad parts and can remind us that we are lots of different people in one person. Looking at your astrology will definitely help in that arena also. You will be able to see your own challenges and strengths. You have to become aware of these in order not to project your Shadow, Anima and Animus onto others. No one is born with a perfect horoscope. In our next chapter, we will examine the 7th house and what it means to each of us as we are all unique.

> *Playfully, you hid from me.*
> *All day I looked.*
> *Then I discovered,*
> *I was you,*
> *and the celebration*
> *of that began.*

LALLA

(A reference is not available for this quotation as it came from a personal note card.)

Looking at your astrology will definitely help in that arena also. You will be able to see your own challenges and strengths.

Notes to Myself:

_____

_____

_____

_____

_____

_____

_____

_____

_____

_____

_____

_____

_____

_____

MORE SHADOW WORKSHOP EXAMPLES

As in Part One, all names and identifying information have been changed to protect client privacy.

EXAMPLE 1: We Cannot Change Our Parents.

Audience: Well, as I was listening to you I felt like you must be reading my mail. I kept reflecting on all these people that give me a charge. The thought I had was what do you do to confront that? I know how I can confront it in myself, but how do you resolve it, especially in the circumstance where you have a person who it might be difficult if not impossible to talk with.

Rebeca: If you can't communicate with somebody, then you are not in a relationship.

Audience: What if you say it's your father? As far as you can get into the conversation is just to acknowledge that there are polarities, and then he shuts down. What do you do with that?

Rebeca: Well, I don't think we can change our parents, and I really don't think we can change other people. We can only change ourselves and how we relate to them. Notice that what you don't like about your father might be a clue as to what you aren't aware of in yourself. With our parents that is usually the case.

EXAMPLE 2: Preferences and Miscommunication vs. Projection

Audience: My wife and I are polarizing. I want to have more sex and she doesn't. Is that Shadow also?

Rebeca: No, that is not Shadow. That's a preference. If I say to you, "I like red cars" and you say "I like blue ones," then that is just a preference. The Shadow is characteristics and qualities of a person's character. In regard to sexual compatibility, I would ask or find out if there is something she would like that would enhance sex and give her more pleasure; then maybe she'd get more into it. I remember at the beginning of my marriage, I didn't want to ask for what I needed so as not to hurt my husband's ego. I believe that honest discussions between partners can help when sex has waned. Usually something is not being communicated. It may have nothing whatsoever to do with sex. They may be mad about something and are therefore withholding sex to get even.

EXAMPLE 3: Marrying Dad

Audience: I swore up and down I would never have the marriage my parents had. My dad was a pack rat, and my mom put up with it. He had boxes and boxes of computer parts. Now my husband

---

Notes to Myself:

has three closets full of computer parts. This is amazing. I married my dad!

EXAMPLE 4: The "Good" Mom and "Bad" Dad

Audience: My mom is really awesome. She's my best friend. We talk about everything. She guides me in a lot of my decisions with men. I don't like my dad at all.

Rebeca: You could be living out her life instead of yours. You will someday have to see who you might be and make your own mind up about things or you, too, will marry your dad. The parent we couldn't stand is the one most dominant in our unconscious.

EXAMPLE 5: The "Good" Father

Audience: My girlfriend and I are polarizing. I want her to get a job and contribute. I had to buy her a car, pay for her gas, and it's getting old. What's my Shadow here? I don't understand.

Rebeca: You are being the good father in the relationship, and she gets to be the child. If you stop paying for everything, then she'll have to get a job, won't she? Sit down with her and tell her that you don't want to be her father anymore. You want to be her partner. She needs to grow up, and you have to let her. You may want to look at how irresponsible you are being to yourself to let someone live off of you. You've attracted her to see something about you and vice versa.

Audience: I guess I've always taken care of everyone, even my parents, but probably especially my mother.

Rebeca: So could you still be trying to get your mother to grow up and take care of you?

Audience: Wow! That sounds like it could be true about me.

Rebeca: This sounds simplistic, but it is deep. Some things are so buried in us that we have to attract these mirrors to see what it is we need to see about ourselves. It's too easy to point the finger and say something is wrong with you! It's usually both people who need to change, but it takes two to tango, so to speak. Talk to her.

EXAMPLE 6: She Is Always Depressed.

Audience: My wife is always depressed. I come home, and it hangs in the air. It's hard to even want to come home as I never know for sure if she'll be depressed or who she'll be.

Rebeca: I would take a look at whether you may be repressing your deep feelings of grief and sadness. You may be forcing optimism and happiness on everyone around you because you refuse to let things get you down.

You may want to look at how irresponsible you are being to yourself to let someone live off of you.

Notes to Myself:

If it's about us, I guarantee you it will repeat. That's how you know it's your Shadow. We take ourselves everywhere we go.

Notes to Myself:

_____

_____

_____

_____

_____

_____

_____

_____

_____

_____

_____

_____

_____

_____

_____

_____

Audience: But why would I want to be a pessimist? That doesn't sound very healthy. I like who I am. I don't let things bother me like she does. I don't understand how this would help me.

Rebeca: No one can be happy all the time. If you are repressing your own sadness or grief, she is probably carrying that energy for both of you. Start to notice when you have a legitimate reason to be sad and you talk yourself out of it. If she is a Saturnian person, it is a part of her nature. If you can talk with her about this and even admit to her from time to time your own sadness and despair, then you may be able to help her see the part of her you are carrying since you are her opposite.

EXAMPLE 7: Overdoing the Guru to Others

Audience: I don't like it when someone acts like they are my guru or my savior. I have a friend who will call me and in a bossy way say to me, "You have to read this book." It really turns me off to where I've begun to avoid him. He is trying to force-feed me his beliefs. Is this my Shadow?

Rebeca: Not necessarily. You might just have to tell him you want to do your work on yourself in your own way. Communicate that with him if that is how you feel. It sounds like he might be identified with the archetype of the savior or healer. We do that when we think we have all the answers for someone else. Then again, there are times when a person is receptive to a book or tape being recommended to them and times when they are not. Someone else might not be offended at all by his suggesting a book. This might be one of those buttons you have about not liking for anyone to tell you what to do. You have to determine which it is for you. This is either about having boundaries and preferences, or if it's repeating in your life and you've walked away from several of these self-appointed gurus, then it could be a part of your Shadow. I recommended an astrology book to my doctor the other day, and she actually emailed me and asked me to send her the title and the author. Go inside yourself and ask "Where else might this same feeling come up for me? Has it happened to me before?" It could be the pushiness that's bothering you. Think about that.

Audience: I don't think this is repeating. I don't recall anyone else trying to force-feed me their beliefs like he does.

Rebeca: Then communicate that to him and let it go. Each incidence is unique to our situation. If it's about us, I guarantee you it will repeat. That's how you know it's your Shadow. We take ourselves everywhere we go.

EXAMPLE 8: Sexuality Taboos in Our Culture

Audience: I have had a very strict, religious upbringing and have always been taught that anything sexual is taboo — evil — a sin, etc. For some reason, even when I am in a very satisfying relationship, I seem to attract men who constantly make sexual advances toward me even though I let them know immediately I am unavailable and uninterested. This excites me. I don't think this shows, but why else do they continue to flirt with me? This is a huge puzzle to me. What is my Shadow here?

Rebeca: Sometimes our "upbringing and strict religious" attitudes about sex get compensated for in the Shadow. You sound like you answered your own question when you said, "It excited me." What part of you gets excited? The Shadow side, of course — since you are identified with your strict religious side. Everything in the psyche is in pairs. The unconscious will have to carry the other extreme for you until you come into balance, which I would imagine would be noticing the signals you are unconsciously putting out to these men. We keep secrets from ourselves when we don't know all the parts. That is the beauty of Shadow work, as these parts come into visibility.

EXAMPLE 9: Selfish vs. Selfless

Audience: You know a lot about me since I have had several readings with you. Why do I find out over time that the person I am dating is very self-centered and selfish and then I'm so surprised by it? Am I supposed to identify with the unconscious selfish part of me? I feel very guilty when selfish, self-centered thoughts enter my mind. I disregard them and do as I always do. Should I stop doing it? How do I stop while retaining self-respect? I'm very hard on myself if I think I wasn't nice, respectful or see myself as selfish. Where does this come from? Does my unconscious want me to be selfish sometimes?

Rebeca: It's your Shadow. Remember that whatever you believe strongly about yourself, the exact opposite is building up in your Shadow. The psyche has to compensate unconsciously for your imbalance. If you know something about a Leo Moon, which you have, it is very self-centered, and maybe your three planets in Virgo won't allow that into your consciousness. It's a part of you, and you have to accept it because it's probably operating behind your back. You can't change something you can't accept. I have Leo Rising and a Leo South Node, so can you imagine? I am very self-centered, BUT I know it, so therefore I can work with it. If you can't admit something or become aware of your own behavior, then you will have to project it, and it gets bigger and bigger and bigger OUT THERE to the degree that you will not own it. Does that make sense? Everyone needs to be selfish sometimes or they become lopsided in the opposite extreme. That is not healthy either. It's balance and consciousness that works. So dig in there and love that part of you, OK?

What part of you gets excited? The Shadow side, of course — since you are identified with your strict religious side. Everything in the psyche is in pairs.

Notes to Myself:

123

EXAMPLE 10: Masculine and Still Sensitive

Audience: I always knew I had a soft part of me, a gentle side of me. I think a guy feels that if he expresses the feminine side of himself, it will make it harder to have the kind of relationship with a woman that he wants. He is concerned that women want a macho man and if he expresses the nurturing side of himself, he will undermine himself in her eyes. It's a sad situation, but I tried to suppress for fear that it...

Rebeca: ...would take you over, make you become effeminate?

Audience: Yeah, yeah, but then I started relaxing. If I'm gentle, it means I can relate more. I can enjoy that and at the same time, the masculine side of me can be expressed, too. It doesn't have to be forced. It can be natural, but I need to attract someone who understands. That's what I would want, as that's the only way that I am going to be comfortable. I need the feminine part of me to be accepted.

Rebeca: I can relate. Learning to be both our masculine and feminine sides is the Aquarian Age goal. I believe that is what real love is about — accepting someone for their total self. Think about it. If a magnet seeks its opposite, if both people embrace their opposites, the spark ignited is love, but it's within and without at the same time. That's the divine marriage, what alchemists call the *coniunctio*. It's not just getting, it's giving because you lose your fear. The biggest fear is if I give you love, I'll be left out because what if you won't love me back? I can't really give to you unless you give to you, too, so we have to stay in balance and each person has to own their Shadow. Projection is so divisive. More relationships end because of Shadow projections being thrown back and forth. Real love is what they will have if they can both see the value of doing this work, but it takes two.

Audience: I think you're right.

Rebeca: In the end, it's about freedom to just be. Non-attachment. No illusions. No romantic delusions. That means you have to take back your projections, each person owning his or her Shadow as well as their Anima or Animus. Can you live like that?

Audience: I hope so.

A Woman Shared Her Story.

Audience: I got the same message when my husband died. I thought that he was my soul mate and he completed me. When he died I thought that part was ripped out of me. First I swore to myself that I'd never love again, but gradually, after about five years, I got it that I'll never love that way again. What I saw as love was completely fantasy and what I'll bring to the next

---

I always knew I had a soft part of me, a gentle side of me. I think a guy feels that if he expresses the feminine side of himself, it will make it harder to have the kind of relationship with a woman that he wants.

relationship, if there is one out there for me is not that we need each other for completion, but that we choose to be together while we work on our own completion. A good analogy is two logs going down the river. They each have their individual path, but that doesn't take away from the fact that each log is going down the river. No matter how close those logs get to each other, if they bump up against each other, they are still on their own individual journey. And something about that shared journey has to complement the individual journey. If it takes over, it never works, because then it throws both people out of balance and it can't work. You have to have that individual accountability, and if you put God on a person, then they will do whatever it takes to keep that intensity and glow alive, but a part of them has to die to do so because they can't really be themselves. They can't be true to who they are, and their Shadow will be more and more split off because they need you to love them as the magnificent person you've dreamed them up to be.

Rebeca: Yes, that makes sense now. One guy kept saying to me, "You don't know me," and it took years for me to understand what he was trying to tell me. We have to tell each other the truth even when it hurts to do so. We want to know who that person really is, not who they're pretending to be for their sake as well as ours. At the same time, we have to make commitments to our relationships for there to be a safe place to do Shadow work.

A Couple Spoke Up.

She: The biggest fear is what if their commitment isn't equal to mine? It takes a long time to realize you really know that you can be your total self and they will not leave you. Even when we fought, we would get physically ill, unable to sleep, gurgly stomach, and we wouldn't want to go to sleep until we worked it out. Now with time, we can disagree on something and we're fine. I tell him, "Sure, whatever, go to sleep."

Him: I'll still snuggle up to her, and then I feel OK, I can go to sleep now even though we haven't made up. That took time.

Rebeca: You've made it! Congratulations! That's what's possible. Having someone really see you — your total self — and love you.

Practicing the Process Continued

Now that I've given you more examples, let's do some more Shadow work. The six processes on the following pages were written to help you go deeper into your own unconscious. Through our introspection and self-honesty, we are contributing to the evolution of our cosmos. We are all connected to each other by the collective unconscious.

Now with time, we can disagree on something and we're fine. I tell him, "Sure, whatever, go to sleep."

Notes to Myself:

125

Our parents are in us. They have affected us deeply.

We have all said this statement to ourselves: "I will never be like them." Which parent did you swear you would never be like? Chances are you are a little bit like both of them.

As the saying goes, the apple never falls very far from the tree. Positive and negative characteristics or qualities, deeply ingrained patterns of behavior, and archetypal predispositions are passed down from one generation to the next. We will often unconsciously pick partners to help us understand these unresolved issues with our parents. Write about your parents and what you saw in them.

Characteristics I like in my mother:

1. _____

2. _____

3. _____

4. _____

5. _____

Characteristics I dislike in my mother:

1. _____

2. _____

3. _____

4. _____

5. _____

Characteristics I like in my father:

1. _____

2. _____

3. _____

4. _____

5. _____

Characteristics I dislike in my father:

1. _____

2. _____

3. _____

4. _____

5. _____

Falling in love is seeing a projection of yourself in another person you hardly know, while loving a real person is a conscious choice that takes place over a period of time.

Whatever is unconscious in you will be highly attractive in a partner. You begin by idealizing some of their characteristics and qualities because it seems that they have something that you don't. What brought you to this particular person is a gift if you'll make it conscious in yourself.

Have you ever fallen madly in love with someone who didn't feel the same way? They may have said to you, "You don't even know me." Write about this person. It can be someone you are with now, or it can be someone that you loved and lost. If he or she is no longer with you, you will still feel a sinking sensation in the pit of your stomach and tears will well up in your eyes when you think of him or her. These strong emotions are a definite clue that this person represents a part of your Shadow that you are still missing.

_____

_____

_____

_____

_____

_____

_____

_____

_____

_____

_____

_____

_____

_____

_____

_____

_____

_____

_____

_____

Our partners will show us our own Shadow traits begging for acceptance and integration.

Relationships are like seesaws. The farther two people move toward opposite ends, the more ups and downs they will create together as they seesaw back and forth.

What characteristics or experiences are you polarizing with your spouse or significant other? Are you acting out one extreme, while he or she is acting out the extreme opposite polarity?

1. Write down three pairs of opposites that keep you on this Shadow Dance seesaw. Can you embrace both parts for the sake of your own wholeness? _____

_____

_____

_____

_____

_____

_____

_____

_____

_____

2. Now that you are more conscious, what changes could each of you make to come toward the middle? It takes two partners who are committed and willing to communicate to make a relationship work.

_____

_____

_____

_____

_____

_____

_____

_____

_____

There is pure gold in our Shadow.

Often we will highly admire and respect certain individuals whom we put on pedestals. This is also called the "halo" effect. We want to be around them as much as possible.

These people can be teachers, bosses, coworkers, friends, lovers, etc. Describe these individuals and what you admire so highly about them. This will be part of your own Shadow. Your highest potentials (parts you don't even realize you already have and also parts that are undeveloped) can be secretly tucked away in the mirrors that these people are holding up for you to see.

1. _____

_____

_____

_____

_____

2. _____

_____

_____

_____

_____

3. _____

_____

_____

_____

_____

4. _____

_____

_____

_____

_____

5. _____

_____

_____

_____

_____

Dreams will often compensate for our conscious intentions or beliefs about ourselves. They will show us Shadow figures within our own psyche.

Keeping a dream journal is a highly effective way to see what is unconscious in ourselves. Study your dream characters. Why are they there? Which parts of you do they represent? What are they trying to tell you?

When you first try to remember your dreams, you may not succeed. Tell yourself before you go to sleep that you want to learn from your dreams and remember them. Then take time to record them. You will find that you are soon remembering more and more.

Dream characters who are opposites represent me. They are...

_____

_____

_____

_____

_____

_____

Dream characters or situations that keep repeating are...

_____

_____

_____

_____

_____

Things my characters do in dreams that I would never do in my real life are... _____

_____

_____

_____

_____

_____

Families are a repository for Shadow figures. Our brothers and sisters may have to suffer the experience of carrying our unacceptable and hidden parts.

When family members who can't stand each other are polarized, they will act out some of the parental issues still dormant in the unconscious. With self-honesty and love, siblings can become safe containers to work out each other's darkest selves.

How do you know whether it's your sibling you can't stand or a part of yourself you deny or need to embrace? You can tell by the repulsive feelings and the high negative energy you allot to their characteristics. Other people will not find these qualities so incorrigible. That's when you know it's about yourself — by your emotionally charged reactions to whatever they do or say. To become truly conscious of our Shadow means we have to acknowledge these situations. This is often a painful discovery that, once accepted, can give us more choices to make about our own behavior.

I am constantly repulsed by the actions of my sister. She... _____

_____

_____

_____

_____

I can't stomach being around my brother for too long. He...

_____

_____

_____

_____

Are you afraid to be like your brothers and sisters? Maybe you need to be more like them. How do you see yourself benefitting from this awareness? _____

_____

_____

_____

_____

_____

NOTES PART TWO:

1) Edited by Connie Zwieg and Jeremiah Abrams, *Meeting the Shadow, The Hidden Power of the Dark Side of Human Nature*, Liz Greene, *The Shadow in Astrology,* Jeremy P. Tarcher, Inc., 1991, pg 153

2) C.G. Jung, CW 10 - *Civilization in Transition, The Undiscovered Self (Mind and Earth)*, Princeton University Press, Bollingen, 1957, par 74, pg 39

3) C.G. Jung, CW 9 - Pt. 2 - AION, *Research into the Phenomenology of the Self,* Princeton University Press, Bollingen, 1959, par 61, pg 33

4) Edward F. Edinger, *Anatomy of the Psyche, Alchemical Symbolism in Psychotherapy,* Open Court Publishing, La Salle, Illinois, 1985, pg 187

5) C.G. Jung, CW 10 - *Civilization in Transition, The Undiscovered Self (Mind and Earth)*, Princeton University Press, Bollingen, 1957 para 69, pg 37

6) C.G. Jung, *Two Essays in Analytical Psychology, The Synthetic or Constructive Method,* Princeton University Press, Bollingen, 1953/1966, par 78, pg 52

7) C.G. Jung, CW 14 - *Mysterium Coniunctionis,* Princeton University Press; Bollingen, 1963, par 1, pg 3

8) C.G. Jung, CW 10 - *Civilization in Transition, The Undiscovered Self (Mind and Earth)*, Princeton University Press, Bollingen, 1957, par 236, pg 113

9) C.G. Jung, *Two Essays in Analytical Psychology, On the Psychology of the Unconscious,* Princeton University Press, Bollingen, 1953/1966, par 136, pg 86

10) C.G. Jung, CW 16 - *The Practice of Psychotherapy, The Psychology of the Transference,* Princeton University Press, 1954, par 534, pg 318

11) John A. Sanford, *The Kingdom Within,* Harper & Row Publishers, San Fransisco, 1970, pg 167

12) Rev. J. Pittman McGehee, Cassette - *On Becoming Married,* Broadacres Center, Houston, TX 1999

13) C.G. Jung, CW 9 - Pt. 2 - AION, *Research into the Phenomenology of the Self,* Princeton University Press, Bollingen, 1959, par 42, pg 22

14) Jellaladin Rumi

15) Edward F. Edinger, *Anatomy of the Psyche, Alchemical Symbolism in Psychotherapy,* 1985, pg 187

16) C.G. Jung, CW 9 - Pt. 2 - AION, *Research into the Phenomenology of the Self,* Princeton University Press; Bollingen, 1959, par 41, pg 21

17) C.G. Jung, *Two Essays in Analytical Psychology, The Problem of the Attitude Type,* Princeton University Press, Bollingen, 1953/1966, par 78, pg 53

18) Robert A. Johnson, *Owning Your Own Shadow,* Harper San Fransisco, 1971, pg 163-64

19) Edward C. Whitmont, *The Symbolic Quest,* Princeton University Press, Princeton, NJ, 1991, pg 38

20) C.G. Jung, CW 10 - *Civilization in Transition, The Undiscovered Self (Mind and Earth)*, Princeton University Press, Bollingen, 1957, par 74, pg 39

21) Robert A. Johnson, *We, Understanding the Psychology of Romantic Love,* Harper & Row, San Fransisco, CA, 1983

22) Edited by, Joseph Campbell, *The Portable Jung, Marriage as a Psychological Relationship,* Penguin Books, 191, pg 174

23) Edited by, Joseph Campbell, *The Portable Jung, Marriage as a Psychological Relationship,* Penguin Books, 191, pg 173

24) John A. Sanford, *Invisible Partners,* Paulist Press, NY, 1980, pg 14

25) W. Brugh Joy, M.D., *Avalanche, Heretical Reflections on the Dark and Light,* Ballantine Books, NY, 1990, pg 210

26) Eric Butterworth, Cassette - *Forming Relationships and Healing the Hurt,* Unity Church of Christianity, 1991

27) Richard Idemon, *Through the Looking Glass,* Samuel Weiser, Inc., York Beach, Maine, 1992, pg 21

28) The Houston Films, *A Matter of Heart,* a documentary on C.G. Jung, *Live footage of Jung and others,* King Video, 1991

29) James Hollis, *The Eden Project: In Search of the Magical Other,* Inner City Books, Toronto, Ontario, Canada, 1998

30) C.G. Jung, CW 10 - *Civilization in Transition, Mind and Earth,* Princeton University Press, Bollingen, 1957, par 579, pg 301

31) C.G. Jung, CW 11 - *Psychology and Religion: West and East,* 1958, par 131, pg 76

32) John A. Sanford, *Invisible Partners,* Paulist Press, NY, 1980

33) Robert A. Johnson, *Inner Work,* Harper, San Francisco, 1986, pg 137

34) C.G. Jung, CW 14 - *Mysterium Coniunctionis,* Princeton University Press, Bollingen, 1963, par 193, pg 163

35) Cassette - Robert Johnson, *Your Shadow, Friend or Foe,* Sounds True, 1992

36) Irene Claremont de Castillejo, *Knowing Woman, A Feminine Psychology,* Harper & Row, Publishers, NY, 1973, pg 84

37) Irene Claremont de Castillejo, *Knowing Woman, A Feminine Psychology,* Harper & Row, Publishers, NY, 1973, pg 20

38) Marie-Louise vonFranz - *Alchemy, An Introduction to the Symbolism and the Psychology,* Inner City Books, Toronto, Canada, 1980, pg 164

39) John A. Sanford, *Invisible Partners,* Paulist Press, NY, 1980, pg 38

40) C.G. Jung, CW 10 - *Civilization in Transition, Women in Europe,* Princeton University Press, Bollingen, 1957, par 259, pg 125

41) C.G. Jung, *Memories, Dreams, Reflections,* (MDR) New York, Pantheon, 1961, pg 326

3 Signs and Planets in Our 7th House

In a letter written to Hindu astrologer,
B.V. Raman, September 6th, 1947- Carl G. Jung wrote:

"Since you want to know my opinion about astrology, I can tell you that I've been interested
in this particular activity of the human mind since more than 30 years. As I am a psychologist,
I am chiefly interested in the particular light the horoscope sheds on certain complications in the
character. In cases of difficult psychological diagnosis I usually get a horoscope in order to have a further
point of view from an entirely different angle. I must say that I very often found that the astrological data
elucidated certain points which I otherwise would have been unable to understand."

Libra Characteristics Chosen Consciously Can Help Us.

The sign or archetype of Libra is the natural ruler of the 7th house, and Libra is considered
to be the sign most interested in relating to others. Libra is a cardinal sign, active in social
affairs and good at organizing people. Ruled
by the planet Venus, Libra has a flair for art
and creativity and a distinct need for beauty,
symmetry and balance. This need for balance extends into relating skills as it is also
very aware of equality and keeping things
fair. This is a clue to what we all need in
order to have successful relationships. We
all have Libra somewhere in our chart, not
just the people born under the sun sign of
Libra. We have to learn the Libran traits of
compromise, cooperation, recognizing each
other's needs and giving our partners equal
room in the relationship. We have to learn
to be considerate, truly listen to our partners
when they have a request or express their
feelings, reach out when the other needs us
and be willing to show that we need them,
too. Nothing is a one-way street. Any planet
in the 7th house will have these requirements no matter what sign is there.

RULERS IN ASTROLOGY	
HOUSE/SIGN	**PLANET**
1 ♈Aries (Mar 20 - Apr 18)	♂ MARS
2 ♉Taurus (Apr 19 - May 19)	♀ VENUS
3 ♊Gemini (May 20 - Jun 23)	☿ MERCURY
4 ♋Cancer (Jun 24 - Jul 21)	☽ MOON
5 ♌Leo (Jul 22 - Aug 21)	☉ SUN
6 ♍Virgo (Aug 22 - Sep 23)	☿ MERCURY
7 ♎Libra (Sep 24 - Oct 22)	♀ VENUS
8 ♏Scorpio (Oct 23 - Nov 20)	♇ PLUTO
9 ♐Sagittarius (Nov 21 - Dec 20)	♃ JUPITER
10 ♑Capricorn (Dec 21 - Jan 20)	♄ SATURN
11 ♒Aquarius (Jan 21 - Feb 18)	♅ URANUS
12 ♓Pisces (Feb 19 - Mar 19)	♆ NEPTUNE

Libra is also seeking to be objective as it
is at the 180° opposition in the chart, an aspect that describes two opposite urges in the
psyche that will need to stay in proportion to each other. Libra's symbol is the scales.
This symbol implies that in partnership we will be required to consciously create balance
with our significant other.

Libra is also interested in ideas and concepts as it is also an Air sign. It is therefore
very mental in its orientation to life. Thinking, reflecting and becoming objective where

our partners are concerned are very important ingredients to sustaining successful relationships. We also have to differentiate from the beloved and see all of them, the dark and the light, in order to love them as the real flesh-and-blood human beings they are.

Withdrawing Our Projections

When we are projecting our Shadow, the hardest thing to do is to consciously withdraw our projections. It always looks like it is simply the other person's fault. We tell ourselves over and over, we are not like them. THEY do this or that. Yet the roller coaster of love will take us up and down, over and over again, until we can see that there is indeed a mirror that is being held up for us by the other person. Only then are we on the way to healing and possibly embarking on a new journey of deeper relatedness.

Usually the "other" is overdoing something and we are getting irritated by it, or vice versa. For example, in a typical Aries-Libra polarity, if they are overdoing Aries, they want their needs to be met at the expense of our needs. They have no problem with over asserting, being selfish or pushy, even when we've dropped hints that "right now" is not the right time or this is something we don't want to do. We might feel we have to hit them over the head to get them to stop. Or we may ask them for something and they will completely ignore us.

Conversely, when the Libra archetype is being overdone, people are so nice we can walk all over them. They refuse to confront anything that is clearly unfair and will sweep things under the rug instead of telling us where we are out of line. They will accommodate our needs exclusively, sweetly smile and take whatever we dish out. They are pushovers deluxe and fake, too. They will flatter us when we least deserve it until we might think, "Is this person for real? Do they ever get angry?"

To do this Shadow dance work, we need to do exactly what they are doing halfway. Taking back our Aries archetype means we need to ask for what we want and get assertive and specific ourselves if we want to truly be in an equal partnership. No one can have their way all the time. If they ignore us, we have to ask again until they hear us. We have to take responsibility for getting our needs met.

Taking back our Libra archetype means listening to our partner, becoming more objective and less subjective. We have to make the effort to accommodate them, compromise with them and be fair, which every Libra has foremost on their mind. If I give to you, then when it's your turn, I expect you to give back to me so that we can stay in balance. We take turns.

Number one, we don't run away from them, ignore them or put them down for being who they are. If we prematurely run away, we've lost a golden opportunity to learn from the mirror they are providing us. If we are in a relationship with them and we ignore them, they will get angrier and more frustrated and they'll overdo even more. Unconsciously, they may start doing whatever they think will push our buttons. If we put them down, we are not taking our share of the responsibility for the polarization. For a polarization to have occurred, both people had to get out of balance and therefore BOTH are responsible for bringing things back to a state of harmony. Both partners have to be willing to discuss whatever the issue is and change their behavior consciously. We meet each other in the middle. We talk about it. We write things down if we have to do so to get clear with each other. This is not an easy task, as it takes work and cooperation. Both have to agree to be fair with each other and take turns. Taking turns giving in is even important. It all has a lot to do with how we communicate.

I'd like to give the following example from John A. Sanford's book *Between People, Communicating One-to-One:*

> ...Harry is upset because his wife, Susan, is drinking again. One evening he says sarcastically, "Well, I guess this is the way it's going to be now, just one drunken evening after another." Of course his wife erupts angrily.
>
> Later, after thinking about it, he brings the subject up again. This time he begins by saying, "Susan, I have to tell you that when you drink I feel it destroys our relationship. That's why I wish you would stop."
>
> Susan is angry again, but her anger does not last long this time. And she stops drinking, for now she knows how her husband feels that what he values is the relationship, where before she felt he was just hostile and critical toward her.[1]

He also describes communication as a game of catch, where one person throws a ball and the other catches it and throws it back. He says,

> To use our image of communication as a game of catch: When one person throws the ball it is an attempt to begin to work through an agenda with the other person. If the other person will not catch the ball and toss it back, the whole process is aborted. And if the ball is not thrown back and forth long enough, all the items in the agenda are not discussed.[2]

When we are withdrawing projections, it is important to be vulnerable and tell the other person we have done so. I'll never forget an incident with my business partner, Trish, where I had gotten angry with her at something she did that I considered to be passive-aggressive. She left that day calmly insisting that I was being

For a polarization to have occurred, both people had to get out of balance, and therefore BOTH are responsible for bringing things back to a state of harmony.

Notes to Myself:

_____

_____

_____

_____

_____

_____

_____

_____

_____

_____

_____

_____

Communication also requires two people who are willing to play. And when they play, when the ball of communication goes back and forth between them, they are brought into relationship.[3]

JOHN A. SANFORD

ridiculous and it was all about me, but later that evening, she called me. When she called, I was writing in my journal how I saw her as being angry herself only she wasn't admitting it. She called me right at that synchronistic moment as I had just written that in my journal, and she admitted it to me. She took back the projection openly. It was awesome. Now we could meet each other halfway and discuss the issue. Our bond only increased more and more through tackling each situation as it came up, and our love and affection for each other grew. There's nothing worse than knowing and feeling intuitively that something is amiss and the other person is evasive and refuses to be honest and vulnerable. It creates an even bigger gap between partners, and nothing gets resolved. Adults can discuss issues that come up and reach a compromise. It may be that this time we will do it your way and next time we will do it mine. We both agree to take turns. People who are seeking Mom and Dad's approval or the exact opposite, rebelling against Mom and Dad's disapproval, will start acting out like little kids, refusing to communicate, pointing fingers and blaming, instead of discussing their problems like reasonable adults. Communication is everything. I can't repeat that enough.

Our Astrology Will Give Us Details.

Astrology can really help out here. If we look at our astrology, we can see exactly the areas that are giving us and our partners trouble. This is the pure GOLD in this information. Having an astrological report for each person and a compatibility report for the two of them is invaluable. There are many well-written reports that can be purchased including the ones I sell on my Web site. (See reports available at the end of this workbook). Each report will give a different perspective on the same energy. A reading can be set up with an astrologer. I prefer doing one person in a couple, then the other, and then the two together. I listen to them each give their perspective of the relationship. It is too revealing to have someone read your chart in the presence of another person, so I do them separately. I have found that when both partners are in the room, neither will be completely honest for fear of vulnerability. (As Trish, my partner, once said to me, "You feel unmasked but it's enlightening at the same time.") I also write extensive notes so that when I put the two of them together in the third session, I can show them where they are projecting their own energies and where they are each out of balance. Many of the couples' charts I have seen have very similar energy. Usually, they have split it up between them. Some have what the other lacks and overcompensate for their partners. Eventually both will resent it.

Whatever we're doing is pretty ingrained. We'll repeat it over and over with whoever comes into our life to teach us that we need to learn *some of the opposite if we want to grow.* Growth takes two people cooperating with each other.

Many people get in relationships where they will do exactly what their partner wants all the time, thinking that this is how to keep the peace. It's a false peace which will erupt sooner or later because the psyche is striving to be whole and complete. In *Modern Man in Search of a Soul,* Jung says,

> ...nothing is more unbearable than a tepid harmony in personal relationships brought about by withholding emotions.[4]

In the *Tavistock lectures,* he explains,

> You see there is perfect harmony here; but do not make the mistake of thinking that this harmony is a paradise, for these people will kick against each other after awhile because they are just too harmonious.[5]

More important than anything we do in this life is the need to become ourselves and not what anyone else wants us to be. We have to make the honest effort to balance who we really are with a partner if we want to be in a healthy relationship. Chances are the unconscious has chosen the perfect person for us to do this with. If there is no attraction, we will not grow with that person. The

Many of the couples' charts I have seen have very similar energy. Usually, they have split it up between them.

Notes to Myself:

_____

_____

_____

_____

_____

_____

_____

_____

_____

_____

_____

_____

_____

_____

Astrology can paint a picture for you of what you are required to integrate within yourself in order to meet the other halfway.

effect that others have on us is purposeful. The teleology of life is bringing them to us for a reason. The healing powers of the unconscious are symbolized by flowing water. This water (our feeling nature) is best expressed in love of others and loving ourselves by doing Shadow work with our partners. The astrological data of each will give both a tool to work with.

The 7th - the House of the "Other"

With conscious effort we can choose to become the signs and planets ruling or in the 7th house. For insight, we can also look to aspects to our Venus, the planet that symbolizes the desire for union, giving and receiving love. The Moon, our emotional nature, is also important as is Saturn because relationships that truly last will have strong Saturnian aspects. Our North and South Nodes are also strong indicators for relationship patterns. Even Mercury will help us understand our particular way of communicating. Astrology is quite comprehensive. It is not vague or fuzzy at all. Astrology can paint a picture for you of what you are required to integrate within yourself in order to meet the other halfway.

The 7th house, being the house of partnership, is the house of equality. Only two equals, standing side-by-side, can create a solid container for the relationship which is the divine marriage *(coniunctio)* taking place within each one. The King and Queen of your inner life are the reward. Every marriage or partnership presents us with this opportunity. If two people are committed to their relationship, growing and becoming conscious, when the projections wear off, an opportunity arrives for both people. Both can now discover and embrace their missing halves. This is not an easy task. It takes work and often involves a painful encounter with the Self (with a capital "S"). In his book, *Mysterium Coniunctionis,* Jung says that an experience with the Self is always a defeat for the ego[6] but that the death of the ego (the self as you knew it) allows one to be reborn into one's own wholeness as projections are taken back. The more we can recognize when our ego is getting in our way, and that we have to open ourselves to the flow of life as it unfolds even when it's decidedly painful, the more we will move toward our inner marriage to the divine.

When each person can learn about their partners' astrology, look at a synastry interpretation of the two of them together, the insights revealed are very healing. I recently made friends with one of my suppliers. The first time I had lunch with him, he told me he and his wife were going through some turmoil in their relationship. After four years of being together, they had reached that stage that married couples often get to where the spark is gone and no one is being honest anymore. We talked about astrology, the Shadow and

Notes to Myself:

unconscious collusion between couples. He was very receptive to looking at himself. I printed a report for him and gave it to him the next time we met. The planet Uranus was transitting his 7th, so it would indicate that it was the right time for them to become more objective and see who each other actually was. The transits (where the planets are right now) to the 7th house are usually dead on. They are like clockwork. The next time we met was one month later. We had decided to have lunch once a month since we were doing business together. He told me his partner had decided to read his report, and read it aloud to him. He said, "Rebeca, it was me! It was remarkable. She was able to understand me in ways she had never seen before. I was so impressed." He promptly wanted me to run a report for her so they could read hers and discuss it. I also gave them a synastry report and they are talking to each other with more intimacy (in-to-me-see) than they had for a very long time.

When we have a thorough understanding of our astrology and our partners' astrology, we can understand so much more who the person we are in relationship with is. Our differences will be spelled out as well. Our imbalances will be revealed. We can take back our projections and realize where we are actually a lot alike, too. Now it's on paper. Astrology is so accurate and detailed. It's hard to deny this is who we are, especially in the face of someone who lives with us day in and day out. The value of taking back our projections is that we can now see and accept our partners for who they really are — not who we wanted them to be, not who we wish they would change into. We can love them not for what they can give us, but for who they are. The love that can now grow between two partners is profound because it is REAL. Real love, unlike projection, is a willingness to see and support another person to be their own unique, separate self. This will untangle us from seeking in them the perfect parent-mirror image of ourselves. ***As long as we are still seeking to be completed by another person, we will not allow them their own autonomy or individuality.*** As the Rune "Partnership" describes it, two separate and whole beings — equals in the true sense of the word — can help each person feel their own union with the Divine within instead of through projective identification with their partner. As the love between them grows and expands to the entire cosmos, this kind of love gives each partner their freedom — the greatest gift of all. As the duet sung by Barbra Streisand and Celine Dion professes, "LOVE will be the gift you give yourself."

Astrology is so accurate and detailed. It's hard to deny this is who we are especially in the face of someone who lives with us day in and day out.

Notes to Myself:

_____

_____

_____

_____

_____

_____

_____

_____

_____

_____

_____

_____

_____

_____

_____

Tell Him, sung by Barbara Streisand and Celine Dion, released as the first single from Dion's Let's Talk About Love and Streisand's Higher Ground album, on November 3, 1997. (Source Wikipedia)

Too Young for Shadow Work?

It seems to be a second-half-of-life experience to understand both the Shadow and the Anima/Animus concepts, because by then we have experienced a few relationships, and we are aware of a repeating pattern. Still, there are young people who are striving to become conscious and are drawn to this information. My son, who is a Libra also, has grown up with this information. I've been learning and talking with him about it since 1990. He brought me one of his friends to talk to who at 23 years of age was experiencing a repeating pattern. After talking with my son, this young man wanted to ask me questions. Several of his friends congregate on my deck to discuss their relationships. Young people are interested, as these young people are the Pluto in Libra and Pluto in Scorpio generations, so it is an essential part of their astrology.

One of the men who came to me for an astrological consultation, who is in his early 60s, told me he thought this information should be taught to people in high school. I agree. We are seeing more and more divorces, and I would attribute much of that to the fact that we live in a "fast food" kind of relationship world. We want intimacy with someone to happen fast. We want to have that "in-love" feeling (which I believe is mostly lust and infatuation) so most people don't take the time to get to know another person. They rush into a relationship expecting that this time it will be different. To paraphrase Edna St. Vincent Millay, "Life is not one thing after another. It's the same damn thing over and over."

Steps to Strive for as We Get into Relationships

Acquaintance - friendship - dating - commitment, then sex is the order that I feel is important for a relationship. We can't skip any of these steps. When we are exploring friendship and dating, we find out a lot about the person. We may or may not want to continue into a committed situation. After being good friends and dating for a long period of time, only then are we ready to deal with commitment and sexual intimacy. Otherwise we are having sex with a stranger. As we saw in Part Two, when we prematurely become sexually intimate, this actually prevents us from getting to know people. Too much fear enters the situation. We start to come from a space of how we can feel secure in this situation instead of how we can get to know who this person is or whether we have a good partnership.

When we are compulsively or magnetically drawn to anyone, it is inevitable that there is an element of projection. Each must also ask themselves, how much more can I learn about myself through this person? No one knows everything there is to know about themselves. So much of our character is unconscious. It is a life's work to

When we are compulsively or magnetically drawn to anyone, it is inevitable that there is an element of projection.

Notes to Myself:

142

become all of who we are meant to be. Becoming conscious of ourselves and individuating is our gift to the cosmos. If we can approach our relationships as catalysts for healing and growth, then we have to take more time to learn about the person we have fallen in love with. Both partners have to be willing to remove their masks/personas slowly as they communicate honestly with each other. Both must be willing to see the light side and the dark side.

There is no perfect person out there who will magically fulfill our every fantasy. Only a child expects perfection. Relating as a conscious adult, we have to learn to compromise and to accept some of the unacceptable in others. They will have to accept us, too. In that space of loving acceptance, people change. We grow. Now both have an opportunity to love a real human being, and this takes maturity and consciousness.

Looking at relationships this way gives us a lot more choices. We learn tolerance and compassion for our mistakes and those of others. If a person can't say they are sorry ever, they have major issues. We learn to say we are sorry since no one is perfect or right all the time. Striving to become conscious of our total selves, we allow our partners also to be themselves. We come to the middle with them, communicating honestly, recognizing when we are polarizing with each other. This is real love.

The other kind of love is only romantic images and ideals we all have. These can only ultimately disappoint us because no one out there is perfect and neither are we. When we put our Anima or Animus on another person, this is a huge burden to put on anyone unless we can own it ourselves. Robert Johnson in his book, *Owning Your Own Shadow*,[7] says it is actually inhuman to expect this of anyone. If we do have a real relationship with a person we have projected ourselves onto, the projections will inevitably fall off, and we will find they are sometimes the ideal we pictured them to be and sometimes they, too, will annoy the hell out of us. They will no longer provide the constant magic for us that we thought we would have when we married them. They become real in our eyes.

Conversely, if we never have a relationship with them, then we can go our whole lives thinking they were Prince Charming or Sleeping Beauty. As myth shows in each of these romantic stories, this is the part of us that needs to awaken inside of ourselves, not outside in someone else. Mythological motifs are much like characters in our dreams. They each represent a different aspect of our many selves.

We are becoming more of who we are when we take this information seriously. We change on the inside. This, too, is one of those paradoxes of life. We want to be loved for who we are, and yet we are all growing and changing all the time. No one stays the same

If we do have a real relationship with a person we have projected ourselves onto, the projections will inevitably fall off, and we will find they are sometimes the ideal we pictured them to be and sometimes they, too, will annoy the hell out of us.

Notes to Myself:

_____

_____

_____

_____

_____

_____

_____

_____

_____

_____

_____

_____

_____

_____

It is only when we feel with our heart that we actually evolve. Otherwise we are animal or purely instinctual (in lust), and animals cannot choose.

for very long. You'll know it is love to the degree that you are willing to grow and change with your partner. Love is feeling your feelings and emotions and sharing them with your partner in the little mundane ways that living day in and day out can provide. It is the kind word when someone is down, the spontaneous touch passing through the kitchen or offering to help when the other is burdened by responsibilities. It is "You have work to do. I'll cook tonight." These little things are the stuff love is made of. These shared experiences that in time build trust are what open our hearts to another human being. It is only when we feel with our heart that we actually evolve. Otherwise we are animal or purely instinctual (in lust), and animals cannot choose.

Not All Relationships Are Meant to Last; Some Are Only Lessons to Be Learned.

There are some people who are just not compatible. I will not naively say that you should be able to accept and get along with everyone, because there are some people who are toxic to each other. They are constantly criticizing each other, have zero in common, so they therefore do not understand the other person's feelings, needs or dreams, and they destroy the relationship. This happens when we marry someone who is the extreme polar opposite, such as an introvert marrying an extrovert. Maybe the earthy, pragmatic individual marries an intuitive, adventurous risk taker. At first, each is the complimentary opposite and they feed off of their differences. Sooner or later, Jung says,

> But now they turn face to face and look for understanding —
> only to discover that they have never understood one another.
> Each speaks a different language. Then the conflict between
> the two types begins. This struggle is envenomed, brutal, full
> of mutual deprecation, even when conducted quietly and in the
> greatest intimacy. For the value of the one is the negation of value
> for the other.[8]

Not all relationships are negotiable when they have no bridge to each other's inherent way of being. When two people are constantly hurting each other, the love between them is not given a fertile garden to grow in. People of very different types are not going to be able to understand where the other is coming from, so constant misunderstandings occur. Two people may have nothing in common, and their relationship may have begun purely on an outer physical level without first getting past their projection/fascination. Those who hold their true selves back in order to win another person can't make a relationship work because they never really knew the person they married anyway. They didn't take the time. Real

Notes to Myself:

love takes time. It doesn't happen overnight or in one instant as you see someone across the room and are physically attracted to them. Our true soul mates are those who can go the distance with us. Some of our closest friends are also soul mates for us. The relationships we have with these people will lead us to our souls. That's what soul mates are about.

I was talking to a friend of mine ending her 10-year relationship as I was ending my 6-year relationship. She said, "I am so angry. I wasted 10 years of my life. I think of all the people I might have met if I had just seen it years ago."

I said, "Angry at whom or what? Angry with him that you couldn't get him to be someone other than who he was? Or angry with yourself because you knew he was not who you wanted him to be? Who are you angry with? I was angry, too, until I realized there wasn't anyone or anything to be angry about... or with. They were who they were. We are who we are. They didn't want us to be who we were either. My boyfriend wanted someone else. Yours wanted someone else. You and I wanted someone else. There it is. That is the truth. The truth will always free you up."

She responded. "Amen! Just angry at not trusting my gut... after all, we both knew, deep down. I thought that this was a life lesson for me to learn to work out my differences instead of leaving. The ironic thing is that even if I had been able to change myself into a frugal, non-pet-loving, emotional and financial slave — it still wouldn't have worked! If there's a next time, I'll be able to recognize it because it will fit better and naturally. Neither one of us will be asked to give up our core values and so much of who we are just to be together." Amen. If we have to give up who we are to be with someone, then we are not fulfilling our contribution to the cosmos. We have to be ourselves. Someone will love you for yourself. There's a saying that goes like this: there is a lid for every pot.

Rejection Can Be a Gift, if You Change Your View of It.

As I said at the end of Part Two, and it bears repeating, if someone leaves you or rejects you, it's an opportunity for you to love yourself more. If we are being mirrored by our partners, then the mirrors they are holding up for us have something to teach us about how we treat ourselves. After a bit of grieving and sadness (because it will hurt to be rejected since we are human) this can turn out to be a real gift. If you can get objective and clear about what a relationship meant and why you drew that particular person to you in the first place, you will see the way the Self in us is always supporting our growth, whether we can see it at first or not.

Notes to Myself:

When we can get to a place where we can genuinely thank the other person for leaving us and we know it was necessary for our soul's growth, we are healing.

As Jung explains,

> Tears, sorrow, and disappointment are bitter, but wisdom is the comforter in all psychic suffering. Indeed, bitterness and wisdom form a pair of alternatives: where there is bitterness wisdom is lacking, and where wisdom is there can be no bitterness.[9]

When we can get to a place where we can genuinely thank the other person for leaving us and we know it was necessary for our soul's growth, we are healing. We may have lost ourselves to the other person or made the relationship more important than our own life. That never works. We have to meet the "other" only halfway in order for us to live out our 7th house with self-love.

Even a nice guy or a nice girl who is typically giving and loving will start to take a "too nice or too eager" person for granted. Some people will bend over backwards to get you to love them until they have nothing left for themselves. I once left a guy because he brought me roses every week. He wanted me too much and was calling me four times a day. Although it was flattering at first, it quickly became boring. His attention started to drive me nuts. I found out what that looked like when I gave too much to someone else and became a doormat. We have all been on both sides of this situation. I once heard someone say, "If we put anyone up on a pedestal, all we'll get to kiss is their feet." I don't remember who said it, but I agree. It doesn't work to give up who we are, or to pretend to be Mr. or Ms. Wonderful to be loved by another. When we love ourselves first and take care of ourselves, then we can receive love from someone else and not before. We can also give love because we are no longer in fear. We have ourselves. We cannot give our love to anyone if we are afraid of them. Fear means we want something that they cannot give us. A wise therapist, Joann Tangedahl, once said to me, "Keep your eggs in your own basket and keep your heart open."

> *In the figures of animus and anima lie the deepest mystery,*
> *and it is through them that one can truly see how relationships*
> *are a path of inner development and the living embodiment*
> *of a journey to the deepest center of one's own being.[10]*
>
> LIZ GREENE

My teacher, Rev. J. Pittman McGehee, said to me a long time ago, "When the inner marriage takes place, the outer one will also." This is the alchemical union of opposites that is symbolized by the GOLD. That Gold is why we valued them so much in the first place. They were carrying our Gold. To be a whole person, we are destined to take our Gold back. We can still be in a committed relationship, only in this scenario that I am talking about, we have to take back our Shadow and our contrasexual image from our partner.

Consciousness Is the Secret Ingredient.

The real key to a truly successful relationship is that both people are working together to become more conscious. This can only happen when two people genuinely love each other and have enough in common to enjoy each other's company — not just during the courtship phase of their relationship but day in and day out. As best friends, both are communicating honestly, especially when it's uncomfortable to do so. They are striving to be authentic — **real** with each other. Owning their own Shadows will help each to accept each other as unique, separate persons. They can both grow and together create the balance and trust that is needed to successfully live together in the 7th house. Their partnership will be a two-way street. Neither will expect more from the other than they are willing to give themselves. In fact, commitment to the partnership is achieved as each person is willing to share of themselves completely with the other person without losing their individual identity or core self.

When partners do their own Shadow work, there is not too much each can accuse the other person of doing. They know, if they're really being honest with themselves, that they are just as capable of doing whatever it is the other person is doing or they need to learn how to do it halfway. We have to be vigilant in our self-reflection. We have to notice when we act the exact way we are accusing our partner or our friend of acting. If we can't be ruthlessly honest with ourselves about our patterns, which repeat, then we will have to keep doing the same exact Shadow dance with whoever else shows up in our life, and the universe will certainly oblige us. Now let's look at the planets.

Planets in or Ruling the 7th House or in Aspect to Venus

Astrology helps us look at how each of us projects the planets and signs in or ruling our 7th house or in aspect to our Venus placement. The following descriptions include some suggestions on how it can look when things are out of balance and suggestions of what we can do to come to the middle with our partners and live out our 7th-house energies together. The projections explain how we see them. Usually our partners will be overdoing whichever planet or sign is in the 7th. The planet or sign on the cusp is destined to be an important aspect of your relationship life. It will work out best when you and your partner are each giving and receiving your fair

They know, if they're really being honest with themselves, that they are just as capable of doing whatever it is the other person is doing or they need to learn how to do it halfway.

Notes to Myself:

_____

_____

_____

_____

_____

_____

_____

_____

_____

_____

_____

_____

_____

Notes to myself as
I recall my own
experience with this
planetary influence.

share of whatever the planet or sign represents, with each partner making the effort to consciously stay in balance. There are often several planets or archetypes in or ruling the 7th house, and each one of these will be uncannily represented in our partners.

The transcendental planets (Uranus, Neptune and Pluto) are difficult to experience as they are energies that are liberating us from our personal ego needs. They symbolize higher states of consciousness. Uranus is higher mind, Neptune is higher love, and Pluto is higher power. When any of these three planets are significators for the 7th house or in aspect to Venus or the Moon, something more is being asked of us. We are to evolve to a higher consciousness, and our ego needs have to be transcended in our capacity to love and relate to others. We, of course, always have the choice to live these out destructively or constructively. It's all in knowing you have a choice.

The first step in understanding planetary influences is to get a copy of your birth chart and your partner's. You do not have to be married. All of our relationships will benefit when we know who we are. Our 7th house is about ourselves in partnership with others. Remember, we cannot change others, but we can be aware of our own needs in relationships and honor our unique selves in this way. There are several places online to get your chart: *starguidance.com/readings/free_chart.html.* I have also provided a symbol legend on the back cover and in Part Four for use in deciphering astrological symbols.

Now I also want to stress that this part — the 7th-house character — is only one part of you or the other person. The house where the Sun falls is also very important to each person's identity. The other planets and house descriptions will tell you a lot more about a person's individuality. So when we are looking at the 7th house, this is only the part of us that symbolizes who we are when we strive for union with others. Therefore everything in the following descriptions will not fit because of other influences. I can guarantee you that the energy of the sign and the planets in the 7th will definitely be a distinct part of us that we are destined to live out, with, and through, our significant others.

Sun (Leo) Aspecting Venus or the 7th House When Projected

When the Sun is being projected and overdone by our partner, we will see them as self-centered, egotistical and narcissistic. They will be boring braggart's always talking incessantly about their accomplishments. A person with particularly strong Leo energy will tell you how everyone loves them, as they are constantly seeking praise and recognition. They are always on stage and want everyone's full attention on them. They dominate conversations, talking incessantly about themselves. These people are great actresses and actors, and you wonder who they are when they are not performing. They like to be the life of the party.

They tend to have big plans, big dreams, but do nothing concrete about it. They just like to talk about what they are going to do. After a while, you may see them as people with big mouths and not a lot of substance. They are unrealistic and cocky about these big dreams. For instance, they will tell you they are going to own a restaurant. Instead of working in restaurants to find out what that is really like and learning from the ground up, they think they can just talk about it, spend money and do it with no plans or experience. Maybe they are going to be a professional singer and start a band, but they refuse to look at how many people really make it in the professional world of music. They are so sure that they are "special" and everything is just going to land in their lap instead of starting out by singing in smaller venues and getting their feet wet out in the real world. There is always a big deal right around the corner that never materializes.

If you offend their big egos, they become drama queens or kings. Men do this, too, not just women. They become arrogant self-aggrandizers, demanding, expecting respect when they have done nothing to merit it. You are just supposed to treat them like a queen or king. They have tremendous pride and cannot back down and admit they are part of a problem. They want you to adjust to them and cannot tolerate differences.

They are bossy. They want you to do this or that, but don't you dare question them as if that is not right for you. They've already decided it is right for you and will tell you so. This attitude can make you feel like they just need subjects to boss around and dominate. They can be loud and overbearing.

With this energy strong, these are the people most prone to needing to be mirrored by instead of related to their partners. They want you to be a reflection of them and want to show you off to others as if they have won a prize instead of loving you, the real flesh-and-blood human being that you happen to be. They want to be "in love" and are stuck in the "puppy love" type of relationship that adolescents are prone to. They behave like teenagers when they are in love. Starry eyes, walks on the beach and made in heaven romance is what they dream about, which of course doesn't exist forever. Once the "new" wears off they are off to search for the next perfect knight or the perfect princess. Their loyalty is only to themselves. You are inconsequential once they are off to search for the next mirror. They tell you they love you, but they are not "in love" with you as they ride off into the sunset.

Notes to myself as I recall my own experience with this planetary influence:

*Notes to myself as
I recall my own
experience with this
planetary influence.*

Let's Do the Sun (Leo) Together.

Doing the Sun together, means being especially supportive of our partner's efforts at creativity and offering genuine praise and applause. A couple can also share creatively together, as in karaoke singing together as a couple. Sharing anything creative shows each one has his own unique talents. As a team, they can take watercolor classes, do sculpture or even build sand castles on the beach. Building sand castles is truly an art. I know a couple who thoroughly enjoy doing this. They enter their sand castles for competition on the beach, and they put a lot of effort into learning how to make sure the castles are sturdy and don't fall over. I know another couple who take dancing lessons and travel to compete in tango dancing all the way to foreign countries like Argentina. They have fun together. A key element is that they like to play together and truly enjoy each other's company.

Doing the Sun together means wanting to bring out the best in each other. Be best friends who can share the spotlight and each radiate self-confidence and self-respect. Being each other's best cheerleader means giving each other recognition. Really genuinely like as well as loving your partner. Seeing each other's individuality. Be devoted to each other and give generously of affection. Treat each other as "special" with flowers, gifts, poems, surprises, etc. They will say to you, "I really like that you don't ignore me. You treat me like I am worth something." Each person is doing that for each other and never taking each other for granted, even in a long-term relationship where others may have become bored after a while.

The Sun placement is where we want to shine our light. If we have the Sun in the 7th or in the sign of Libra, we will be particularly interested in being a part of a partnership or marriage. That's who we came here to be and what makes us feel we are being true to ourselves. We want to relate to and cooperate with others. We actually want to share in someone else's happiness and fulfillment. We did not come here to be alone.

We will want to be each other's hero or heroin, and this will be appreciated and respected by both people. When partners are committed and their love is heart-centered, we feel their warmth, their generosity. They want us to have what we want for our lives. They ask us what our dreams are for ourselves. They want to know what is important to us. Their efforts to express adoration and accept our individuality will be sincere.

One couple I karaoke with has been married for 13 years. I'll call them Jane and Joe. We all go to a local club to sing on Friday nights. As they approached the table where we were all sitting last week,

Joe expressed to another friend sitting at the table, "Can you move over one seat? I want to sit next to my wife." He didn't just sit down anywhere at the table, he made room for her, the love of his life, his marriage partner. Even after 13 years, these two do not ignore each other or take each other for granted. This is a good example of doing the Sun together.

Moon (Cancer) Aspecting Venus or the 7th House When Projected

When the Moon is being projected onto a partner, we may view them as needy, emotional vampires or overly clingy big babies. They want their partners to be responsible for their feelings. Crab-like, they will go into their shell and become distant and cool or moody, sulking and pouting when they don't get what they want, especially in regard to nurturing. They may throw little-boy or little-girl temper tantrums until we end up doing what they want just to appease the situation and keep the peace. They want to be taken care of so their partners end up being Mommy. Needing constant approval, their need for emotional assurance seems to be insatiable. We can't pamper them, compliment them or give to them enough. They are emotionally draining, like a bottomless pit. When they are emotionally overwhelmed, they can be prone to overwhelming emotional outbursts. They will need partners to calm down their crazy feelings. You will hear, "Please take care of me." They can overindulge in food when upset — milk, ice cream, anything sweet or white that symbolizes Mother.

Unable to keep a steady career for long, they seek older, wiser or hard-working, responsible people to take care of their needs for a home and family. Their partners end up having to support them as they cannot support themselves. These are the classic codependent relationships because a symbiosis is set up from the very beginning. One person is the baby, and the other one is the parent. There is no equality here when the Moon is overdone.

They are edgy and overly sensitive to criticism — seeing criticism when you are talking to them where none was implied. Seeing you as Mother, they want unconditional love and acceptance even when they are displaying traits of dependency and not willing to fend for themselves. Their partners end up feeling they want all the mothering for themselves and have none to give. Partners are also afraid to leave this person as they become one of the children instead of a true partner. Overly sensitive and moody, they will be mad if we pay too much attention to our children or even a pet. You will hear statements like "You don't have time for me. You have to fit me in. I don't want to share you with other people. They are taking up too much of your time." They can't see that what you do

Notes to myself as I recall my own experience with this planetary influence:

151

Notes to myself as
I recall my own
experience with this
planetary influence:

_____

_____

_____

_____

_____

_____

_____

_____

_____

_____

_____

_____

_____

_____

_____

_____

_____

_____

_____

_____

_____

_____

_____

_____

_____

with others might also be important to your well-being or happiness. So you end up adjusting frequently to accommodate them.

Childlike, they want you to provide a roof over their heads. They do not contribute their fair share financially. They have no goals for themselves and no intention of being self-supportive. They are dependent. You end up feeling guilty if you leave them. Who will take care of everything for them? What will become of them if you aren't there to meet all their needs?

The Moon out of balance creates a strongly codependent relationship. Both people contribute to this emotionally draining situation. Usually you will find that one or the other has a lot of control issues or a strong need to rescue others in order to attract such a dependent partner. Instead of being the one who is needy, the controlling partner can be too nurturing, too smothering. They may remind us of our own mother. They give too much emotional nurturing, protecting us from the real world or from growing up. They may overdo sympathy, compassion and understanding. They want to keep us dependent and encourage that, but there is usually a fear of abandonment driving this symbiosis.

Let's Do the Moon (Cancer) Together.

Doing the Moon together, each partner can tune into the other's needs to feel safe, secure and nurtured. There is a balance between loving them and loving yourself. If the scales get out of balance, you are able to say to them, "It's too much. I need some time out." They would be understanding because they would know that the supply wasn't exhausted. They would see you wanted to share time with friends, with kids or just your own hobbies and that they still matter. The bumps in the road would not become earthquakes. You know that you can be your total self with them and that they will not leave you. You are completely safe and secure. True acceptance will be reciprocated and felt by each partner. Each takes turns providing comfort and understanding when one or the other is having a rough time. Empathy is shared and reciprocal. Partners protect each other in ways that are supportive such as listening to each other sympathetically.

Partners with the moon in balance will cook for each other, or cooking together will be enjoyed. When one is sick, the other will offer to make soup, go for medicines, whatever they can do to make the other more comfortable. One couple told me they enjoy rubbing each other's feet. Each person feels the other's concern and constant care as interdependence is a way of life for them.

Both people physically take care of their home together and come up with ways to share chores and money. They arrive at what is important together. They will run errands for each other. No one has to remind the other when it's their turn to help, to give, to be nurturing — they do it automatically.

Doing the Moon together means appreciation for how much home and family mean to each other. Both will enjoy each other's families and willingly get involved in family get-togethers at holiday time. Children will be a mutual responsibility and a shared joy. Both people truly like being parents together and are willing to participate in their children's and grandchildren's activities.

Both partners are willing to listen. One may make a statement the other doesn't get right off the bat. Instead of jumping to conclusions or tuning out, both open up a dialogue and ask each other what was meant or what are their feelings about such and such.

Moon in balance means learning to know your mate well. Make the attempt so that you don't feel threatened if attention is distributed elsewhere. Just because one partner plays with the grand-kids, the other shouldn't mind. When one person is very giving, the other should strive not to take advantage. Express appreciation and ask what you can do to reciprocate. Each notices and strives to be in balance. They both honor when time is needed apart. They both give each other breathing room and emotional space when needed. They experience each other as interdependent and supportive but not at each others' expense.

Mercury (Gemini/Virgo) Aspecting Venus or the 7th House When Projected

Scatterbrained, flaky chatterboxes who don't know when to stop talking describes Mercury overdone. These individuals won't shut up! They want to be heard, but they don't listen. It's not an exaggeration to say they will call on the telephone 3-4 times a day, so communication can be overdone. It's annoying when they interrupt constantly just to chit-chat. They talk incessantly, but do not ask their partner anything about themselves. Very subjective, they need to learn to be more objective and to listen as well as speak.

Bored easily, Mercury overdone is a person who is flighty and fickle, often a big flirt unwilling to be committed to one person. This can turn into the unavailable man or woman that is a constant challenge. Restless, nervous energy, always on the move, going somewhere, so it's hard to tie them down or make plans to do anything. They will say, "I don't know right now. Can I get back with you later?" The partner is left feeling that maybe they are waiting for something better before they commit. At times, getting them to follow through on something they promised they would do is difficult. They dislike routine or anything that is too serious or binding. Try to talk to them about serious subjects and they make a joke and refuse to talk about anything deep. They change the subject

Notes to myself as I recall my own experience with this planetary influence:

often as their mind is skittish, and they will keep the conversation on a superficial level. This becomes mentally annoying after a while.

The moral codes of society are not something they adhere to. They may not be trustworthy and can be into spreading rumors based on hearsay. Con artists deluxe, there is a duality to their nature that is complicated. One minute they are one person, and the next they are another. Easily distracted, they can be saying one thing to you, and midway they start saying the exact opposite and don't even realize it.

They can be childlike and immature to a fault. They do all they can to avoid being responsible adults, wanting their partners to take care of everything for them. They have difficulty in making decisions. Always making up excuses or blind to the consequences of their actions, they can get in over their heads and expect their partners to bail them out. Peter Pans and Puellas, their worst character flaw is they refuse to grow up.

From the Virgo side of the Mercury function, they will be overly analytical, exactingly critical and fault-finding. They overdo seeking perfection in their mate. This criticism becomes a revolving door as each becomes critical and carping which is so decisive.

Let's Do Mercury Together.

Mercury partners in balance are curious about life and have a great mental rapport. They find each other mentally stimulating as they seek variety and companionship based on mental exchange. Communication is like food to them. They both have an unusual capacity for light banter, teasing each other and using witty words to play with each other. Sharing thoughts and ideas comes easily, as conversations are never strained. Communicating what is going on with them, such as touching base to see how the other is doing, is part of their everyday activity. Diplomatic and tactful, 7th-house Mercurial partners are concerned with being fair to each other and keeping a balance between them as each one is considerate of the other's needs.

Rational, logical and flexible, they like playing word games such as Scrabble, Sudoku or Bunko. Working on crossword puzzles is something both enjoy. Even putting puzzles together, which takes mental concentration, can be a shared pleasure. I know a couple who enjoy doing this. They take turns choosing the puzzle they will work on together. They actually both did this when they were single and were excited that they had this form of play in common when they met.

With Mercury in the 7th house, you can attract a brilliant partner who is well read and gifted with words, possibly a writer or an eloquent speaker or a professor. They enjoy mental competitions that involve impromptu speaking, such as Toastmasters. Mentally clever and quick with words, they are good debaters as they are masters at seeing both sides. Curious about many subjects, they are information gatherers, especially about current events. Jack-of-all-trades, they know a little bit about everything which makes them really interesting partners. They respect each other's thoughts on a variety of subjects, so each can have their own interests. Reading is definitely a passion, and books will be throughout their home. They particularly enjoy reading aloud to each other.

They both listen as well as speak, so they are perceptive and discerning where their partner is concerned. They really look forward to talking to each other at the end of the day. They may even check in with each other during the day from time to time as constant communication is shared and welcome.

Taking short trips for pleasure will also be enjoyed. Every other weekend, they may head over to their lake house to relax and read or head over to a city within driving distance to play and explore for the weekend. One couple I know goes to the Kerrville music festival every year. Being flexible and adaptable, they both enjoy taking off on short notice and are spontaneous about these little side trips and willing to go with each other.

Socially adept, there are no strangers to them. These folks can easily talk to anyone everywhere they go, from the person standing in line at the post office to the teller at the bank. Witty and charming, they'll be the last to leave a party or social event as they go around talking to everyone in the room.

The Virgo side of Mercury wants to be a helpmate to their partner, each serving the other in practical ways. There is also a love of order in their environment, and both value good health habits. Both are perfection-or detail-oriented in their work and careers.

Venus (Libra/Taurus) Aspecting Venus or in the 7th House When Projected

When Venus is projected onto a partner, we may only see skin deep. We may look for the most beautiful woman or the most handsome man. Attractions are prone to the infatuation stage of relating. Loyalties are not based on the essence of each person but on what they look like or how they are able to flatter by being a mirror. They can be in love with love; therefore their ideals about mating are not about real people. Superficial, fickle and unreliable, their connections with others lack depth. Prone to love addiction, they give all their power away to the person they are "in love" with. They can

*Notes to myself as
I recall my own
experience with this
planetary influence:*

lose themselves to revolving in an unhealthy manner around a partner they have put on a pedestal without taking the time to know the person first. Attachments are shallow and don't develop into anything concrete. Butterfly-like, they are off to their next admirer, always seeking to be mirrored instead of relating to the whole person.

Self-indulgent Venutians tend to spend more than their share in the partnership and may run up credit cards excessively to their partner's dismay. Lazy, they may expect their partner to deal with their extravagance and refuse to be accountable for maintaining their fair share of financial support. They want to be taken care of and use charm to get their way with others.

A partner with Libra overdone is seen as weak, wimpy and too placating. Indecisive, wishy-washy and fence-sitting, Libra out of balance has difficulty making decisions. Overcompromising or being an overgiver is common when this energy is overdone. All the while they resent it. Sooner or later, they will attack you or undermine you in a passive-aggressive way and then deny any responsibility for their actions or words. In order to keep the peace superficially, no one is being honest. Overdoing Libra everyone is being "nice," therefore negative emotional responses and feelings are hidden. Evasive, they can't stand conflict and run away from confrontation. The harmony they create is fake instead of a natural manifestation of core values and the essence of who each person really is.

The Taurian side of Venus is possessive and controlling. They do not like to share. They can objectify their partners, viewing them as a part of their asset base. If they give love to others, their partner sees it as depleting their love source. They can't see that love can flow freely to everyone. They are more interested in how much money you make and what you can give them, so financial gain is a part of why they choose a partner. Lazy, stubborn, stick-in-the-mud types who resist change and will not budge even when it's in their best interest to try something new.

Let's Do Venus (Libra/Taurus) Together.

Much of what I wrote at the beginning of this chapter about Libra is the same for Venus in the 7th. Cooperation, mental compatibility and meeting each other halfway is the hallmark of this fortunate placement. Partners are loving, gracious, diplomatic and kind to each other. Each does a part to maintain the equanimity in their relationship. They cooperate and compliment each other easily. They are concerned with being fair to each other and no one has to remind the other when it's their turn to give, to help, to pay for their share or when it's their turn to give in. Both want to please their partner and will do loving things to keep romance alive even after years of being together. These are the people who do not take their partner for granted because they value partnership above all concerns. First and foremost, they are each other's best friend so they'd rather be together than apart.

These partners share in activities that are ruled by Venus, such as art, creativity and beauty in all its forms — painting, stained glass work, music, the arts, etc. Cultured, they regularly dress up and go to plays and theater together. They enjoy watching others perform and perform together themselves. Here the partners may both love to sing, for instance. They may sing duets and harmonies with each other to the pleasure of everyone watching them. They are very social, charming others as a couple and enjoy hosting parties together, each doing their part to entertain their guests. This extends to networking abilities, and both are popular with their social contacts.

When Venus is shared, each makes their home a place of beauty and everything from their furnishings to their art shows aesthetic taste. They enjoy going to antique shows or art galleries, shopping together, as beautifying their home is a shared experience. Their home is an expression of their shared love of art.

Conflicts and disagreements are worked through as each is striving to see the other's view and reach an equitable compromise. Balance becomes the cornerstone of all their interactions. They love their partners for who they are, not how he or she makes them feel, and they accept each others' differences.

The Taurean side of Venus gives relationships constancy, sensual and physical pleasure, as well as security and safety. Each is a reliable person whose ideals are exhibited in the reality of their everyday interaction with each other. In other words, they don't just talk about being fair and seeing both sides, they are.

Mars (Aries) Aspecting Venus or in the 7th House When Projected

When Mars energy is not owned, a partner can be overpowering and domineering. The extreme played out usually attracts a bossy, angry, aggressive partner who will compete with them for dominance. This can create some nasty scenes where two people are constantly fighting, throwing things around and even beating each other up. When you hear of a partner being violent and picking fights constantly, Mars is out of balance. This makes the battered wife syndrome possible. This is also the partner who is pushy, forcing outcomes. When a partner isn't willing to do what they want,

Notes to myself as I recall my own experience with this planetary influence:

they bully them. They will make insulting and condescending remarks. Projecting Mars, they will see others as doing all of this, but not themselves. Often, they will pick on each other, not realizing that their own passive-aggressive behavior, can attract overly aggressive behavior, and this is not gender specific.

Mars projected can also be the too independent partner who won't compromise and won't commit — free spirits. A partner can also be restless and bored easily or impulsive and impatient.

This is the person who comes on really fast and scares you. They try to pull you over when you are driving to come on to you. They don't realize an accident can happen that way as they are reckless, self-focused and rambunctious.

Relationships can start rather quickly. Jumping in head first is often observed with Mars in the 7th. Immaturity manifests through passionate and all-consuming infatuations because Mars can't wait for anything and wants it now! This can lead to a marriage and divorce of partners who hate each other when they separate, attacking each other and hitting below the belt to wound.

Self-centered to the core, Martians out of balance believe everything is your fault. They are never wrong. Everything has to go their way, the only way. They won't take turns or share in responsibilities for the relationship. They want all the power. Extreme Martians also take advantage of their partners and expect to be catered to. They want everything right now. Irritable and quarrelsome, they can't stand to see weakness. They will punish it by withholding sex or with selfish sex, where only their own sexual needs are being met.

Let's Do Mars (Aries) Together.

Shared competitive Martian energy allows both people to challenge each other in constructive ways like chess, Scrabble, Backgammon or engaging in sporting activities that require stamina and action, like tennis, racquetball or skiing. They can become black belts together, and the challenge of sparring is physical and stimulating to both. I know of a couple who took Jazzercize® together. The husband did not feel the least bit intimidated by the fact that mostly women take Jazzercize. He was right there with her three to four days a week.

Dancing is another shared Martian outlet. One person told me, "I love the exhilaration of spinning on the dance floor. It's a skill that's difficult to do because not only am I spinning in place, but I am doing multiple circles within a circle. I lose count after 30 spins. Doing that with my partner requires precision and technique, and each person has to be physically fit to keep up." There's a leader and a follower, but dance requires trusting your partner to be in sync, as each movement has purpose for both people.

Exploring and adventure are other ways to use Martian energy. Going crystal mining, hiking in the mountains, kayaking down a river — anything where both are interested in trying a new adventure or activity can be enjoyed by a couple doing Mars together.

Independence is encouraged and accepted. "I don't want to go camping, but you can go if you want. Take the kids while you're at it!" There is a sense of freedom for each person's individuality. There is a balance between togetherness and doing things on your own. Each person can do their thing without being guilt-tripped by the other person.

Sexuality between Martian partners means no one is on top all the time. They take turns, and sexuality is exciting, passionate and constant. Each asserts his or her needs and there is a desire for change and variety that both contribute to.

Both put their partner first in their life. You are numero uno with your Mars partner. You admire and respect their spunk, their audaciousness, their initiative and spontaneity. They are inspirational, and you respect them for the courageous Martian attitude of "I can do anything." Their vitality and tough-as-nails outlook is contagious and exhilarating.

Martian partners can also fight for a cause together. They get into politics, promoting their favorite candidate or physically getting involved in community projects or organizations like Habitat for Humanity, or whatever requires decisive action and physical strength.

Learning to fight fairly is also a way to share and balance this energy. When this energy comes into play, neither can refuse to fight or think that fighting is too petty for them. They have to learn to fight without hitting below the belt and attacking each other. No one wins or loses. They learn to compromise and meet each other halfway. They cooperate and share power so that issues become a win-win for both people. This is something Mars partners can work toward together.

Jupiter (Sagittarius) Aspecting Venus or the 7th House When Projected

When Jupiter is being projected, a partner can be a self-appointed guru, know-it-all. They can be overly dogmatic and opinionated and expect you to share their opinion about everything. Arrogant if you challenge their authority, they tend to have an exaggerated

Notes to myself as I recall my own experience with this planetary influence:

sense of their knowledge. They will only see their own views and not be willing to see yours. Refusing to meet you halfway, Jupiter out of balance becomes overbearing, dogmatic and self-righteous. This is the patronizing partner who knows better than you do and is closed-minded. Everything is black and white to them. They are always right, and you are always wrong, according to them. As one man said to me once, "End of discussion," as there was none. He would not discuss anything.

Overly Pollyanna in their outlook, they can be unrealistic and expect everyone around them to be "happy." Anything too heavy turns them off, and they will avoid those who are undergoing a life crisis. In this way, they can ignore their partners' feelings of genuine sadness or disappointment, wanting them to snap out of it.

This person can at times exhibit excessive egotistical behavior. Many times they will take their partner for granted yet expect understanding, even when they are being thoughtless and inconsiderate. They will say, "I promise you this or that," and then forget. Poor planners, they often promise more than they can actually deliver because they have much too much going on at once.

This person can be prone to sentimental, weepy, theatrical and melodramatic behavior. They seesaw between extreme optimism and pessimism and will dramatize that nothing is working out for them. Manic highs or lows can be a part of their emotional make-up. Short-tempered and short-sighted, too, they can be hurtful, overly blunt and rude. They will tell you they are just being honest when they hurt your feelings.

Jupiter projected is the hedonistic person who overdoes, overgives, overextends themselves and refuses to set limits. The *Puer* or *Puella*, the archetype of the Peter Pan, is also common with Jupiter in the 7th. They are the child who refuses to grow up, so you end up having to take care of their mundane needs. Wasteful, impractical and extravagant, they spend every last dime they get, living beyond their means. They don't know how to save or bargain hunt. They buy whatever their whims at the moment dictate without regard for the future. They spend money before they have it, counting on the next "big deal" which hasn't manifested yet. It's only in their imagination. In this way, they have a hard time dealing with the reality of a situation. Their lack of common sense causes them to make mistakes by being overly optimistic, taking risks and gambling without first securing facts to back up their "big dreams."

Restless, this person can also look at relationships and binding commitments as too restricting. Often they are unwilling to recognize how their love of variety keeps them in shallow and temporary relationships with many people who are basically strangers. This is the "one foot out the door syndrome."

Let's Do Jupiter (Sagittarius) Together.

Jupiterians love learning and are especially open to philosophical and spiritual pursuits such as studying comparative religions or experiencing metaphysical or self-help workshops. Loving anything that ex-pands the mind and encourages consciousness, they seek out mentors or shamans in order to grow. They also make great teachers themselves, wanting to share what they've learned and inspiring their partners. They are seen as interesting companions. Their conversations are stimulating, educational and enlightening. They help expand each other's philosophies of life. They share a "live and let live" philosophy and allow for differences of opinion in their spiritual beliefs. They are both open-minded.

Jupiter partners recognize each other's humanity and are honest with and loyal to each other. Lacking pettiness, they will be charitable, tolerant and forgiving when either one of them makes a mistake. They pick themselves up and go on, knowing they had something to learn from their experiences. Life is seen as a series of lessons and opportunities that bring them understanding. "Everything happens for a reason" is their favorite mantra for living life.

Warm and generous with affection and blessed with a great sense of humor, Jupiterians are happy-go-lucky and very popular with many people. They love entertaining in a big way. Loving to meet people from all walks of life, they go out of their way to make sure everyone feels at home and is having fun.

They are usually also quite fortunate and lucky together. They encourage each other by being each other's best cheerleader. Risk takers, born optimists, they share a philosophical belief that they will always be blessed and life obliges them, as many of those risks pay off in spades. They are not only generous with each other; their generosity with others contributes to their prosperity and good fortune as people want to give back to them. They are also fantastic salespeople and have a knack for sales and marketing because of their high-spirited and contagious enthusiasm.

Traveling is a passion as they enjoy learning about and visiting other cultures. Even spontaneous, spur-of-the-moment exploring together is fun and exiting. "Just put me on an airplane and I'm happy because I'm going to go see something different," I heard one of these people say. It's actually a requirement for Jupiterians to travel regularly, as this is what recharges their batteries. Their idea of rest is adventure, especially if it's out-of-doors, as they love new scenery and fresh air. They come back ready to tackle life again rejuvenated.

Notes to myself as
I recall my own
experience with this
planetary influence:

Future-oriented they are always setting new goals for themselves. This is what makes life exciting and adventurous for them. As a visionary couple, they will accomplish a great deal together.

Saturn (Capricorn) Aspecting Venus or the 7th House When Projected

Saturn often brings in the partner who is older or much younger, so there may be an age difference. As a relationship planet, when Saturn is being projected, partners are seen as distant, cold and unresponsive emotionally. Like a negative father figure, they will make excessive demands that a partner do or be what they want that person to be. There is an element of control going on that is unbalanced. They can be very demanding. They may say "I expect you to call me tomorrow" after you've had one date with them!

You feel you are constantly having to prove yourself to get their affection. It is not freely given. You have to be perfect for them to love you, and they constantly remind you by putting you down. When they say, "You are not perfect, mister," their intent is to keep you on the ground at their feet.

This is the person who sets limits on intimacy. For instance, he or she can see you only on the weekend for one night, and that is it. Overly Saturnian partners leave you feeling rejected and unloved. An example is getting involved with folks who are married to someone else, so they have to leave you after making love. They may be workaholics with no time to have a personal life. You cannot feel a sense of security or safety with their affections because they are not really available. Something else is always more important. You get only a certain amount of their time, and you have to adjust yourself to their schedule. You never feel safe because the situation itself is not a reliable and healthy situation. With this placement, the fear of trusting another person with your heart and emotions is immense. Each will mirror back and forth this inability to establish trust.

These people are users. Saturn projected is the parasite whose mantra is "gimme, gimme, gimme," but they have nothing to give in return. At the same time, they are very concerned with keeping up with the Joneses. Their image in society determines who they will associate with. They are caught up in being "an aristocrat." It's a sign of inferiority masked as superiority. You end up being "the daddy," instead of the partner to this person — male or female.

There is also usually a feeling of unworthiness, constant depression and pessimism about outcomes when Saturn is aspecting Venus or in the 7th house. Saturnians will make statements like "I am good at business, but I am not good at relationships, so I give up." Fear is a strong part of this, because wherever Saturn is placed, we have the most fear of inadequacy and inferiority. There is a great fear around being vulnerable, as Saturnians want to be in control. Our Saturn placement is our Achilles' heel. We have to work harder to measure up to whatever sign or house Saturn is in. With Saturn in the 7th, it always looks like limitation and frustration comes through the marriage partner. Both people hold back and therefore their relationship is indeed a mirror.

Let's Do Saturn (Capricorn) Together.

Balanced Saturn, the partners work equally toward a good relationship. This happens over a matter of time and is not done overnight. They move toward each other slowly, and their timing is good with each other. Each person is responsible to the other in ways that are healthy. Keeping up with their end of a commitment helps each feel safe and secure, knowing their partner is reliable. Trustworthiness is an aspect of both of them. Each can be relied upon to keep their word. If one is running late, they will call and say, "I am sorry I'm running late. I am on my way. I'll be there soon." They are constantly communicating and checking in because they want to be considerate of their partner. They apologize when they cannot live up to what they said they would do. They do not sweep it under the rug. Mature in their outlook, each person makes an effort to be in integrity with the other. Patient, persistent and disciplined can describe the characters of both. Trust in each other is established through being there for each other in good times and in bad. Both can deal with life's disappointments and frustrations. They know things that happen are just part of life, and they don't expect everything to be perfect. They are both realistic about outcomes and go out on a limb emotionally for each other. Their agreement is explicitly stated as, "No matter what part of you comes out, I will not leave you." They are each completely committed for the long run.

Doing Saturn together means making joint practical decisions such as how to raise kids, how to save or spend money or where to live. No one has the upper hand or is the boss. If the partners do not agree, then nothing is done until they are both happy with a major decision. They are truly equals in the partnership.

These partners may even meet through their careers and/or work together in some capacity, perhaps even owning a business together. Each of them will do their part, and they can achieve many goals together, as each is hard working and dedicated to the success of the partnership. Respect and commitment is important for long-term relationships, and they both know it.

Notes to myself as I recall my own experience with this planetary influence:

Uranus (Aquarius) Aspecting Venus or the 7th House When Projected

When Uranus is being projected, the extreme played out means freedom needs are polarized and can get real uncomfortable for both people. This person is always attracted to people who cannot make commitments, who rebel at sharing responsibility for the relationship or who connect and disconnect constantly. Their relating style can be described as a push-pull or on again, off again situation. Yes, I want you. No, I don't. They refuse to be accountable for your feelings. This person will be cool, aloof and detached emotionally. They have difficulty in expressing any emotion and ignore the emotional needs of others. "It's your problem if you are hurt," is one of their favorite statements. Abandonment becomes a part of their relationships, as each person is not in sync with the other's needs for space and autonomy. They run hot and cold so you never know which one to expect. Indifferent to emotional displays, they can be hard to connect with once they've decided to cut you off.

Here's where you will often hear the famous words "I love you, but I'm not in love with you." Yet erratically, they will continue to say they love you, so you are not really sure half the time what they really feel. These are the ones who want to be only friends, while they expect the benefits of lovers and partners. Communication is not completely honest, and resentment builds because of this lack of authentic communication and true expression of feelings. Indifferent to commitment, they cannot bear possessiveness and are addicted to the excitement and limerence in the beginning of a relationship. This is "the grass is always greener" syndrome.

Erratic and restless, they are independent to a fault and usually unpredictable, too. You'll invite them to an event, and they will say, "I'd like to come if I can remember to. Thanks for inviting me." They always have a way out so they don't have to be committed. Absent-minded professor types, they conveniently forget what they said or the plans they made with you. "Did I say that?" or "I might do this or that." They call you at the last minute or not at all, and you have to call them to find out what's up. Then they wonder what you are upset about if you call them on it and expect them to be considerate and let you know what they are doing. They consider it to be infringing on their freedom to explain, instead of just common courtesy or good manners.

Extreme Uranians are flaky, spacey, weird, kinky, strange and odd ducks. Willful and obstinate, with fixed-dogmatic thinking, unwilling to cooperate, they rebel for the sake of rebellion and mainly to shock others by their adolescent, self-centered behavior.

Let's Do Uranus (Aquarius) Together.

Uranus at its best is the planet that symbolizes individuality and freedom. Freedom and space are important aspects of the Uranian relationship. There are many ways to live this out constructively, but first, it requires two people who openly communicate their desires and expectations and then consciously cooperate with each other. When both people are aware, this can work quite well. One person traveling a lot through their work is an expression of Uranian relating. This fulfills their need for freedom and change, as they have periods of time away from each other that are natural and even welcome. Partners can also live in separate houses or have separate parts of a house they both share where each has his own space. Both agree to let each other be alone when needed. This can lead to some unusual and nontraditional living arrangements where a couple has homes in two cities and goes back and forth, sometimes living together, sometimes living apart.

Each person is unique in their character, and they each honor uniqueness. I know of a couple with Uranus in the 7th where the wife decided to go to law school two years after their twin boys were born. She is married to an Aquarian — true to the planet in her 7th house as Uranus is the ruler of Aquarius. Her partner supported her decision wholeheartedly. She was free to choose what she wanted for her individuality despite conventionality which would have determined she should stay home until her kids were in school. This is Uranus at its best. These people are each other's best friend. They are nonconformists when it's important to their relationship and not concerned with "what people think." They are still married 25 years later. Independence is encouraged, and friendship is a key part of how they came together.

Uranus is also called the "Awakener." As a couple, these partners enjoy getting involved with organizations or groups, whether it's church involvement or just a cause both want to contribute to. They encourage each other's participation in collective advancement. They want to better humanity in some way, and they share similar values or ideals with the groups they get involved with.

Uranus is a very idealistic planet, and it's considered to be the higher octave of Mercury, so it's very mental. Partners are attracted to brilliance. Uranus shared is an exciting exchange of mental stimulation for both. They are always learning something new from each other. They are evolving.

Each has friends of both sexes, so they trust their partner's commitment to the relationship and allow the freedom to have a variety of people in their lives. Uranians know their partner is their

Notes to myself as I recall my own experience with this planetary influence:

165

best friend, so they are not concerned with possessiveness or the usual jealousy of conventional marriages. They don't have to ask each other permission to socialize or get involved with whatever or whoever is interesting to them. Freedom is encouraged and accepted.

Both people have to acknowledge their ambivalence about being committed since freedom needs are so dominant. Then they have to be willing to give each other equal amounts of space and time for intimacy, while honoring the uniqueness of each partner. These are all ways to live out the energy of Uranus together.

Neptune (Pisces) Aspecting Venus or the 7th House When Projected

When Neptune is being projected, it can be pure fantasy and grand illusion, having a relationship in their mind with someone who is actually not even there and/or someone who doesn't have a real relationship with them. They only imagine they do. They can be married to someone else, live halfway across the country or be of a different sexual orientation than them. The imaginary partner can even be a glamorous figure like a rock star, musician or a movie star, since Neptune rules theater, music and art.

Because Neptune is the planet of compassion and idealism, these virtues can be overdone. The person can get involved with people they are trying to heal or to save like drug or sex addicts, alcoholics and escapists deluxe. These people can't deal with the real world, so they are wounded in some way. The person who has Neptune with Venus/7th house may feel they are the only ones who can understand this person, always forgiving them their faults and seriously not having their boundaries respected. The person they try to rescue usually has no interest in being saved or healed, so it's a dead-end street that can leave the Neptunian very disillusioned and feeling victimized when it's over.

Neptunians wear rose-colored glasses, not accepting the reality of the person they are with. They also attract romantic dreamers who need to be rescued, who always have problems of some kind or other, or who never make it in the world of reality because they aren't grounded. This is the person who can look you straight in the eye and lie to you. Since they are big liars and very deceptive, something about them is always hidden from view. They may be unfaithful cheaters, having secret affairs or still be pining away for a previous lover behind their partner's backs, all the while pretending to be loving and kind. The Neptunian will forgive their unfaithfulness over and over again. Loving too much and playing the martyr is an aspect of this energy even when it is a clear violation of each person's self-respect and dignity.

This is also the classic con artist. These people live off of other people's sympathy, needing money, needing help, needing more than is the Neptunian's fair share to give, so the Neptunian sacrifices constantly for the relationship. They will take your money or even borrow your credit card and charge $4000.00 on it and then split. It can be rather devastating to find out the truth about these people. The Neptunian can then become cynical about love after a few of these people show up in their lives.

One man told me a story about his wife's father becoming ill, so he had to move in with them. She quit working to take care of her father. Then, after he passed away, she refused to go back to work. She then allowed her son and his three children to move in because her son's wife had left him with the kids. Next thing he knew, this man was taking care of all of them and no one was contributing. He felt cheated and used. Eventually he left this situation and got a divorce. It was devastating to him that his wife could not see that she was being unfair and taking advantage of his kindness. Extreme Neptunians can be kind to a fault until, after several of these experiences, they realize that they are sacrificing themselves, and it never works to do so.

Priests and ministers are also fantasies to this person, as they are seen only in a holy light with no Shadow. The Neptunian projects their God image on these people. If you really got to know religious leaders, you would find out they are flawed and imperfect like everyone else, but to the Neptunian they are perfect. In having affairs with ministers and priests, one very obvious thing is overlooked. These people of the ministry willing to have affairs are liars, cheaters and of questionable integrity. They can be the most romantic of people, swooning in your presence and pulling out your chair before you sit at the table, opening doors and whispering sweet nothings in your ear. All the while, they are only disguised in their holy garb.

Another manifestation of Neptune is the person who is always confused. They don't know what they want. They fall in and out of love constantly and are never satisfied, like a bottomless pit. The classic chronic discontent of Neptune is no exaggeration. No matter what you give to them, nothing makes them happy for long. They are in a constant fog and have unrealistic expectations of nothing going wrong, so they are impractical and unrealistic. They can be vague and illusive, hard to pin down to anything real. Clandestine relationships are more their cup of tea as they are not concrete with responsibilities that would tie them down to reality.

Let's Do Neptune (Pisces) Together.

Doing Neptune together means kindness, compassion, total

Notes to myself as I recall my own experience with this planetary influence:

*Notes to myself as
I recall my own
experience with this
planetary influence:*

_____

_____

_____

_____

_____

_____

_____

_____

_____

_____

_____

_____

_____

_____

_____

_____

_____

_____

_____

_____

_____

_____

_____

_____

acceptance and loving devotion are shared. Sacrifices are made, but not at the expense of either person's core values. Compassion and genuine concern for each partner's well-being are shared equally by both partners. Both have a sense of attunement to each other. When the other is hurting or in need, each can actually feel it, as there is a psychic bond felt by both. Partners make allowances for each other's idiosyncracies, so forgiveness is easy. They make statements to each other when one or the other makes a mistake, like "That's only one part of you. There are so many good things about you. Forgive yourself." Total acceptance and generosity of spirit is mutual.

Spiritual and metaphysical subjects are a part of their daily relationship. Meditation, masterminding together, prayer or church or temple worship is done together as a couple. Oneness with God within or individuation is a goal for both, and devotion to their spiritual unfoldment or communion is jointly practiced.

Creativity is enhanced and shared through music, photography, poetry or dance. All these Neptunian delights are jointly expressed. Both partners can be very talented, maybe even singing in a choir together. I know a couple who both enjoy painting and singing. They also share a love of the ocean, so they bought a beach house and a sailboat, where they spend their leisure time. The ocean is ruled by Neptune.

Altruistic volunteer work for those less fortunate is non-egoic and nonpersonal. This is a form of giving back to God and the Universe, expressing their joint love for the planet. They do not overextend themselves in their giving. It is kept in balance with their relationship to each other and to their own children.

Their relationship can withstand fateful blows like losing a child, losing a job or having to share financial burdens, one or the other being sick and needing to be there for each other. These are all sacrifices made with love and devotion. They bring out the Christ consciousness in each through their abiding love.

When Neptune is shared, both people are thoughtful of each other. Little things they do for each other are reminders of their love. An example would be that there partner likes gummy bears so they remember and give them occassionally with a sweet note or a card. These two can be very romantic, and their romance can last years and years because they do not take each other for granted. They are heart-centered and devoted to each other. These are soulmate unions in the sense that they touch each other's souls. Each can see the soul in their partner even when he or she is not exhibiting their best self. Neptunian partners bring to mind the words

"Love is patient. Love is kind. Love bears all things, forgives all things."

Pluto (Scorpio) Aspecting Venus or the 7th House When Projected

Power struggles, compulsive obsessions and triangles are a difficult manifestation of Pluto ruling or in the 7th house. The Plutonian feels they have no choice as their emotions are overwhelming and obsessive. Betrayal, intrigue and secrets can be a difficult part of the relationship.

Plutonians can project their capacity for ruthlessness and manipulative behavior, seeing the other as doing these things and themselves as innocent. This partner can be coercive, withholding emotionally to control for spite and revenge. They can be overly controlling, with convoluted motives. Game playing sees power thrown back and forth as some kind of a prize, which inevitably leads to hurt feelings as power is being misused by both. One person may be overwhelmed psychically by the other person, and individual differences are not accepted. Both will tell the other person what to do, what to wear or whom they can be friends with. There is a dominance of power that is challenging. One woman expressed to me, "The weapon he would use was money and intimidation to win me over. It was a constant power battle, and he had to win. I felt out of control." The mirror is emotionally intense as each struggles to hold their own. Both will experience their share of emotional and psychological abuse as they vie for who is going to run the show.

Plutonians can manipulate by being self-destructive or threatening to commit suicide, as death is ruled by Pluto. Death or paranoid fear of death can be a part of the relationship. One may have to suffer that their partner actually dies. In some way they will go through many deaths and rebirths of consciousness as they learn about each other, often blaming each other for devastating situations and entanglements.

Ruthless and jealous, they can set themselves up for huge vendettas. One man told me his wife was so hateful after they got divorced, she threw bricks at his car and burned his photography portfolio. Another's revengeful wife who was a lawyer, decided that although she'd been married to him for only one year, she would try to take his business he had owned for 15 years away from him. These are the very nasty divorce court battles over who gets what where lawyers have a heyday.

Intensely smothering, they can try to buy their partner by always giving presents to make the other person feel obligated

Notes to myself as I recall my own experience with this planetary influence:

instead of allowing their love to come from volition. Emotionally when their will is thwarted, they are prone to brooding silences.

They are always probing. What are you doing? Where are you going? Who are you going with? What are you feeling? Only they never reveal anything intimate about themselves. Secretive and silent when they are upset, they withhold emotions or sex for spite and to keep an upper hand. One lady told me she did this on purpose because that is the only way she could get her needs met. That would be manipulation deluxe and zero honesty.

Sometimes Pluto partners will experience traumatic and intense experiences beyond either of their control. An example of this would be losing a child or having a car accident. These experiences, instead of bonding them through hard times, turn them against each other as they blame each other.

Let's Do Pluto (Scorpio) Together.

Doing Pluto together means having the capacity for each person to share power. Both do Shadow work together, revealing their fears, failures or painful wounds. In the revealing, healing takes place on a deep psychological level. Sadness, grief, anger, lies, loss, betrayal, fear, shame over past events real or imaginary, everything is easily discussed with their partner. There are no taboo subjects. They can be a therapist for each other in this way by telling each other everything because their trust in each other is so strong. Power is used for healing and transformation instead of to control.

Both are interested in working with their unconscious, helping each other to be more in integrity with their truest selves. The bond is not easily broken because of the tremendous intimacy that is shared. Trust is implicit once the relationship has undergone the test of time, and they know their partner will not leave them no matter what is revealed. This is relating through the deepest core of each person. Both go into the underworld, Pluto's domain, willingly. Psychological deaths and rebirths are experienced in the presence of another. Empowerment and wholeness is the result of their being together. They become more authentically who they really are just from being in each other's lives.

Intensity and passion are valued as each of them shares openly and deeply about sexual desire and preference. They have nothing whatsoever to hide from each other. Each makes an effort to stay connected spiritually and emotionally, which connects them sexually in a very deep way. Due to this ability to be radically honest with each other, sex is erotic and fulfilling.

Forgiveness and empathy for each other's weaknesses and mistakes are acknowledged through recognizing their own Shadow. They both realize they are capable of anything they might see in their partners and are both willing to see the whole person instead of just the part. Love and acceptance are choices they make with the conviction that their partnership is dedicated to the spiritual evolution of each. Their relationship is healing, as it is always changing and growing as each person learns the importance and value of vulnerability and sharing power.

Forgiveness Is True Forgiveness.

We have now looked at each planet in light of how all affect our 7th house in relationships — both strengths and weaknesses. If we are honest with ourselves, we know we've done some of both the positive and negative aspects of our 7th-house planets and signs, although for the most part we've projected these energies onto our partners.

Keeping in mind that the 7th-house planets and signs are the most foreign to us, we experience these energies in our significant others or whomever we are close to. That can even be our boss, our siblings or our friends. Therefore, an important aspect of any loving relationship is that forgiveness is exercised as a spiritual faculty. Just a shift in attitude, and your feeling nature will go right along with you. Instead of focusing on what your partner does wrong, focus on what they do right. That puts everything into perspective so that you can forgive them. A very good friend once brought me a beautiful container, and she said, "Start writing down all of the good things he does for you, or says to you because someday he will disappoint you and you will need to read those little notes to yourself to remind yourself of all the good things he's done." That was great advice for both of you.

If we're seeking perfection, at the first sign of a person's doing something wrong, we give up. Too easily we might give up on a relationship. If we try to remember the good things the person is or has done, then bumps in the road wouldn't turn into mountains. They are just bumps in the road. That is life. *We can never be all another person expects us to be if we are to be true to ourselves. This kind of forgiveness is real.* We don't hold a grudge or punish each other by withholding sex or affection. We talk things out. In every situation, if we can stand in another person's shoes, we can relate to what they were experiencing from their point of view. We may not always agree with everything, so we agree to disagree, but there's no shaming or attacking involved. If we make a mistake, we apologize.

By contrast, love cannot grow when someone is denying their own needs just to stay in a partnership. Ask for what you want and

Notes to myself as I meditate on forgiveness and how it helps me heal the past:

_____
_____
_____
_____
_____
_____
_____
_____
_____
_____
_____
_____
_____
_____
_____
_____
_____
_____
_____
_____
_____
_____
_____
_____
_____
_____
_____

"Just shower the people you love
*   with love*
Show them the way that you feel
Things are gonna work out fine if
*   you only will*
Shower the people you love with love
Show them the way you feel
Things are gonna be much better
*   if you only will"*

Music and words
by James Taylor

Quan Yin - Goddess of Mercy and Compassion

be honest. If you can express your feelings, then a real relationship will happen. The more both express both positive and negative feelings, the better off both will be. Then we are relating to a real person. They will know who we are, and we will know them.

Many people stay together because of financial security or children or whatever excuse they choose. If they are not staying together because they want their relationship to work, unconscious wounding gets passed back and forth. Some people won't let you get close to them, and have walls that are too big to get past. You have to recognize them for what they are and move on when it becomes obvious. We can't fix anyone or be compatible with everyone. We know we can love, and we keep on keeping on. Choose to become the energies of your 7th house and see what miracles take place. You will finally be more loving to yourself.

For we know in part and we prophesy in part; but when the perfect comes the partial will be done away. When I was a child, I used to speak as a child, think as a child, reason as a child; when I became a man I did away with childish things. For now we see in a mirror dimly, but then face to face; now I know in part, but then I shall know fully just as I also have been fully known. But now abide faith, hope, love, these three; but the greatest of these is love.

I CORINTHIANS 13: 9-13

Many years ago I had a dream. In the dream I was in my parents' house. I was alone with them, although I have five siblings. It was raining outside, and water came all the way up to the lawn (flooding, which in alchemy is a *solutio* process). I went with my mom and dad to the window. Out on the lawn as the water subsided was a large piece of what looked to be very old wood. I said to them, "It looks like a piece of an old ship. Let's go see if there is buried treasure in it." They both went with me outside, and we started to pull the wood away. After a while they both gave up and went inside. They told each other there was nothing there. I did not give up. I took one more pull, and there indeed was a box in a crevice in the wood. I opened the box, and in it were blue jewels and gold coins! I took them inside to my mom and dad and Mom exclaimed, "There was a treasure!" When I studied alchemy and found out that what we are looking for is ourselves, this dream made perfect sense to me. The alchemists had many names for this, but one was the *lapis,* or the alchemical Gold.

I had inherited my parents' Venus Neptune energy. I had also inherited many of their characteristics, both the light and the dark, of that I was clear. They were not able to see that they were split into two parts, conscious and unconscious, so they lived it out through projection. I was destined to see the meaning of what they went through and what many couples face. I knew that in my own marriage I had run away from large parts of myself.

We come together to be a mirror for each other, to lead each other to our own soul, and this is what soul mates are to me. We help each other see our own divinity, and we allow each other to be human, to have differences and to truly be individuals. This is freedom in its highest form through the path of relationship. This is the ultimate experience of the astrological 7th house in the Age of Aquarius.

Notes to myself as I reflect on dreams of my own, my parents and my partners:

173

Libra and Aries, King and Queen, Male and Female, Sun and Moon are all symbolic of the mystical marriage, the *coniunctio*. This balance of opposites is what we are all heading toward. This is what Shadow work will lead to if we are sincere. The alchemists always said that when you undertake this very sacred task, you have to be sincere and honest with yourself. You have to know what the left hand and the right hand are doing in every situation. Things will repeat until an "AHA" blows through you and you see it all as a dance. The alchemists called it the Golden Game. In *The Tavistock Lectures,* Jung says,

> I call this *fourth stage* of the therapy of transference the *objectivation of impersonal images.* It is an essential part of the process of individuation.[2] Its goal is to detach consciousness from the object so that the individual no longer places the guarantee of his happiness, or of his life even, in factors outside himself, whether they be persons, ideas, or circumstances, but comes to realize that everything depends on whether he holds the treasure or not. If the possession of that gold is realized, then the centre of gravity is in the individual and no longer in an object on which he depends. To reach such a condition of detachment is the aim of Eastern practices, and it is also the aim of all the teachings of the Church.[12]

> [2] See *Psychological Types*, Def. 29, and *Two Essays*, pars. 266ff. [Also 'A Study in the Process of Individuation' (C.W., vol 9, i).]

We have to know the Gold is within us and direct our love and our energy to others in a detached way, not a detachment that doesn't care about the other person, or their well-being, but a non-attachment born of knowing that we are each individuals with our own relationship to God within us and to our own souls. When we withdraw our projections from each other, we can love a real person. We will want to know who they are as a unique and separate individual. What are their dreams? What do they feel about their life? What makes them happy? Our relationship to them will resemble more like a best friend who is not intent on possession or engulfment but in an abiding love and devotion that emphasizes the Aquarian freedom to be.

A Symbolic Life

There is so much more to learn from Jung's work. I continue taking classes at the Jung Center. Some of it is very complicated and it will probably take the rest of my life, and maybe several more to understand it all, but I am determined to make these concepts a part of my every day life, and to have what he called an experience of the Self with a capital "S" as my most valued goal as I strive to grow. As he discovered, the more we pay attention to the symbols around us, and the constant synchronicities occurring, we will have an experience of the divine working in our lifes.

I also started to have what the Sufis, a mystical sect of Islam, and the Hindus call a relationship with the inner beloved. Instead of hearing love songs and feeling sad that there was no one for me to be romantically involved with, I started singing and hearing them as if God was singing to me or me singing to God. My favorite song for God is the Rod Stewart version of "Have I Told You Lately That I Love You?" I encourage others to do this, as it fills your heart with love on a daily basis. One time I got in my car as I was singing a love song, and turned on the radio, and the song was playing in the exact same place!

One year, a guy I met gave me a dozen red roses and two of the roses started growing in the vase! I had never seen this happen before, so I decided to forfeit the blooms, and I planted them in a pot. One of those roses made it, and it's almost a 3-year-old plant now. This experience said to me that I was growing from what had transpired in that relationship. These are the symbols and synchronicities that bring meaning and joy, and we can feel our own connection to the divine.

Songs to Sing, Words That Heal

I have always used music to guide me. When I am hurting or feeling alone, or when I am happy and feeling hopeful, I ask God to give me a song to touch me and show me what's next. I will even get in my car and say to myself the next song on the radio has a message for me. This is no different from a Tarot reading, using the I-Ching or pulling a Rune for guidance. I love to sing, so this is my way of doing the very same thing. Sometimes a song won't leave you alone! It will keep playing over and over again in your mind. This song has something to say to you. A song I found recently says everything I want to say to those of you who truly want better relationships. It's called "Til We Ain't Strangers Anymore," a duet sung by Bon Jovi and LeAnn Rimes. The words of this song describe beautifully that what we all want is to love each other and come out of the dark (the unconscious) in order to do so. We have to own our Shadows and be willing to be fully known by another.

Till We Ain't Strangers Anymore, lyrics by Bon Jovi and performed by Bon Jovi and LeAnn Rimes

It might be hard to be lovers
But it's harder to be friends

Notes to myself as I read the words of this song:

_____
_____
_____
_____
_____
_____
_____
_____
_____
_____
_____
_____
_____
_____
_____
_____
_____
_____
_____
_____
_____
_____
_____
_____

Baby pull down the covers

It's time you let me in

Maybe light a couple candles

I'll just go ahead and lock the door

If you just talk to me, baby

Til we ain't strangers anymore

Lay your head on my pillow

I sit beside you on the bed

Don't you think it's time we say

Some things we haven't said

It ain't too late to get back to that place

Back to where we thought it was before

Why don't you look at me

Til we ain't strangers anymore?

Sometimes it's hard to love me

Sometimes it's hard to love you too

I know it's hard believing

That love can pull us through

It would be so easy

To live your life

With one foot out the door

Just hold me, baby

Til we aint strangers anymore

[Solo]

Its hard to find forgiveness

When we just run out of lies

It's hard to say you're sorry

When you can't tell wrong from right

It would be so easy

To spend your whole damn life

Just keeping score

So let's get down to it, baby

There ain't no need to lie

Tell me who you think you see

When you look into my eyes

Let's put our two hearts back together

And we'll leave the broken pieces on the floor

Make love with me, baby

Til we ain't strangers anymore

We're not strangers anymore

We're not strangers

We're not strangers anymore

The next section of this workbook has graphics of symbols, key words for the sign and planets in the 7th house, the meaning of the houses and correspondences for the archetypes called the zodiac. Once you have your own chart, you can also look at the tools in Part Four to learn more about your own relationship requirements by studying the key words and correspondences.

You can get your chart online for free at *starguidance.com/readings/free_chart.html.*

Notes to myself as I recall my own experience with this planetary influence:

_____

_____

_____

_____

_____

_____

_____

_____

_____

_____

_____

_____

_____

_____

_____

_____

_____

_____

_____

_____

_____

_____

_____

_____

_____

NOTES PART THREE:

1) John A. Sanford, *Between People, Communicating One-To-One,* Paulist Press, New York, Ramsey, 1982, pg 8-9

2) John A. Sanford, *Between People, Communicating One-To-One,* Paulist Press, New York, Ramsey, 1982, pg 12-13

3) John A. Sanford, *Between People, Communicating One-To-One,* Paulist Press, New York, Ramsey, 1982, pg 2

4) C.G. Jung, *Modern Man in Search of a Soul, The Problems of Modern Psychotherapy,* A Harvest/HBJ Book, Harcourt Brace Jovanovich Publishers, San Diego, New York, London, 1933, pg 34

5) C.G. Jung, CW 16 - *The Practice of Psychotherapy, The Problems of Modern Psychotherapy,* Princeton University Press, Bollingen, 1954, par 158, pg 77

6) C.G. Jung, CW 14 - *Mysterium Coniunctionis,* Princeton University Press, Bollingen, 1963, par 778, pg 546

7) Robert A. Johnson, *Owning Your Own Shadow,* Harper Collins Press, San Fransisco, CA, 1993

8) C.G. Jung, *Two Essays in Analytical Psychology, The Problem of the Attitude Type,* Meridian Books, NY, 1953, para 80, pg 54

9) C.G. Jung, CW 14 - *Mysterium Coniunctionis, The Personification of the Opposites,* Princeton University Press, Bollingen, 1963, par 330, pg 246

10) Liz Greene, *Relating, Living With Others on a Small Planet,* Samuel Weiser, Inc., North Beach, Maine, 1978, pg 120

11) C.G. Jung, CW 18 - The Symbolic Life, *Analytical Psychology: Its Theory and Practice, The Tavistock Lectures,* Princeton University Press, Bollingen, 1935, par 377, pg 166

4 Symbols, Correspondences and Key Words

...the unconscious is guided chiefly by instinctive trends, represented

by corresponding thought-forms — the archetypes.[1]

CARL GUSTAV JUNG

Once you have your birth chart, you can use this chapter's references to interpret your own 7th house and aspects to Venus. The experience of reading about yourself is enlightening and ultimately healing because the validation of your inherent character through astrology is unsurpassed. Astrology can show you what you and your partner have in common, as well as where your energy is different. Your partners and/or repeating patterns in relationships will be described clearly in the keywords for the 7th house. This will help you see your own Shadow as these descriptions will be those you least identify with as well as our own royal road to wholeness.

Zodiac Symbols

This graphic helps you read the symbols as well as see the natural wheel of the zodiac.

Keywords for the 7th House (Rising Sign and Ruler Descriptions)

These four pages describe your rising sign, or ruler. The keywords on these four pages describe your 7th-house energy, i.e, your Shadow. It always looks like these keywords describe your partner and not yourself. The transcendental planets in or ruling the 7th or in aspect to our Moon or Venus are especially challenging for our growth and evolution.

The Houses

This graphic shows keywords for the meanings of each house (area of our lives).

Archetypes and Correspondences

Each of the 12 archetypes in the zodiac are described by a sign, a planet and a house.

There are also:

- Modalities (cardinal = action oriented - outgoing, fixed = stable - determined, mutable = flexible - changeable)

- Elements (earth = sensation, air = thinking, fire = intuition and water = feeling)

- Perspectives (personal, social/interpersonal and collective/universal)

- Polarities (yin and yang, similar to Jung's introvert and extrovert)

- Various correspondences to the archetype itself (actions, characteristics, professions, etc.)

EARTH
Taurus
Virgo
Capricorn

- negative / yin

AIR
Gemini
Libra
Aquarius

+ positive / yang

MC
SOUTH

10   9

11   8

Capricorn
(cardinal)
♑

Sagittarius
(mutable)
♐

Aquarius
(fixed)
♒

Scorpio
(fixed)
♏

transpersonal signs

interpersonal signs

Pisces
(mutable)
♓

Libra
(cardinal)
♎

12   7

AC
EAST

The Zodiac Archetypes

DC
WEST

Aries
(cardinal)
♈

Virgo
(mutable)
♍

1   6

personal signs

Taurus
(fixed)
♉

Leo
(fixed)
♌

Gemini
(mutable)
♊

Cancer
(cardinal)
♋

2   5

3   4

+ postive / yang

- negative / yin

NORTH
IC

FIRE
Aries
Leo
Sagittarius

WATER
Cancer
Scorpio
Pisces

KEYWORDS for the 7th - Marriage House
(Marriage, Partnerships & Open Enemies)

So if you have:

ARIES RISING - LIBRA/or Venus in the 7th - The PEACEMAKER

+ characteristics: seeks equality/balance, diplomatic/tactful, considerate/fair to others, kind, sociable, easygoing, good taste, able to negotiate, seeks intimacy/relatedness/partnership, just, cooperative, artistic talent, intellectual, refined, harmony-seeking, loving/romantic/affectionate, willingly shares what one has with a partner, gracious, mediator, objective, peaceful, pleasing appearance, reconciles, includes, aligns, affiliates, agreeable, courteous, charming, great host or hostess, tolerant, grace, softness, expresses appreciation, accommodating

- characteristics: vain, lazy, devious, uses flattery to get one's way, unwilling to confront/make waves/passive-aggressive, sometimes overaggressive, sometimes uses nonaction to control, indecisive, inconsistent, extravagant, superficial, trying too hard to please, critical, judgmental, shallow, wishy-washy, fence-sitter, equivocating, placating, indirect, acquiescent, compliant, indulgent, meddles, justifies for appearance's sake, self-deprecation, frivolous, codependent

TAURUS RISING - SCORPIO/or Pluto in the 7th - The DETECTIVE

+ characteristics: powerful, transformation-oriented, feelings and actions are in alignment, intriguing, mysterious, penetrating, instinctual, sexy/exotic/magnetic, attracts others easily, analytical mind, deep, intuitive, fortitude, loyal, intuitive/perceptive, investigates, passionate, intimate, resourceful, life changing, healer, strength in a crisis, lets go, recycles, self-motivated, thorough, regenerative, involved, resilient, backbone, influential, unafraid of taboo subjects

- characteristics: revengeful, vindictive, game-playing, obsessive, manipulative, controlling, extremely intense/emotional, punishes, secretive, uses silence (withholding) and sarcasm as weapons, possessive, stubborn, fixed opinions, annihilator, guarded, suspicious, paranoid, brooding, coercive, intimidating, subversive, bargains, complicates, addicted to extremes, compulsive, probes, jealous, destructive, condescending, seductive, exploits, overpowers, makes mountains out of mole hills, autocratic, relentless, uncooperative, cruel, ruthless

GEMINI RISING - SAGITTARIUS/or Jupiter in the 7th - The PHILOSOPHER

+ characteristics: optimistic, philosophical, inspirational, humorous, fun-loving, outgoing, nature-loving, sports-minded, naturally curious about the Universe and the meaning of life, prophetic, student/teacher, adventurer, explorer, philanthropic, trusting, high-minded, theoretical, truth-seeker, strong convictions, adventurous, lover of travel both physically and mentally, goal-oriented, prosperity-conscious, idealistic, freedom-oriented, jovial, generous, lucky, welcomes everyone, honest, moral, ethical, positive, benevolent, honorable, blessed

- characteristics: opinionated/self-righteous/preachy, dogmatic, overdoes, overpromise, overextends one's resources, restless, fanatical, dislikes routine/responsibility, hot temper, blunt, tactless, rude, arrogant, argumentative, overindulges, judgmental, intolerant, restless, inconsiderate, extravagant, grandiose, pompous, permissive, opportunist, flamboyant, takes advantage, cynical, boastful, greedy, inflated, exaggerates, impractical, hypocritical, game player, rover, groupie, proselytizer, inconsistent/unreliable, constantly running late

CANCER RISING - CAPRICORN/or Saturn in the 7th - The FATHER

+ characteristics: patient, ambitious, responsible, efficient, reserved, traditional, organizer, serious, dutiful, resourceful, long-range planner, integrity, punctual, gives confidence to others, wisdom from experience, protects, self-disciplined, managerial talent, stoic, dependable, introspective, shrewd in business, formal, conservative, earns respect, accountable, accomplished, strives for excellence, authority, results-oriented, focused, mature, methodical, trustworthy, self-control, frugal, economical, professional, established, realistic, cautious, diligence, worldly

- characteristics: insecure, overly perfectionistic/cautious/suspicious, austere, difficulty showing feelings/emotions, cold/unresponsive, judgmental, intolerant, isolated, user, opportunist, demanding, limiting, harsh, too strict, critical, overexacting, rigid, loner, despair, anxiety prone, contracts, inhibited, parsimonious, cuts nose off to spite face, prone to depression, pessimistic, restricted, unimaginative, worried, stiff, severe, archaic, calculating, fearful, punishing, overly conservative, backwardness, autocratic, defensive, controlling, guilt

KEYWORDS for the 7th - Marriage House
(Marriage, Partnerships & Open Enemies)

So if you have:

LEO RISING - AQUARIUS/or Uranus in the 7th - The HUMANITARIAN

+ characteristics: objective/detached or exhibits non-attachment, independent, truth seeker, genius, inventive thinker, beats his/her own drum, original, group/goal-oriented, friendship-and freedom-oriented, innovative, avant-garde, open-minded, revolutionary for a cause or to impart wisdom or understanding, loyalty to truth, intelligent, needs space and allows it to others, idealistic, seeks to change/reform anything stagnating progress, awakener, seeks enlightenment, intuitive, progressive, unusual, social, exciting, experimental, insightful, humanitarian, friendly, non-conformist, brilliant, ahead of their time, different, tolerant, iconoclastic, unconventional

- characteristics: unpredictable, unreliable, rebellious, stubborn, aloof, cold/icelike/unfeeling, impersonal, eccentric to alienate/likes to shock people, can't commit/difficulty with intimacy, radical, controversial, unorthodox, disorganized, forgetful and absentminded, refuses to play by the rules, inconsiderate, bizarre, weird, strange duck, inappropriate, odd, maverick, fixed values, nervous, fidgety, antagonistic, unreasonable, won't follow directions, irresponsible, flighty, disrupting, perverse, detachment to an extreme, anarchist

VIRGO RISING - PISCES/or Neptune in the 7th - The VISIONARY

+ characteristics: compassionate, sensitive/psychic/in tune with others, imaginative/creative/poetic, idealistic, adaptable, self-sufficient, unassuming, congenial, intuitive, sacrifices, spiritually-oriented/mystical, dreamy, ethereal, saintlike, rescues others, romantic/loving/kind, cosmic consciousness, versatile, gifted, adaptable, prophetic, heroic, visionary, emotional, sympathetic, artistic or musical talent, subtle, psychological, aesthetic, requires alone time to meditate/replenish energy, mystic, introverted, universal love, empathic, forgiving, angelic

- characteristics: escapist/unfocused, self-sacrificing to a fault, martyr, impressionable, hypersensitive, changeable, insecure, chameleonlike, confusing, chaotic, indecisive, secretive, vague, moody, spacy, evasive, deceitful, procrastinator, spineless, gullible, enabler, fraudulent, daydreamer, lacks boundaries, makes excuses, weak, misguided, drug/alcohols addictive, illogical, unrealistic, impractical, spacy, self-pitying, fake or illusory, guilt-ridden, capriciousness, prone to prevarication, rationalization expert, delusional

LIBRA RISING - ARIES/or Mars in the 7th - The PIONEER

+ characteristics: courageous, explorer/adventurer, enthusiastic, leader/high energy, honest, independent, daring, a warrior, audacious, knight in shining armor, noble, naive, innocent, action-oriented, inspirational ideas, direct, passionate, ardent, childlike, self-confident, bravado, demonstrates integrity, pioneering, playful, ambitious, vitality, masculine strength, spirited, exuberant, lively, assertive, fiery, athletic, outgoing, demonstrative, affectionate, responsive, enjoys competition, vivacious, winner, survivor, gutsy

- characteristics: selfish/self-centered, argumentative battler, touchy, irritable, impatient, frustrated, defensive, cocky, aggressive/pushy, arrogant, impulsive, hot temper, rash, insensitive, inconsiderate, antisocial, discourteous, restless, blunt, jealous, uses force to get their way, impetuous, reckless, careless, foolhardy, headstrong, imprudent, ill-considered, precipitous, hurried or rushed, devil-may-care attitude, hotheaded, explosive, rude, competitive, hostile, rascal, violent, rival, wild, attacking

SCORPIO RISING - TAURUS/or Venus in the 7th - The BUILDER

+ characteristics: patient, persevering, reliable, security-oriented, loyal, trustworthy, accumulator, slow to anger, productive, grounded, stable, quiet, artistic, enjoys sensuality, affectionate/loving, calm, lover of beauty, earthy, quality-seeking, solid, protector, collector, desires touching and being touched, attractive, unshakable, assuring, peaceful, likes to relax and take their time, careful, methodical, maintains, persistent, practical, steady, talent with musical instruments or singing, seeks to give and receive pleasure, tranquilly, nature-lover, tenacious, sensuous, comforting, doesn't discourage easily, dependable, esthetic tastes, culinary talent

- characteristics: stubborn, overindulgence in food, sex or drink, lazy, slow, rageful when angered, extravagant, jealous, possessive, stick-in-the-mud, set in routines, resistant to change, greedy, boring, dense, dull, conservative, plodding, immovable/rigid, resists, territorial, indulges, grasping, self-indulgent, acquisitive, passive, apathetic, lackadaisical, careless, stodgy, humdrum, monotonous, stagnating, gluttonous, unyielding, materialistic, tiresome, repetitive, trying, frustrating, overprotective, covetous, mundane, pack rat

KEYWORDS for the 7th - Marriage House
(Marriage, Partnerships & Open Enemies)

So if you have:

SAGITTARIUS RISING - GEMINI/or Mercury in the 7th - The COMMUNICATOR
+ characteristics: interesting, great conversationalist/thinks quick on his or her feet/articulate/intelligent, jack-of-all-trades, perceptive, logical, friendly/sociable, amusing storyteller, lively/charming, humorous, flexible or adaptive, knowledgeable, agile, curious, facile with words, clever, mimics, informative, studious, adaptive, youthful, interactive, dexterous, curious/interested in others, androgynous, versatile, unbiased, talkative, factual, educating, teaching, writing, idea man or woman, salesmanship

- characteristics: contradictory, fickle, unable to commit, two-faced, inconsistent, emotional detachment, immoral, changeable, nervous, fidgety, restless, unable to concentrate, easily bored/variety-seeking, talks too much, chatterboxes, too literal, scattered, devious, cunning, crafty, sly, two-faced, tricky, double-dealing, unscrupulous, dishonest, liar, Machiavellian, nervousness, antsy, easily agitated, fragmented, *puer* or *puella*, superficial, babbler, game player, unreliable, cheater, evasive

CAPRICORN RISING - CANCER/or Moon in the 7th - The MOTHER
+ characteristics: caring, supportive, sensitive to feelings, loyal/protective, emotionally warm/tender, industrious, responsible, thrifty, frugal, ambitious, sociable, action-oriented, vulnerable, psychic, memory-retentive, inclusive, home-oriented, nurturing, gentle/kind, intuitive, patriotic, close ties to family, sentimental, responsive, expressive, remembers important days, (i.e., birthdays, anniversaries, etc.), personal, dependable, sympathetic, thoughtful, imaginative, instinctive, maternal, subtle, sweet/loving, loves children, reflective, nostalgic, sincere

- characteristics: childish, moody, needy, argumentative, self-centered, oversensitive/touchy, overemotional, unstable, smother love, holds grudges, clams up when angry, clingy, maudlin, insecure, self-protective, inconstant, reactive, covert, brooding, doubtful, habitual, self-indulgent, hoarding, defensive, needs constant reassurance, codependent, uses children to get even with partner, issues about food, helpless, devouring, passive, clannish, carping, clings to the past, regressive, holds on tight

AQUARIUS RISING - LEO/or Sun in the 7th - The ENTERTAINER
+ characteristics: inspiring, enthusiastic, popular, loves to entertain and host parties, magnanimous, humorous, loyal, ambitious, leader, creative, spontaneous, generous, optimistic, grateful, warm-hearted, dramatic/regal/dignified, desires recognition, vitality, fun-loving, captivating, noble, confident, outgoing, plays, embraces, loves with passion, romantic, expressive, infuses life with joie de vivre, cheerful, makes an impact, amusing, self-esteem, impressive, brave, protective, honorable, powerful, optimistic, sincere, talented, funny, distinctive, fiery, happy-go-lucky, affectionate, energetic, proud, shines like the sun, vivacious

- characteristics: domineering, demanding/bossy, self-centered, overly dramatic, closed-minded, conceited, willful, aggressive, arrogant, self-glorifying, snobby, self-indulgent, excessive pride and touchiness, egotistical, grandiose, self-aggrandizing, boastful, player, overbearing, excessive, needs a lot of attention and flattery, unadaptable, stubborn, childish, spendthrift, braggart, showoff, superiority, patronizing, wants to be the center of attention, blows things out of proportion

PISCES RISING - VIRGO/or Mercury in the 7th - The HEALER/SERVANT
+ characteristics: helpful/service-oriented, health-conscious, industrious, hard working, practical, earthy, reliable, considerate, accurate, analytical excellence/active mind/intelligent, craftsmanship, flair for organizing, healer, detail-oriented, factual, quiet, efficient, seeks better ways to accomplish/fix things/useful, productive, modest, discriminating, responsible, orderly, skillful, industrious, observant, logical, reserved, cautious, neat environment, precise, sensible, particular, unassuming, humble, natural

- characteristics: critical/fault-finding, worrier, cranky, self-critical, perfectionistic, nervous, finicky, skeptical, tendency to become hypochondriac, picky, afraid to make mistakes, discontented, carping, doubting Thomas, uptight and aloof, prissy, nitpicking, narrow vision, exacting, can't see the forest for the trees, nagging, constantly complains about everything, holds back emotional expression, fussy, inconsistent, intolerable, pedantic, can't leave well enough alone, workaholic, nagger, hair-splitting

KEYWORDS for the 7th - Marriage House
(Marriage, Partnerships & Open Enemies)

So if you have: THE TRANSCENDENTAL PLANETS (Uranus, Neptune & Pluto) in the 7th HOUSE or in aspect to VENUS or the MOON)

URANUS/higher mind - The MAGICIAN

+ seeking illumination, appreciates intellectual challenge from a partner who will liberate/awaken them to their own intuitive knowing, offers friendship/freedom to partner; needing space within their relationship, strong beliefs about equality, honors principles and exhibits honesty in communicating, altruistic and farsighted in their thinking, loyal to the relationship, non-possessive loving, differences accepted and encouraged

- cannot bear possessiveness, willful and obstinate to rebel, complains about others' selfishness/coldness, indifference and not acknowledging their own, refuses to acknowledge emotional pain in others, fear of abandonment strong so "I will abandon you before you abandon me" attitude, addicted to excitement and this creates havoc in relationships, erratic and restless, fixed-dogmatic thinking, unwilling to cooperate, anything too routine cages them in, fear of intimacy, cool, impersonal, distant, aloof, inconsiderate, keeps one foot out the door

POSITIVE MANIFESTATION TOGETHER - can enjoy independence and authentic communication with their partner, who will also be their best friend; both want to change the world to make it a better place through philanthropic pursuits, travel and learning together to expand their minds and learn metaphysical/spiritual truths; creative solutions to living arrangements; give each other space and freedom, can enjoy a wide circle of friends without jealousy, possessiveness or guilt-provoking, honoring their right for each to be a free bird

NEPTUNE/higher love - The ROMANTIC DREAMER

+ seeking to transcend the physical plane with unconditional love; seeking God and higher states of consciousness with their partner; devoted; romantic and compassionate; able to forgive; psychic attunement with a partner; sensitive to their partner's emotional pain; gives others the benefit of the doubt, affectionate, gentleness, concern, caring, thoughtfulness, altruism, sympathy, self-sacrificing for the relationship but each keeping the balance by reciprocating this kind of unselfishness when necessary, taking turns being understanding or charitable

- seeking God in the partner; the "perfect" partner which of course does not exist on the earth plane, discontent, denial about other's behavior, sacrificing oneself when there is no reciprocity, confuses sympathy for love, deceptive in relationships, absence/fantasy/escapism/addiction/feeling unworthy, unconscious guilt, platonic relationships with the one they love/sex with someone they do not love, wears rose-colored glasses, unrealistic expectations, dreamer, has difficulty setting limits or having boundaries with partner, kind to a fault, justifies, capricious

POSITIVE MANIFESTATION TOGETHER - can enjoy creativity/music and spirituality with a partner, impersonal helping/healing and devotion to a higher power/spirituality together/soulmate unions/seeing each others divinity, kindness and devoted love for each other, flexible to each others needs/schedules, consideration for each other, keep romance alive through their gifted imaginations, overlook each other's faults, idiosyncrasies, tenderness, kindness and compassion, charity begins at home with these two lovebirds

PLUTO/higher power - The THERAPIST

+ seeking transformation through merging with significant other; needing to develop one's own power and ability to change not fix each other; healing ourselves from past pain and trauma through real vulnerability; deeply committed to supporting each other's growth/experiencing deep feelings/sexuality/sharing; Shadow work that heals them both, renewal and regeneration through the partnership, shamanic experiences, depth psychology

- crisis through relating, chronically insecure, seeking to control and manipulate by overgiving of oneself and material things no matter what it costs, painful emotions such as possessiveness, jealousy, vindictiveness in relating, lack of trust, never getting enough from partner, suspicious, usually involved in triangles through emotional denial and underestimating their own vulnerability, sex, money, power misused and exploited, teases, withholds, secretive about motives, says the opposite of what they actually feel to deceive, vengeful, cruel

POSITIVE MANIFESTATION TOGETHER - can enjoy merging/sharing power/deep emotional sexual union with a partner, plumb the depths (Shadow work) together and eliminate/destroy the shameful pain/hurts in each other's past, be a channel of power in the world for healing/transformation of the planet/the wounded healers, transformative and honest communication, loyal to the death and nothing in the outer world can destroy their commitment to their transformational bond

The Houses

Each house in the astrological chart describes an area of our life and our psyche. When a person is born with several planets in a particular house, the meaning of that house will be a strong focus in their life.

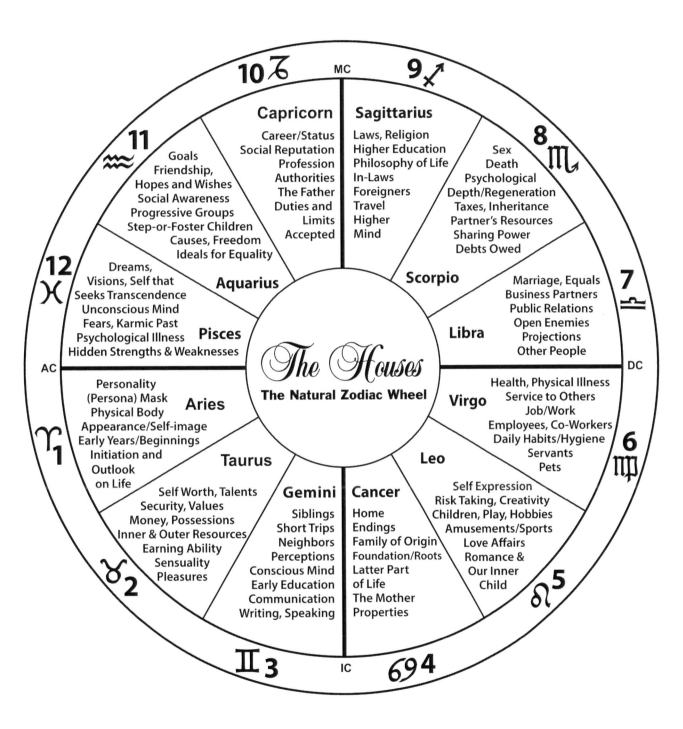

10 Capricorn — Career/Status, Social Reputation, Profession, Authorities, The Father, Duties and Limits Accepted

9 Sagittarius — Laws, Religion, Higher Education, Philosophy of Life, In-Laws, Foreigners, Travel, Higher Mind

8 Scorpio — Sex, Death, Psychological Depth/Regeneration, Taxes, Inheritance, Partner's Resources, Sharing Power, Debts Owed

7 Libra — Marriage, Equals, Business Partners, Public Relations, Open Enemies, Projections, Other People

6 Virgo — Health, Physical Illness, Service to Others, Job/Work, Employees, Co-Workers, Daily Habits/Hygiene, Servants, Pets

5 Leo — Self Expression, Risk Taking, Creativity, Children, Play, Hobbies, Amusements/Sports, Love Affairs, Romance & Our Inner Child

4 Cancer — Home, Endings, Family of Origin, Foundation/Roots, Latter Part of Life, The Mother, Properties

3 Gemini — Siblings, Short Trips, Neighbors, Perceptions, Conscious Mind, Early Education, Communication, Writing, Speaking

2 Taurus — Self Worth, Talents, Security, Values, Money, Possessions, Inner & Outer Resources, Earning Ability, Sensuality, Pleasures

1 Aries — Personality (Persona) Mask, Physical Body, Appearance/Self-image, Early Years/Beginnings, Initiation and Outlook on Life

12 Pisces — Dreams, Visions, Self that Seeks Transcendence, Unconscious Mind, Fears, Karmic Past, Psychological Illness, Hidden Strengths & Weaknesses

11 Aquarius — Goals, Friendship, Hopes and Wishes, Social Awareness, Progressive Groups, Step-or-Foster Children, Causes, Freedom, Ideals for Equality

The Houses
The Natural Zodiac Wheel

Correspondences/Archetypes/the Zodiac

21 March - 20 April	21 April - 21 May	22 May - 21 June	22 June - 22 July	23 July - 23 August	24 August - 22 September
Aries	**Taurus**	**Gemini**	**Cancer**	**Leo**	**Virgo**
Mars	**Venus**	**Mercury**	**Moon**	**Sun**	**Mercury**
Yang	**Yin**	**Yin**	**Yin**	**Yang**	**Yin**
Fire	**Earth**	**Air**	**Water**	**Fire**	**Earth**
Cardinal	**Fixed**	**Mutable**	**Cardinal**	**Fixed**	**Mutable**
Personal	**Personal**	**Personal**	**Personal**	**Social**	**Social**
1st House	**2nd House**	**3rd House**	**4th House**	**5th House**	**6th House**
Self-Awareness	Money	Environment	Home and Family Life	Entertainment	Health
Physical Body	Physical Body	Communications	Personal Unconscious	Creativity	Work/Service
Personality	Personal Resources	Early Education	Foundations/Roots	Self-Expression	to Others/Coworkers
Persona/Mask	Possessions	Siblings/Neighbors	Instincts	Gambling/Sports	Daily Mundane Duties
New Beginnings	Security/Safety	Short Journeys	Real Estate	Children	Self-Improvement
Survival	Productivity	Duality	End of Life	Love Affairs	Discrimination
"I AM"	"I HAVE"	"I THINK"	"I FEEL"	"I WILL"	"I ANALYZE"
Pioneer	Builder	Communicator	Nurturer	Entertainer	Servant/Healer
RAM	BULL	TWINS	CRAB	LION	VIRGIN
Head, Red Blood Cells	Neck, Throat	Arms, Shoulders,	Breasts, Bodily Fluids,	Heart, Head	Nervous System
Muscles, Adrenal Glands	Thyroid Gland	Hands, Lungs, Brain	Lymphatic System, Stomach	Back/Spine	Intestines
			SEA GREEN	GOLD	NAVY BLUE
RED	PALE BLUE	YELLOW	SILVER	ORANGE	GRAY
ORANGE	MAUVE				
			SILVER	GOLD	MERCURY
IRON	COPPER	MERCURY			
			PEARL	RUBY	SAPPHIRE
DIAMOND	EMERALD	AGATE			
			white rose	sunflower	nutbearing trees
red chili	rose	nut-bearing trees	geranium	marigold	morning glory
cayenne pepper	daisy	lily of the valley	lily	saffron	pansy
thorn-bearing trees	poppy	lavender	all white flowers	rosemary	forget-me-not
capers	foxglove	maidenhair	tarragon	laurel	buttercup
honeysuckle	cypress	fir/fern	cabbage	citrus trees	oak tree
thistle	fig/apple tree	marjoram			
peppermint	violet		restaurants	amusement parks	small domestic pets
		books	water	games/casinos	vitamins
heat	coins	newspaper	home	nightclubs	calculators
wounds	furniture	letters/messages	lakes/ponds	plays/dramas	toothbrushes
blisters	statues	phone	family	cinemas	mouthwash
weapons	art objects	mobile phone	pearls	gifts/toys	combs
sharp instruments	houses	radio/television	glass	fun	libraries
war/battles	cattle	copiers	collections	parties	vitamins
competitions	jewelry	posters	bathrooms	picnics	first aid kits
injuries	wheat	butterflies	kitchens	courtships	diners
fireplaces	treasures	automobiles	souvenirs	playing cards	closets
acne	wallets/purses	siblings	containers	castles	nutrition
caps	music	highways	boats	felines	textiles
aloes	windpipes	desks	food	ballroom	studies
brimstone	karaoke	computers	breasts	crowns	pantries
brick	gum	trains	mementos	emblems	photos
wood carving	art		comforts		
		bookkeeper		cartoonist	secretary
athlete	architect	advertising	farming	broker	maid
military	banker	mailman	caretaker	goldsmith	dentist
salespeople	cashier	cab driver	historian	entertainer/actor	civil service
hairdresser	confectioner	novelists	gardener	circus clown	chemist
welder	artist	clerical work	patriot	director	editor
soldier	art dealer	neighbor	housewife	fatherhood	librarian
physical therapist	singer	reporter	milkman	gambler	accountant
military	sculptor	passenger	nurse	romances	nurse
metallurgical engineer	farmer	the press	obstetrician	contractor	minister
karate master	gardener	printer	real estate agt.	jeweler	masseur
fireman	golfer	computer tech	plumber	creativity	dietician
gangster	seamstress	messenger	women	sculptor	critic
butcher	stock broker	postal clerk	psychologist	dancer	craftsman
surgeon	real estate	salesmen	cook/chef/baker	politician	inspector
steel worker	builder	journalist	collector	stock broker	veterinarian

Correspondences/Archetypes/the Zodiac

23 September - 23 October	24 October - 22 November	23 November - 21 December	22 December - 20 January	21 January - 18 February	19 February - 20 March
Libra	**Scorpio**	**Sagittarius**	**Capricorn**	**Aquarius**	**Pisces**
Venus	**Pluto**	**Jupiter**	**Saturn**	**Uranus**	**Neptune**
Yang	**Yin**	**Yang**	**Yin**	**Yang**	**Yin**
Air	**Water**	**Fire**	**Earth**	**Air**	**Water**
Cardinal	**Fixed**	**Mutable**	**Cardinal**	**Fixed**	**Mutable**
Social	**Social**	**Universal**	**Universal**	**Universal**	**Universal**
7th House	**8th House**	**9th House**	**10th House**	**11th House**	**12th House**
Marriage/Partnerships	Transformation	Religion/Laws/Ethics	Father	Social Interaction	Transcendence
Open Enemies	Sex	Philosophy of Life	Achievement	Group Awareness	Spirituality
Networking/Socializing	Joint Resources	Higher Education	Authority	Goals/Dreams	Karma/Atonement
Contracts/Agreements	Death (physical	Understanding & Wisdom	Public Standing	Wishes	Parapsychology
Lawsuits	or symbolic)	Foreign Travel	Reputation	Liberation	Confinement
Art/Aesthetics	Taxes/Inheritances	Advertising/Publishing	Administrator/Mgr.	Progress/Change	Sacrifice
"I BALANCE"	"I DESIRE"	"I SEE"	"I USE"	"I KNOW"	"I BELIEVE"
Peacemaker	Detective	Philosopher	Father	Humanitarian	Visionary
SCALES	SCORPION	CENTAUR	GOAT	WATER BEARER	FISHES
Kidney, Buttocks	The	Hips,	Knees/Joints	Ankles, Calves,	Feet, Pineal Gland,
Veins, Lower Back	Genitals	LIver, Thighs,	Bones, Skin,	Electricity in Body,	Endocrine System
	Adenoids	Arteries	Teeth, Right Ear	Blood Circulation	
BLUE					PALE GREEN
LAVENDER	CRIMSON	PURPLE	DARK GREEN	ELECTRIC	TURQUOISE
	MAROON		BROWN	BLUE	
COPPER		TIN			PLATINUM
	PLUTONIUM		LEAD	URANIUM	
OPAL		TURQUOISE			AQUAMARINE
	TOPAZ		GARNET	AMETHYST	
rose		narcissus			fig
bluebells	chrysanthemum	holly	ivy	orchid	pussy willow
daisy	hawthorn	dandelion	pine/elm/yew	fruit trees	jonquil
almond trees	crustaceans	mulberry	aspen/poplar	daffodil	water lily
apple tree	rhododendron	birch/oak/ash	pansy	primrose	white poppy
hydrangea	geranium	carnation	poppy	elderberry trees	chickory
ash/cypress	honeysuckle		comfrey	golden rain	cucumber
		horses		kiwis, star fruit	
beauty parlors	cemeteries	lucky charms	bruises		chaos
boutiques	reptiles	altars	ashes	astrology	anesthetics
contracts	morgues	archery	abandoned places	aviation	aquariums
dressing rooms	autopsies	ceremonies	basements	technology	churches
divorces	eagles	institutions	cement	gases	escape
flowers	phoenix	universities	cryogenics	inventions	distilleries
furriers, luxury	feces	courts of law	excavations	radiology	drugs
grace	dumps	customs	dungeons	wireless	liquids
harmony	cesspools	commerce	dirt/gravel	bizarre	film
refinement	chemistry	travel	leather	batteries	imprisonment
martrimony	operations	literature	old age	lightning	hospitals
pianos	sewers	prayers	honors/awards	instruments	convent/monasteries
warfare	funerals	passports	mountains/stones	scientists	submarines
weddings	poisonous plants	races	government	friends	art/paintings
social gatherings	reincarnation			gases	myth/symbol
boudoirs	espionage	politician	manager	electronics	
	laboratories	teacher/professor	chiropractor		nurse/doctor
pianist		interpretor	civil engineer	humanitarian	nun
artist	detectives	judge	contractors	group-oriented	bartender
decorator	magicians	minister	government service	politicians	clairvoyant
cosmetician	pharmacists	philosopher	watchman	revolutionaries	charlatan/fraud
golfer	laboratories	clergyman	traffic manager	physicists	alcoholic/addict
lawyer	chemical labs	lawyer	organizers	avante garde	poet/dreamer
jeweler	gynecologist	jockey	orthopedist	altruist	prison guard
dressmaker	doctor	hunter	loner/pessimist	genius	dancer
diplomat	surgeon	guru	politicians	associates	musician/pianist
florist	mortician	sportsmen	osteopath	inventors	savior/messiah
interior designer	garbage collector	wise men/women	accountant	pilots	photographer
receptionist	insurance agt.	veterinarian	mathematician	announcers	mystic/saint
graphic designer	tax collector	travel agent	conservative	radio and television	martyr/victim
fashion model	psychologist	gambler	hospital administrator	different/unique	fisherman/sailor
social director	researcher	foreigner	president	salesmen	psychotherapist

(PLEASE NOTE: dates will vary slightly from year to year as to when one sign ends and the other begins.)

NOTES PART FOUR:

1) C.G. Jung, CW 10 - Civilization in Transition, *The Undiscovered Self (Mind and Earth)*, Princeton University Press; Bollingen, 1957, par 545, pg 113

FURTHER STUDIES:

Go to the Jung Center in your area to learn more about Jung in order to apply his wisdom to your daily life.

Once you start looking into astrology and are impressed with the self-knowledge you receive, you may want to take classes and learn more about it. So I am recommending the following schools for further study.

ASTROLOGY SCHOOLS:

In Houston, Texas

I highly recommend Kimberly McSherry, professional astrologer and owner of Houston Institute of Astrology, in operation since 1980. Kim teaches an intensive two-year curriculum intended to provide the student with a basic knowledge of astrology. The course is modeled after the mystery school tradition, focusing on astrology as a tool for self-awareness, insight into one's own nature and personal evolution.

LEARN ASTROLOGY ONLINE at:

astrocollege.org
International Academy of Astrology, the oldest online astrology school. We offer live online classes, workshops, and lectures with real instructors covering every level of astrological education. Our comprehensive diploma program is recognized by astrological organizations worldwide. Plus we have an ever-expanding video library featuring lectures and mini-courses on a wide variety of astrological topics.

aaperry.com
Founded in 1987, The Association for Psychological Astrology (APA) is dedicated to the integration of astrology and psychology. Our purpose is twofold: (1) establish general guidelines for the application of astrology to the fields of counseling and psychotherapy, and (2) enrich the field of astrology through the systematic integration of psychological concepts and practices.

astrosynthesis.com.au
Brian Clark, is the creator of the Astro*Synthesis distance learning program which has been shaped from his experience as an astrological educator.

He is the author of many student publications, as well as three recent books – *Vocation: the Astrology of Career, Creativity and Calling, The Family Legacy Astrological Imprints on Life, Love & Relationship and From the Moment We Met: the Astrology of Adult Relationships*. His latest book *Soul, Symbol & Imagination* reflects on his participation and practice of astrology as an astrological student, counsellor and teacher over the past 40+ years.

SOFTWARE:

For the PC, I use Kepler which can be purchased at AstroSoftware.com, home of Cosmic Patterns Software, Inc., or call 800-779-2559 or Email: kepler@astrosoftware.com

---

...taking up your sword and moving beyond your basic ground also
holds the promise of greater individuation, greater self-realization
and self-fulfillment, and greater freedom from old patterns and
complexes that have inhibited you and trapped you.[1]

RICHARD IDEMON

Having a consultation with a psychological astrologer can bring a person information that could take years to unravel in therapy. Astrology does not substitute for long-term therapy, but it does shine a light on the parts of a person that are hidden from consciousness. What the individual does with this information after that may (or may not) *require a therapist. I have been Shadow Work Coaching for the last 15 years. The following four consultations give readers an example of my work.*

Astrology Consultations

The planet Uranus rules astrology. As we learned about Uranus previously, this is the planet that is iconoclastic. It beats to its own drum. Its job is to enlighten or awaken us. It is the part of all of us that refuses to conform to convention and accept society rules. Wherever it falls in our own chart, we pride ourselves on being different and unique.

All astrological consultations are different because astrologers themselves are different in their orientation and education. Some astrologers are therapists themselves, having degrees from traditional schools; others are karmic astrologers or do predictions; some are into the body and healing; others are good at business and helping people with timing. There are many ways that astrology can be used effectively to help a person see their karma and their psyche. A session will generally be indicative of the work that a particular astrologer has done on themselves, and you can have a consultation on your birth chart with many different astrologers, and more and more will be revealed to you. I see the astrologer's role as a valuable tool to guide the person into knowing more about themselves.

Being a woman with five planets in Libra, (the sign of marriage) in the 3rd house, and North Node in Aquarius in the 7th, I was destined to be interested in relationships but not in the traditional way of going to a university to become a counselor. The planet Uranus is the ruler of my 7th house, so the way I would go about it would be somehow not the same way as everyone else. I resonated the most with Jung's work because it involved seeing the whole person, the dark and the light. An attempt at balance is required to do the work of what he calls **individuation**. All of my Libran planets are indicative of my need for seeing both sides of everything. My Saturn in Libra in the middle of my stellium (a group of 3 or more planets in one sign) would also mean I would focus exclusively on one particular subject and learn as much as I could about it. I am still learning, as it is a life's work. The following consultations are an example of this work. Many clients have told me how much more they understand Jung once they saw his concepts and archetypes acted out in their individual lives. More than any other section of this workbook, this part shows the Shadow at work and why the studies of astrology and Jungian psychology complement each other so powerfully!

ASTROLOGY CONSULTATION EXAMPLES

The following examples are verbatim from four astrology sessions with clients that I felt really embraced a Shadow aspect of themselves through our work together. These examples can help the reader see that the astrological chart can help a person see a part that has become split off or projected and how that un-lived part of us can work against us. These dialogues are transcribed from tapes, with minor editing for grammar. All names and identifying information have been changed to protect their privacy.

JEAN

Tuesday, July 1, 1958
10:40:00 AM EDT
Pittsfield, Massachusetts
Tropical Placidus True Node

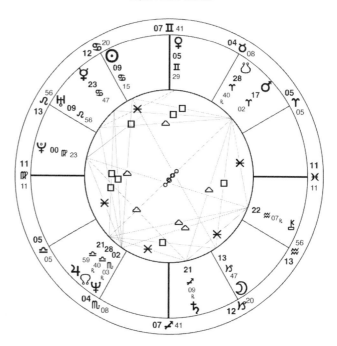

EXAMPLE 1: Jean - A Woman Born with a Strong Animus

When a woman is born with a strong emphasis in masculine energy, she will have to struggle with understanding her male side and how her Animus either helps or hinders her in her life. By masculine energy, I mean she has six or more planets in fire or air (which in Jungian terminology is thinking and intuition) signs or she has a "very strong" Mars. I refer you to my diagram in Part 4 that shows the gender and correspondences of each archetype and sign. A very strong Mars means Mars in its own sign, which is Aries, Mars in an angle (1st, 4th, 7th or 10th houses) or Mars in aspect to every planet in her chart. To be born a woman with this kind of energy is a dilemma, and doing Shadow work is very helpful to deal with it. The following is a story of a woman who came to me for an astrology session after taking my Shadow Dance workshop. Her parental complex took on another scenario. Her story is helpful, and I will call her Jean.

Jean started having dreams right after she took the Shadow Dance workshop. In her dreams, black gooey stuff was coming up from the vent of her car, spilling onto her. She didn't want it to spill on her gym bag. She said the gym bag was representative of her image of herself. She would push away the vent so it wouldn't spray on her, but it just kept coming out. After the workshop, she realized that the black gooey stuff was her Shadow. Our cars are often symbolic of how we go about life, as they are how we get around. Jean's dream made her feel a Shadow aspect of herself was surfacing. She determined this was her lost and rejected feminine self. As a young child growing up, she felt that "being male" seemed to get the most approval, so she squashed her femininity. It went into hiding. She said the discovery that this was a major piece of herself that she was missing was huge, and she wanted to talk about it further.

Jean was about to go visit her parents. She said she knew that her relationship with her parents was a big issue for her. She especially felt she had a major issue with her mother. She wanted to get as much information specifically on that relationship as she could before going home.

Jean: My mom is very ill, so she won't be here much longer, and I want to take advantage of the time left to work on this issue. I want to see why I can't stand her and where that might be in me, because I don't see it. Mom raised a family of eight children, so none of the children got much individualized attention. My mother lived for her family and lost her own creativity and sense of self in her marriage. Now when I go home and see my mother, it makes me sick. My mother is weak, ineffectual and in a wheelchair in her old age. She talks about inconsequential and stupid things. She refuses to answer questions. She lives in her own
fantasy world, and she is now expressing bitterness toward my father that she should have expressed years ago and didn't. She loves playing the martyr, and I can't talk to her. It brings up so much frustration in me that my body revolts at the sight of her. When I go home, it's like an emotional roller coaster.

Rebeca: Your mother and your lost femininity are completely connected. Go on telling me your story.

Jean: I did a little digging in myself to see my weaknesses, and

Notes to Myself:

I ask myself why I can't just love her for who she is. Why can't I accept her in all her frailties, in all her lost dreams? Why can't I just love her because she's my mom, and just let her be without any expectations — without expecting her to come to me now at midlife and love me the way I needed her to love me as a child? I know it's not going to happen. Why can't I let this be and love her just the way she is?

Rebeca: The question becomes apparent, "Why can't we love and accept ourselves the way that we are?" We can't love our parents in their imperfection until we can see how they represent Shadow sides of ourselves. The male side of us says no, we don't want to be weak like them. Strength is what counts in this world of the patriarchy.

Jean: Yes, and when I go home, I love her, but I can't stand her weakness. I get caught in this trap, and I end up leaving as an emotional mess. What do I do with that?

Rebeca: Well, you were born with the Moon in Capricorn. The mother for a woman born with the Moon in Capricorn is exactly what you just described: somebody who was over burdened, had many children, not enough time for any of them or for herself and was critical and maybe even depressed. A woman with Moon square Jupiter, which you also have, is like a child who doesn't want to grow up. It wants to be irresponsible, adventurous and have fun. Then Moon squaring Mars has lots and lots of anger about it all. Well, this is your chart, so these are all components of your psyche as reflected by your mother. The Moon describes your emotional need. It's what you need to feel nurtured. Moon in Capricorn needs to feel that she is strong. She values structure, order, control, practicality. Everything has to be perfect. There's a constant battle with yourself about not being perfect enough and making yourself nuts about it.

Jean: Yes! That's it.

Rebeca: This is something that astrology and doing Shadow work helped me see, because these are parts of us that are not going to go away. These parts that we would rather no one else see, how do we live with them and accept ourselves?

You do get to a place where you realize you are changing. You are growing. If you look back 20 years, you realize you have changed, BUT there are certain parts of your character that are consistent. You are not going to get rid of them. The changes are going to be more in accepting who you are. This is a real strong part of you. The fact is, you need structure, order, discipline, accomplishment, and that's fine. Make that a part of your business world. The other feminine part of you, the Venusian part, needs to be lived out also. The Venusian part in your case is also in Capricorn, and your Aphrodite wants togetherness to be stable, concrete and values form given to feelings. Do you do any art?

Jean: See, that's what's bizarre. In doing this Shadow work, I've noticed bursts of creative energy. I feel I have an eye for photography and a desire to write. My teachers told me I was talented in art, something my parents never saw.

Rebeca: There are great classes at the Jung Center for creative self-expression. I, too, felt I had lost my femininity growing up as the fifth girl in my family. My father wanted a boy. I took a class at the Jung Center, and we were given clay to describe our Shadow. I made a clay mask of a little girl in pigtails. She was my hidden self. My image of me was that I was strong. I didn't need anyone. I could take care of myself.

Jean: Yes, I know you! That's me.

Rebeca: Well, I am fortunate with women friends. I attract to myself women who are teaching me to honor that part of me, to not lose the strength in me, but to give myself a chance to feel my feelings.

Jean: That's really neat that you said that, because I believe my weight has always been a symptom of what is going on inside of me. It's almost as if my male side would say to me, "Eat something, because that way you won't have to feel it." So I would eat all the time to not feel what was going on. I found out about this image inside of me, and I called her Sable. She was the strong, athletic macho side of womanhood, but I saw her as fat and overweight. I started doing some reading on myths and decided there was another part of me, and she was like Persephone. The whole concept of Persephone was that she was stolen away before she could really achieve her maidenhood. Into the darkness of Hades she went, the darkness of the unconscious. There she stayed and remained. Now that I put a name on her as she's coming up from the depths of darkness. Now instead of this overweight girl, she's turned around. She is Persephone, this beautiful girl, the image of beauty, fertility, and now I see her in the same light. There's Sable, and there's Persephone, and they are both part of me.

Rebeca: One of the best things about doing this work is finding out that we are a multiple of beings within one soul and that is what creates the individual. We are vast. It's only when a part of us is not allowed expression that another part gets overdone. It's a compensation, striving to correct the imbalance. In my chart, Mars is very strong as it aspects every planet in the chart. You have a strong Mars, too. Mars for you is in Aries. Aries is the warrior God, the hero, the conqueror. BUT your Sun sign is in Cancer. If after 40 we don't start doing the Sun, we start to feel like we are going nuts.

Notes to Myself:

Jean: You see... it's right on time.

Rebeca: Cancer is about mothering.

Jean: I know!

Rebeca: Maybe, and I hope this doesn't sound judgmental, but maybe part of that journey is for you to start paying attention to your body. Almost as if you are glorifying it, beautifying your body, loving your body. Maybe dress more feminine, even a bit sexier than what is comfortable for you — not gaudy — but just a little more feminine and colourful.

Jean: Yes! It's weird, because ever since I discovered Persephone. there was a woosh of softness that came over me, just by naming her. I'm finding I am looking at women differently. Women who are mothers — I am looking at them with a foreign eye like I've never been able to see them before.

Rebeca: That's the part of you that you were missing, so that's why you couldn't stand that about your mother.

Jean: What do you mean I couldn't stand that about my mother?

Rebeca: You couldn't stand that she was such a mother and that was all that was important to her.

Jean: Ohhhhhh!

Rebeca: She had all these children. She lived for that. She had nothing of her own. You saw her as having no individuality. It was splattered all over these children and her role as a mother. Does that make sense?

Jean: Yes.

Rebeca: That's the part of you that you need to develop.

Jean: So that's why it came out as a projection of dissatisfaction on her?

Rebeca: Right. Because you don't want to be that.

Jean: Oh, that's interesting. That's good.

Rebeca: Our Sun sign is what we need to develop the most. It symbolizes our vitality, our need to shine and what is really important for our center. The Moon sign is what we are instinctively. We come in with it *a priori,* which means it's an inherent disposition. So your Capricorn Moon is that rigid, controlling, perfect and strong woman that says, "I'm not going to be like you." (She laughs.) Your Sun sign is in Cancer. Cancer is about belonging and emotional need. It's about expressing feelings, being vulnerable, wanting closeness and family.

Jean: I have escaped that my entire life. I have denied it, and I didn't even know to what extent that I denied it until one of my friends told me, "I couldn't relate to you from my female side. You were never vulnerable. You never cried. You never did anything to allow me to get close to you."

Rebeca: So you can start now. Express your feelings. Go and have massages. We all need to be touched on a regular basis. Buy yourself flowers. Put flowers from the yard inside your house in every room. These are all things that feel feminine, and they also feel homey. That's a real Cancer thing to make your home real homey. Pillows and needlepoint and candles make it soft and sensuous. Then all of a sudden your voice will start changing.

Jean: Yeah?

Rebeca: Now I am buying myself roses, listening to romantic love songs, and this is how I bring my spirituality into this. I listen to a song, and instead of thinking that a man is going to be singing that to me or loving me, I am bringing that in as spirit. So every song that plays is God singing it to me and/or me singing it to God. Through music I envelop myself in a wonderful space. I don't lose that feminine part of me that needs a garden, that needs nurturing, that needs sensitivity. The more I am able to do that, the more I am able to cry. The more I am able to be emotional and vulnerable with guys. I could never do that before.

Jean: Wow, that's really helpful.

Rebeca: So do you see why we need our Shadow?

Jean: Yes. That part of me was buried.

Rebeca: So, the woman inside of you that wants to nurture and be nurtured can become more acceptable to you.

Jean: That's so interesting. Last week I was watching the movie *The Mummy.* It's not a film I would watch, but in the last scene, where he gathers her in his arms and she rides off on a camel with him, I had a really hard time with that vision because it was "a woman being taken care of" type of thing. It was hard to accept or relate to being like that.

Rebeca: Yet, you need to accept her because she is in you. Eventually you will change your hair, your dress; your body will become more comfortable with your feminine side.

Jean: If indeed you have that strong male aspect, does one carry themselves differently without even knowing? Does it actually turn into projecting out of you a hard, male-looking side instead of that softer self?

Rebeca: I think it does.

Jean: So in a sense, not only your physical appearance, but does what's in here come out and in a way take over your features?

Notes to Myself:

Rebeca: Yes. I think so. I've been working on this, trying to bring in my feminine side for years. I have a strong Mars. It aspects every planet in my chart and is conjunct my Moon so it's like having the Moon in Aries. I've had to continually deal with it. If you look at the transition, how I've changed my dress, even my hair color, lightening it, everything, going to exercise classes, taking care of my body, my health, eating healthy foods. I even go to Jazzercize three times a week, and there are all these women in there who are housewives, and they are all talking about their husbands or their kids. At first I didn't want to be there. It was so uncomfortable for me. I felt inferior to them.

Jean: Did you actually feel inferior, because I felt superior?

Rebeca: Yes. I felt inferior in the sense that — well, I felt superior in that I have a career I love, I drive a Lexus that I paid for and I don't have four kids hanging on me, etc., but I felt inferior because I want to be softer. I want to be a woman, too. I want to relate to men. I want to have relationships with men. I have lots of women friends. I don't have a problem with that.

Jean: Wouldn't you also have lots of men friends?

Rebeca: Yes, I have about four or five really good guy friends, too.

Jean: But at least you have male friends.

Rebeca: Oh, yes, I have both, but I have lots and lots of women friends who have the same problem I do. They are very business oriented; they are very successful in their careers. They've done all that, but they don't have a family and a home with a husband and the white picket fence and all that stuff.

Jean: Right!

Rebeca: But I really don't believe that would make me happy. I wouldn't want all of that, and I don't want to pretend that I do, because I don't.

Jean: It's an outer manifestation of an inner thing.

Rebeca: It's more an inner sense of femininity, regaining the parts of you that you can't stand in women. The more you can be them, even halfway, coming toward that, expressing weakness or need, the more you will be in balance.

Jean: I notice they are getting closer, so they are merging; it's that reconciliation. They want to be reconciled, but they are still two separate entities. I know that they are both there, so it is just a matter of saying to myself, "This is something I am doing to nurture my female side. I know my strong masculine side is still here, but this time I am doing this or that because I accept it. I want it to rise to it's fullest. I want that side to grow. So I am doing this to help my female side."

Rebeca: Yeah. Making decisions in that way.

Jean: And consciously doing it.

Rebeca: Yes. And doing the feminine things like buying flowers and changing my clothes. I've changed a lot of my clothes. I used to wear a lot of black. Now I wear a lot of colors that make me feel feminine. I am really concentrating on feeling pretty and working on that, and my voice started changing.

Jean: Really?

Rebeca: Yeah, guys have told me, "Your voice has changed. I don't know what it is you're doing, Rebeca, but keep it up." Some guys told me that last week at a party. One told me he used to be afraid to talk to me, but he could see that I had changed.

Jean: How interesting. That actually makes sense. The other day I was sitting on the couch, and I was talking to Steve. That's my ex. He said, "What are you looking at?" In that moment I felt like I was looking through softer eyes. They felt softer. My posture was more relaxed instead of rigid. It was just that for that moment I was experiencing that softness, of trying to have compassion for him on that level instead of the strong, rigid one.

I can really see from what you're saying that we hold more maleness in our outer appearance than we're even aware of. It's not to the point where one would completely say I hate men, because there is still that sense inside me that wants relationship but somehow can't let go of the need to control. It's very strong.

But the whole idea of finding Persephone, that beautiful little girl that was robbed away before she had a chance. When I reach for food now, I tell myself, "What are you feeling? Don't be afraid to feel. Feel it. Feel what you're feeling." So I work on what I am trying to feel, and usually the urge to eat goes away. And Sable, the strong, athletic side — when we go to the gym, Sable is totally into image in the strong sense, but now she has abilities. She is showing Persephone how to use the equipment and she's showing her how to work on her body. They can work together. They want to be reconciled. In a sense, that is what spirituality is about, the need to reconcile...

Rebeca: ...both parts of yourself.

Jean: Yes.

Rebeca: To me you don't ever lose your strength, but you come from a different place. When the strength is coming from the Animus, it's harsh, it's critical, it's innuendos, it's opinionated. Notice when it's opinionated stuff and you get on a high horse. Ask yourself, "Did I really need to cut them off? Did I really need to say it like that? Did I really need to do that?"

Jean: I do that all the time.

Notes to Myself:

Rebeca: But you won't as often when you work with the Shadow because in time you will change as you become aware. When you're not aware, you just keep doing it and doing it. Honor that part of you that is asking the questions, because the more you work on it, and it takes time, the more you'll find you will be less and less opinionated. You will still speak the truth when it's necessary. The warrior part of you will come out when it's necessary, because the warrior part of you, that Mars in Aries, needs a place to fight. Work out at the gym, play some competitive tennis, do whatever you can do to live that part of you. It needs to live. It doesn't go away, but it doesn't have to take over your life.

Jean: That's what's really nice about Shadow work when you can say, "I am this, AND I am that" — like you said in the workshop.

Rebeca: Right.

Jean: There's a magical thing that happens in your psyche that releases the fear, because fear almost seems like the Shadow is a part of oneself hidden down. When you bring it into the light, there's freedom to be able to look around, the freedom is...

Rebeca: to be all these parts of you.

Jean: And there is truly a shift in how you look through your eyes.

Rebeca: Now you have a choice when to be weak, needy, yes... needy. I almost think you have to go to the extreme of that in order to come back to the middle where you can just express need instead of "needy," which is an extreme.

Jean: Now let's go back to my mom. I know I can't go back and make that relationship the way I wanted it to be when I was a little girl, but how can I reconcile? Speaking about my mom, they said when she married, it was almost like a Cinderella story. She thought it was going to be like a Cinderella story, and it never happened.

Rebeca: Is that in your Liz Greene report?

Jean: Yes.

Rebeca: That's your Moon-Jupiter conjunction.

Jean: My dad, get this, he studied to be a priest for four years. So he brought huge amounts of spirituality into my being that always has been in the back of me. When he came into the marriage, it wasn't what he expected. We have this facade of this idyllic family, but we're not. We're all screwed up, and now things are coming out that were repressed.

Rebeca: Everybody is.

Jean: What I want to do when I go home this time is to be able to somehow understand what my relationship is with my mother that will help me to see her in a way that I have never seen her before, that will help me to...

Rebeca: Have you ever put yourself in that place? Have you ever been in a relationship where you were weak, where you were overgiving, where you were desperate for that person or wanted them so badly that you gave more than they did and they used you?

Jean: Yes. In my marriage, which lasted eight years. We came together mutually attracting. He had a strong feminine aspect, which makes sense now. We seemed to have all these levels that we connected on. In that sense, I felt like I gave and gave and gave, but nothing was given to me. I put him through college, did all these things just for him. I did it all for him, and I wasn't getting anything back.

Rebeca: Well, who does that sound like?

Jean: OK, let's see... I was giving, giving, giving, and I was getting nothing back. OK, my mom! Oh, my God!

Rebeca: I did the same thing. I put myself in the same exact situation that my mom did with my dad, and it was impossible for me to see that I was just like her. When I finally saw that, I had so much compassion for her. All the negative feelings went away. I used to be mean to her. I would pick on her unconsciously. I wasn't doing it consciously, but when I saw that, I could accept her for who she was because I did the same thing she did.

Jean: When we were in your workshop, and you asked us to write down what we didn't like about our parents, I wrote that down. "She lost her sense of self in her marriage." So are you saying that when we realize that we are like them, is that what begins the compassion? Once we have compassion for ourselves, then it spills out to them.

Rebeca: Yes. As you're looking at her this time, when you go back and you see her doing or saying something that you consider being a martyr, notice. Notice. Think about yourself when you overgave and you sounded like a martyr. It doesn't even have to be just in your marriage. It can be at work, it can be with a friend, it can be with a sister, whomever. Notice that you've done that, but you don't like that about you, therefore you let her be that. You've done it, too, but when she does it, it makes you really mad because you're not aware that it's also in you.

Jean: So when she goes off and does her thing, and the first emotions start to rise up in me, I can say, "Well, you know I've done that too. It's me. I am my mother's daughter in that respect."

Rebeca: This is really awesome that you are here, because three days ago, I dreamed I was in my mother's bed asleep in the same bed. I started a conversation with her and I told her, "I've decided to move. I've been thinking that I don't want to live here anymore and I need my own space." She said, "Well, good, because I don't like to have to clean up after you when you leave dishes in the sink." And I said to her, "Well, you know what? I don't want to clean the dishes in the sink until I want to. So the best thing to do is get my own place." That was my dream, but we were not mad at each other. We were not fighting. It was very peaceful between us. I know the dream was symbolizing the peace that I don't have to be her anymore, but when I am I will know it. If we leave someone and we're still angry with them, then we haven't gotten it yet. We will have to go through it again because we still haven't seen what they are representing to us. Often it is about our parents. My dad died a few years ago. My mom is 80+ years old, and she is going to exercise three times a week. Next month she's travelling with her sister to Italy. She's finally getting to have the life she never had.

Jean: Isn't that weird? My mom is never going to be able to have the life she wanted because she is an invalid. She never got to live out her dreams. She wanted to go to Hawaii and to Ireland, and she'll never have it.

Rebeca: And my mom is a health fanatic.

Jean: Through her entire life?

Rebeca: Yes. She has a Mars-Saturn conjunction in Virgo, so she is a health fanatic, almost like a hypochondriac — taking herbs and vitamins, etc. But what's funny is that is not in my chart, so I don't identify with that, so it never bothered me about her. You see? It's only the things that are also in you that will bother you about your parents.

Jean: Ohhhhh!

Rebeca: What you know about them that doesn't bother you is not about you! Isn't that interesting?

Jean pulls out her Liz Greene report and points to the section on her mother. It's all highlighted. I tell her how mine is highlighted in four different colors because I've read it so many times. (We laughed!)

Jean: OK, it was talking about my having to be very careful not to live my mother's dream that I might be unaware of that.

Rebeca: That's another part, Moon square Mars. A Moon square Mars mother is someone who is or was adventurous, and she didn't get to do that. So you end up overdoing it. Jung says that we are highly susceptible to our parents' unlived lives. You might be living out the adventurous woman who never settles down, who doesn't want roots, because you're afraid to end up like your mother. There is a part of you that is an adventurous person.

Jean: I've had adventure dreams ever since I was a kid.

Rebeca: Yeah, I used to have dreams that I could fly. The archetype is Peter Pan, the *puer aeternus*, the woman is the *puella*. Have you ever read *The Wounded Woman* by Linda Leonard?

Jean: No.

Rebeca: Well, I highly recommend it. It's about healing the Father-daughter wound. Let me show it to you. I also want to show you this book called *Astrology for the Soul,* by Jan Spiller. I recommend this book to everyone whether they are an astrologer or not. I've actually given it to a few friends of mine who are therapists, and they tell me they use it in their practice. See this right here in your chart? This is your South Node in Aries, and it's conjunct your Mars. What it says is that the warrior in you, that masculine, strong part of you, is something that you've been doing for many, many lifetimes. This is your North Node, and it's in Libra. Libra is the sign of marriage and partnership, and your North Node is conjunct my Venus.

Jean: So what does that mean?

Rebeca: Well, Venus is the feminine part of us that loves and receives love. Whenever a person's North Node is conjunct a planet like Venus or the Moon or the Sun, then you have karma with that person, and it's beneficial to both of you. In other words, you're helping me and I'm helping you. This has been good for both of us.

Your North Node in Libra is about balance. This is why you're here. Our North Node is the most important point in the chart. Libra is about cooperation, negotiating and compromising with a partner, balancing the opposites within ourselves. Also, your North Node is conjunct Neptune and Jupiter. Neptune is the planet about spirituality. This is really a fabulous conjunction to have because what you are wanting to manifest in this lifetime is being a seeker of wisdom (Jupiter) and your full potential is about balance (Libra) and recognizing imbalance in your relationships.

Jean: That's why this Shadow thing resonated totally with me.

Rebeca: The spirituality symbolized by Neptune is a real big part of it.

Jean: It's huge.

Rebeca: What you'll come to understand within yourself is that spirituality is a full and total acceptance of who we are.

Jean: I never realized that. It's the Shadow work that led us to even conceive of that very thought.

Rebeca: Right. Because otherwise we'll beat ourselves up for the rest of our lives. Then we'll think, "Everybody else is perfect. How come I'm not?" We are all perfect just the way we are.

Jean: And that compassion and love and acceptance for you only naturally spills out to others.

Rebeca: Absolutely, because the more critical we are of ourselves, the more critical we are of everyone else.

Jean: Exactly.

Rebeca: What goes around, comes around. It's profound. This book, *Astrology for the Soul,* will tell you all about your North Node. It has about 20-25 pages on each Node, and it's all about restructuring how you cooperate when you get into relationships — relationships with everyone including your mother. The only way to forgive our parents is to see how much we are like them. This time when you go home, you can see her in a totally different light. Your dreams will completely change. You'll feel different, not sorry for her, because she chose all that. You have to keep that in mind. She chose the life she is living. That was her choice of how she lived out her energy. We may not understand that completely, but from an evolutionary perspective, if you take a broader perspective, maybe her soul needed that for that part of her evolution. Your soul chose her and your family for this part of your evolution. If you look at it like that, it's not personal. It's just part of fate.

Jean: If someone had told me that even two years ago, I would have laughed at them. The whole concept of reincarnation was such a turnoff to me. Back then I would have said I don't buy it.

Rebeca: Well, it takes time. Most people don't start doing soul work until after midlife. People in their thirties haven't suffered enough yet. They haven't experienced. After 40, we know these things have repeated.

Jean: This has been really helpful. Just since your workshop two months ago, I can feel a shift taking place in me, and I knew that I wanted to come talk to you about my mother.

Rebeca: That's why we have to really look at the parents. You know what I think the biggest fear of all is? The biggest fear is we will be like them, and the biggest release is that...

Jean: ...we don't have to be!

Rebeca: No, the biggest release is that WE ARE!!!

(Laughter bubbles up between us.)

Jean: That's funny!

Rebeca: I know. It's that we are, so we don't have to be afraid of it anymore.

Jean: Isn't that weird? Fear is usually about the unknown. When you know it, then it's not really that fearful anymore.

Rebeca: Right. Because now you know it.

Jean: I like that.

Rebeca: Once you reach that acceptance, there's like a huge shift. It's in that acceptance that you can use it to your benefit.

Jean: That's really good. My sisters are going through the same thing. I have a sister who is one year younger than me. She's so afraid of becoming my mom that it's driving her crazy. Well, yeah. Don't worry. We are. Wow! Just in that statement I already feel a relief. The fear of going home has dissipated.

Rebeca: So now you're free. You're free to choose.

Jean: That's it. This is the "AHA" moment!

Rebeca: Now you can choose. Now you can use both sides of your parents to integrate yourself.

Jean: That is what I wanted. This is what I am working on right now — the Libra part of me, the balance.

Rebeca: Look where the transits are right now. Pluto is the planet that rules the unconscious and transformation and regeneration. It has just crossed the cusp of home and family, the 4th house. So the work that you are doing is deep, and this is only the beginning. More and more will become clear to you.

Jean: Wow. I was ready.

* * * * * * * * *

Notes to Myself:

Notes to Myself:

BETH

Monday, November 1, 1954
12:32:00 AM CST
Eglin Air Force Base, Florida
Tropical   Placidus True Node

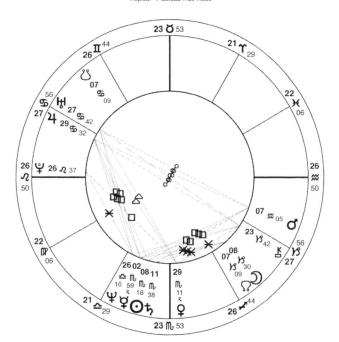

Example 2: Beth - The Case of a Missing Parent

Rebeca: You've had readings before, so I didn't want to just start telling you about yourself as usual for a few minutes. Do you want to talk about the Shadow and how that might be of interest to you in your relationships?

Beth: Is there anything in particular you saw about myself that might be interesting?

Rebeca: Well, I saw several challenges. One would be communication — difficulty with communication, holding things back, being kind of secretive. That's very Scorpio. The Scorpio nature is to be cautious, to be reserved, to wait until you feel that you trust before divulging or being emotionally vulnerable with anyone. You have Mars, which is the planet of action and self-assertion squaring the Sun and Mercury. That would indicate a reticence with communicating because you're afraid you'll speak out angrily if you are upset about something. There would be a tendency to be aggressive at times and at the same time holding back. Is that something that would give you a challenge once in a while?

Beth: Well, yeah it does. I think that that's pretty accurate. OK, into the Shadow. Let's see what the Shadow knows.

Rebeca: Well, often Shadow is everything about us we don't know about. So if you know it, then it is no longer Shadow.

Everybody has squares and oppositions in their chart. Oppositions indicate that one side is doing something and the other side is projected out. Mars is in an opposition to Uranus. So say somebody is exaggerating; that might ruffle you. If they're too independent, they're too detached and you are wanting more emotional connection; that might be a challenge because that is a part of you as well. Now that might be something in your Shadow that you are not aware of, the ability to detach and to be aloof.

Beth: Well, I do tend to obsess about a lot of things. Another Scorpio trait, I guess. I try and recognize it, but it's not easy to control.

Rebeca: Recognize what?

Beth: Obsession. Not the detaching.

Rebeca: So you don't recognize that you detach and you can be aloof yourself?

Beth: Well, I guess I can be at times, but hmmn...

Rebeca: What we identity with, what we are conscious of, what we really recognize in ourself, the exact opposite to the same degree is going to be in our unconscious. This is what constitutes our Shadow. It's parts of us that we are absolutely not aware of, so when we see it in somebody else, it's more apt to get under our skin, so to speak.

Beth: OK, OK.

Rebeca: Doing Shadow work means looking at things about other people. Libra and Scorpio are the two signs in the zodiac most interested in communicating with others, being attached to others and being involved with others. We need other people to fulfill who we came here to be. A Libra needs communication with a partner to fulfill being a Libra, and a Scorpio needs intimacy in a very deep way. Sharing deep, dark facts with another person and being completely vulnerable and having them accept that kind of intimacy is vital.

Beth: Well I do have that with my husband.

Rebeca: That's awesome.

Beth: We have a very good relationship. We've been married twenty-seven and a half years. We had issues, almost divorced at the fourteen year point, but we were both willing to look at ourselves and move forward, but I have a lot of problems with male bosses.

Rebeca: Male bosses. OK, and what are their characteristics?

Beth: Bullying. In my opinion, not really seeing the value of what I'm doing as being important to the overall organization.

Notes to Myself:

Notes to Myself:

Rebeca: That is indicative of the Sun conjunct Saturn. Saturn has to do with authority — responsibility and authority figures. As you just said, valuing and having somebody value you. The Sun is the center of consciousness. It's the most important thing you are here for — Sun in Scorpio — so you want to be identified as someone who is resourceful, someone who has a lot of strength and ability to do things in your job. I don't know what you do, but it probably has something to do with communication, with four planets in the house of the mind. What do you do?

Beth: Well, actually I just quit my job. For the last seven years, I was in government consulting with the Department of Defense mostly. I was doing research and analysis for the defense maintenance program.

Rebeca: That makes sense. "Research" and "analysis" are key words for Scorpio.

Beth: My boss moved me into organizing a worldwide maintenance conference, which was a good fit for me, but I felt that he undervalued the entire project and what I was doing with it. Then I moved from Washington to San Antonio with my husband, who is in the Air Force. I took the job with me. I didn't feel that my boss was giving me the help that I needed, and my stomach was really in knots about the whole thing. I had some health issues, and I felt I just needed to take some time off and focus on them. I chose to not let him step all over me, use me and abuse me. Right now I'm not doing anything.

Rebeca: That must feel wonderful for a change, huh?

Beth: It is. For the last seven years… well, actually it was just the last four years that I was working with this big conference.

Rebeca: Is the conference over?

Beth: Well, I quit in July, and the conference will be next week.

Rebeca: Wow!

Beth: I gave them a month's notice and tried to put together a continuity book and things to help them out. But it's really been very liberating that I don't have to go through that. Last year I spent 90 hours in six days — so about 15 hours a day on the conference. It was grueling. I didn't have the help that I needed. It didn't have to be like that. It's very liberating. I'm spending the time now just trying to work on myself. One of the things I am really interested in right now is I tend to have a weight problem. I've been trying to look back in my childhood at some things that could have caused it. I do have a mental block. I gained weight the summer before the third grade. That was the summer that I remember my mother sent me and my brother to stay with my grandparents for a couple of months. My grandfather was a very stern, unapproachable person in my opinion, and my mother used to say that she was a little bit afraid of him. I think I picked up on her fear or hesitancy of male authority. I keep trying to remember why she would have done that to us if she felt that way. I've asked my brother about it, and my brother's response was, "I don't remember you being there." So he was no help. I was seven years old, and he was nine. He just remembers riding on my grandfather's tractor up there. I'm just trying to trace it back to its roots.

Rebeca: To see where the authority issue came up or began and how that relates to your health and your weight?

Beth: Yes. My husband says I have had a string of bad bosses, and he thinks that this contributes to my weight problem. I tend to want to eat when I get stressed out or nervous. I just can't break this cycle. So I am trying to understand.

Rebeca: Looking at the chart, I can see how that could be happening. It's interesting to hear someone speak their chart. The planet Mars has to do with how we take action in the world, how we assert ourselves, how we go after what we want, and it has a lot to do with how we defend ourselves as well. So every single time you get into a relationship with a boss where they are an authority figure, unless you're willing to step up to the plate and be assertive with your own authority, then you are always going to find people who will dominate, who will undermine, almost force you into that role because it's a part of you you're not accepting or not living. Whatever one doesn't live, lives against one. If we're getting a technicolor pattern of a mirror of somebody who is in a position of authority and is abusing that authority, it means that we're abusing that authority toward ourself. So how can I stand up for myself when I run into this kind of situation? How can I say with conviction and with courage this is what needs to happen and this is what I need? When you were saying, "I needed help and I wasn't getting it," well, there has to be a powerful force within you. With so much water, you have a tendency to retreat instead of being overt, instead of being out there. Then, having a Mercury that is conjunct, all that makes you reticent to communicate. BUT if you believe that you are in a position of power and a position of authority, you don't take that role: "I'm the authority and this is what needs to get done." It's almost as if you take on more of a feminine role than you need to and that now you need to take on your masculine role. It's like we have to all balance a combination of our feminine and our masculine. If our masculine isn't onboard, somebody out there comes into our energy field and portrays the negative father, the negative grandfather, the abusive one, the person who doesn't acknowledge us, the one who won't give us the kudos, doesn't recognize our value. WHY? Because we're not doing it. That's the only reason. When you have Sun conjunct Saturn squaring Mars, that means that is important in the second half

Notes to Myself:

of life. In the first half of life, we develop along a certain gradient. Having so much water, you are more introverted. Besides being very talented at analysis and research and organization, you have tremendous self-discipline and you probably recognize that.

Beth: I feel disciplineless.

Rebeca: You do?

Beth: Yeah, I'm disciplined if I'm backed up against a deadline. Other than that, I tend to scatter my energies. Because of that, I try to focus on just one thing at a time. I've long been an energy scatterer. I have a lot of interests. If I were really that disciplined, then I probably wouldn't have a weight problem. I would get out and exercise more, or I could say I am going to have these couple of hobbies and I am going to only devote x amount of time to each one, or whatever, but because I tend to scatter my energies, I usually try to focus on one to the exclusion of the others. Does that make sense?

Rebeca: Yes, it does, but it's also a part of your path. A big part of your life is to be self-disciplined, to take on responsibility. I would think that you had to from a very early age.

Beth: Well, I have, and I've had a lot of jobs with a lot of responsibility. This last one, I had to be responsible when I moved from just research into planning the conference. I was one of the three major planners, so it was a big responsibility. My other career path, I was an Air Force officer, so I've had responsibility.

Rebeca: OK, so you have been disciplined in that regard?

Beth: Yes, they were things that forced me into it, and I kind of thought I probably went into the Air Force because I needed that type of responsibility. I think that people tend to attract certain careers or jobs, or churches, because they need that type of environment. I was raised in a rather disciplineless home. My father died when I was three, so, single mother, two kids. I think a lot of times she was doing her best to get through it all. I got through school, not because she stood over me with an iron hand, but probably because it's just in me. If you tell me to do something, I'm probably going to do it. But as far as being a good student, I wasn't very disciplined, so college was a slap in the face.

Rebeca: Well, you have four planets in the house of the mind, so I have to dissect them each so you can see the individual parts of you that are mental, that are education, basically. The first one in the pack is Neptune, which is about idealism, which is about dreaminess, which is about poetic, creative, artistic, and that's conjunct your Mercury. Mercury is the mind, how we think, how we relate, how we communicate, and Mercury is also conjunct the Sun and Saturn. Saturn is diametrically different from Neptune. Saturn is the part of you that says, "Well if I have to do it, I have to do it." To me, that's called discipline in the sense that if I'm supposed to do something, then I do it. I'm very conscious of what I am supposed to do.

Beth: Well, I am. I'll agree with that definitely.

Rebeca: Then the creative part, the Neptune part, the dreamy person that's also a part of you. It's wanting to just space out wanting to be vague and not committed to something — that's what's so interesting to me about astrology. We each have all these characters in us, and they all need a voice. There's also something called "Voice Dialogue," which I also recommend by Hal and Sidra Stone, where you dialogue with each one of these parts of you and then you assign them a task or you give them a place in your life. That's what I just love about astrology because we aren't just one person; we are lots of people. Astrology gives you a way of looking at these individual parts and how they need a voice. I would say that if you are attracting on a repetitive pattern bosses or authority figures who do not value you, then you do not value yourself and that also leads to the weight problem. That sounds so simple, but it's profound.

Beth: Yes, I have tried to gain my voice over the years. Before I left the D.C. area, which is where I originally found the job back in 2000, my boss was going over my performance rating with me. He was saying, "You know you've done this well, you've done that well." I said, "Well, let me be honest here about what I feel that I need to do with my work. I need to feel that it's important." He had just made a number of comments. I was trying to get a couple of people on the staff to provide input for this big conference, and they weren't doing it quickly. I was in danger of not meeting my deadline. I went to my boss, and I said, "Well, you know I need so and so to provide this input," and he said, "Well, what they are doing is important."

Rebeca: In other words, it wasn't important that you get those things?

Beth: Yes. They're doing more important things. So I decided I was going to tell him that I need to feel that what I'm doing is important, and he cut me off. He said, "Well, if I led you to feel that I don't think it's important, well, I'm sorry," and then he went off on another tangent. So I was trying to...

Rebeca: ...have a voice.

Beth: Yes, have a voice. I'm tall. I'm 5'10". Sometimes I have problems with men, with the "small man" attitude. This man was small and effeminate. Without even trying, sometimes I just piss people off. Oh, well.

Rebeca: Well, you know what? We all do sometimes. That's just

Notes to Myself:

life. It's hard to get along with everybody, but I think the most valuable thing you're doing is trying to get a handle on why these things would be repeating and how you can improve or change your behaviour toward this kind of situation so that when it does come up again, you're ready. That's what I hear.

Beth: Well I'm 53, so I may or may not get back into the work-force. When my husband retires, we have the option of just retiring completely, but even if I don't get another job, I need to be prepared for this pattern's repeating again. Even if it's not from a boss, it's going to be someone.

Rebeca: It will. It will, because it's a part of you.

Beth: So I need to address what it is that is keeping this weight around me. Maybe I have a feeling that I need to protect myself or something. I was at the doctor yesterday. I've developed some arthritis along my spine, which is not uncommon with weight gain. He was saying it's just willpower, which I thought was a very simplistic approach, and I told him so. It's a matter of why do I feel I need to protect myself? It may be against what I consider to be these irrational authoritarian males. It probably goes back to my childhood somewhere.

Rebeca: Probably, but I would also say that it's inherent within your own psyche to recognize and own that part of yourself. Your own, how did you say it?

Beth: Irrational, authoritarian...

Rebeca: I'm writing it down — irrational, authoritarian male figures. So inside of you, your Animus, your male side, there's a part of you that has an irrational, authoritarian male that you haven't embraced. When I first started doing dialogue work with the Animus, with the inner male (because the outer male is often a portrait of our inner male), I would hear criticism. You're not good enough, you should have said this, why didn't you do that? That kind of stuff was commonplace in my psyche until I started to do voice dialogue with that person inside of me. Jung calls it active imagination. What is it that you want? Go inside yourself and say, "OK, I recognize you're in there. I wouldn't keep seeing the mirror outside of me if it wasn't inside of me. So I know you're in there. What is it that you want?"

Beth: You're saying that the masculine part of my nature is irrational and authoritarian and I need to address that?

Rebeca: Yes. You need to have a voice dialogue with it, go inside yourself, get a pen and a paper, start journalling with this and doing what Jung called active imagination. Robert Johnson has a good book on doing active imagination called *Inner Work,* if you want to read it to get familiar with the technique. There's also the books on Voice Dialogue; they give you a great way of working with your inner parts.

Beth: What is the title of that?

Rebeca: The titles are *Embracing Our Selves* and *Embracing Each Other,* both by Hal and Sidra Stone, Ph.D.

Beth: Actually I wrote down some titles from your Web site. I wanted to buy *Owning Your Own Shadow,* by Robert Johnson the other day at the bookstore. I didn't find it there. I will have to order it, but I did buy a book called something about your unlived life.

Rebeca: I don't know which one that would be. On Amazon.com you can even buy used books. When you have an inner male authority figure that is in there, and you are wanting to work with him and understand. I would go inside, get a pen and a paper and allow yourself to just write whatever comes to you. A few minutes ago you said, "I want to feel that what I'm doing is important." Go inside and ask, "What else is it that I am not giving to myself that I want these other people to give to me?"

Beth: OK.

Rebeca: "How do I give all that to myself, so that they see it and I don't feel oppressed? I don't have to pull to myself an oppressive authority figure. How do I give myself my own authority?" I think that's a lifelong lesson for most people, but especially for you with Sun conjunct Saturn squaring Mars. On my Web site I also sell *Psychological Horoscope Analysis Reports* by Liz Greene. I highly recommend those and my Shadow DVD to work with the inner figures, including reading books. Working with our Shadow is a process. It's so rewarding because those characters that we see parading in front of us are US! If we can take those qualities and embrace them in our own psyche, then we come off different. Our energy field is different. We will attract different situations because we've changed, not because they've changed. It's easy to see that if someone in our life would just change, then we would be happy, but we really have to do our own work. I really acknowledge you for recognizing that you're wanting to work with this pattern, and it probably will change your weight issue as well.

Beth: In dealing with this boss, I went out and bought several books. I bought, *I'm OK, You're OK,* on transactional analysis, which I think is great. Another one was *How To Win Friends and Influence People.* I wish I had had that back when I was 15. I think they should make that required reading back in elementary school. Another one was *How to Deal with People You Don't Like.* I realized there were some things that I could change in myself. But I just got to the point where I guess I was so weighed down with it that I needed a break. This is where I

Notes to Myself:

am right now, trying to process all of this, find out what it was could learn from it and move forward. I guess the goal of astrology is to be able to become the entire zodiac or to be able to use all of the energies as we need to.

Rebeca: Exactly.

Beth: I find it fascinating. I have a computer program where I ran a natal chart on myself. Of course, I've just scratched the tip of the iceberg, but I do have four planets in the 3rd house, and I know that your specialty is the 7th house, in which I have nothing. (She laughs.)

Rebeca: See how your Mars is in the 6th house and it's squaring that Sun-Saturn? The 6th is the house of work, and it's in Aquarius, which is about community affairs and group situations which you described. The Sun conjunct Saturn in the 3rd house with Mercury in a very tight conjunction is squaring that Mars. A square is indicative of two parts of the psyche that are conflicting. In squares, the conflict is that we will be one part or the other. We have to come to terms with the struggle inherent in that square. That square is indicative of a temper, aggressiveness, a selfishness, maybe asserting, maybe it's about timing... like finding the right time to go forward and maybe seeming to be awkward at times you might have asserted yourself where you might best have left it alone.

Beth: OK, I can see that.

Rebeca: So a timing would be involved, instead of your being irrational, like — OK, I need to assert myself right now or it's not going to get done — and getting all upset. It's about taking that Sun-Saturn and being in control. How that might look would be telling yourself, "Ok, I'm in control of this; it's not going to control me." Being strategic, kind of like a game of chess. What is the best way for me to get the results that I want and come off as the person who is in charge and who is the boss here? Then you become your own authority. Instead of looking for the authority to empower you, you've already empowered yourself because you've taken control of the situation. You've made your own decisions, and you recognize that timing is involved. It's important to approach people when they are not stressed or when they are available, so make an appointment. When you say, "I need an appointment to talk over something or some issues that I want clarity on." It's not coming from a position of weakness and irrationality, and therefore you wouldn't get that same response.

Beth: OK, I can see where I've done that.

Rebeca: So taking that Sun-Saturn part of you, say, "I am the authority that I want. I am the person who is capable. I'm responsible here. This is my conference. This is my party. This is my event. This is my project. Whatever." It might even be at a church for that matter. "I am part of the group because I enjoy group dynamics, and I prefer to be the leader."

Beth: I think that it's probably very accurate what you're saying, that I look for authority outside of myself. So I need to look within.

Rebeca: I would venture to say that the self-discipline that you did not identify with earlier is inherent. It is absolutely inherent in your character and in your nature. Embracing it and having a dialogue with that would lead you to get your weight to a place where you are happier. That might sound simplistic, but it's also psychological. I think our mind and our body are connected. Our body is going to respond more when our mind is in sync with what we want, what we've decided, where we're going. I have this fabulous cleanse I can send you a jpg file of. It's fabulous for me, and it takes a lot of discipline, but if you do it, it really does get you "kick started" to getting rid of excess weight.

Beth: I mentioned I was just at the doctor's office yesterday because I have arthritis of the lower spine. Part of what I want to do is yoga, which I definitely believe in. I think what I need to do is, as you say, embrace the self-discipline which is already there.

Rebeca: Oh, yeah, it's there.

Beth: And quit telling myself I'm not disciplined.

Rebeca: Yes, quit telling yourself that.

Beth: Yeah, OK, OK, good point.

Rebeca: Because it is. Your Moon is in Capricorn. That's descriptive of somebody who is extremely disciplined, because the Moon is instinctual. I think that the way that you've been doing it is doing the negative father. The negative father is "You should. You didn't. Why didn't you? Who are you? You're not good enough." That's the negative father complex within us.

Beth: OK.

Rebeca: It's also that Sun conjunct Saturn, so the negative father will show up outside of you because you're doing it to yourself anyway. Sooner or later that person is going to show up, too.

Beth: That's interesting that you mention that. I said my father died when I was three, so I don't remember him at all, but some years back I had my eyes read, which is called iridology. That man said that my father would have been very critical, very demanding and unaccepting.

Rebeca: Exactly. That's indicative of the Sun-Saturn square Mars.

Beth: I'm sure from what I hear from relatives, he was a very nice

Notes to Myself:

Notes to Myself:

man, but just looking back on the little bit that I do know about his life, I could see that he could be that way. So it's interesting that you mention the negative father.

Rebeca: What's interesting to me is that the chart is symbolic of us, and it isn't necessarily our personal father, but it is the father inside of us, and what's inside is outside. That's the alchemy of astrology. What's inside is going to show up outside.

Beth: Right, OK.

Rebeca: Whether your father was there or not, Sun conjunct Saturn can also indicate that I lost my father or that he wasn't very available. I had to develop my own authority, my own strength, my own ability to make decisions and plan. Everything that a father would do for a child would be to empower that person to go out in the world and make something happen. The mother is the more nurturing, loving, feminine side, and, because you have so much water, you're very loving. You have a strong loving, maternal side. Jupiter is in Cancer, so you value home and family. That's really strong in your nature, and you are also a very compassionate person.

Beth: You mention developing this father. There have been numerous times throughout my life where I didn't trust my inner voice. I undervalued my opinion.

Rebeca: Right.

Beth: Why shouldn't I press this issue, when I thought that it should have been this way? No. No. I'll listen to my husband. I'll listen to my boss. I'll listen to so and so. I ended up hitting my head on the wall when I should have listened to myself.

Rebeca: Exactly. But you know that's how we learn. If you didn't have anything to look back on to compare it to, then you couldn't move forward. I have a teacher at the Jung Center that I've been studying with since 1990. His name is Rev. Pittman McGehee. My favourite statement that he said to us was "What kept us alive in the first half of life will keep us from living in the second half of life."

Beth: Yeah, I guess that's what Robert Johnson says in this book that I am just now reading. He's saying basically the same thing. He says in the first half of life you are climbing the ladder, being socially acceptable. You don't address your unlived parts, your unlived dreams. As you say, you don't move forward.

Rebeca: Yes, and it will work against you. You know why I haven't heard of that book? It's because I haven't read it. It's new, so I need to get it.

Beth: It's called *Living Your Unlived Life, Unrealised Dreams and Fulfilling Your Purpose in the Second Half of Life,* by Robert Johnson and Dr. Jerry Ruhl.

Rebeca: Well, I am going to have to get that book. I know I'll love it. I have all of Robert's books.

Beth: Well, what else do you see?

Rebeca: Your North Node is conjunct the Moon in Capricorn, and the North Node is very important in our second half of life. What North Node conjunct the Moon would tell me is that you would be very valuable working with women. The Moon is symbolic of women. Consider something where you are expressing your creativity and advancing women's issues or empowering other women, helping women see that they can be disciplined, that they can make something of themselves, maybe empowering young people, because it's in the 5th house of children. I don't know what your goals are for your future or what you want to embrace, but those are things that would be also inherent in your character.

Beth: Well, I think as you said it's just embracing the self-disciplined part of myself and stopping the negative speech of telling myself that I am not disciplined, so I think I'll practice that definitely. When I read stuff, it's *Psychology Today* or anything on personality development. I am just fascinated by it. One of the things I like about astrology is it gets into the energy. I find that totally compatible with psychology. Anything else you see?

Rebeca: Well, let's see. By transit, which has to do with where the planets are right now, the planet Saturn is in your first house, which means that you want to grow up.

Beth: Oh, no. (She chuckles.)

Rebeca: It means you are wanting to be your own father. The next year and a half it will be easy for you to lose weight as you embrace this father part of yourself, which is exactly what's happening.

Beth: Interesting, OK.

Rebeca: The planet Jupiter, which is about luck and abundance, and the planet Pluto, which is about intensity and transformation, Shadow work and healing, have moved into your house of children, creativity and romance. Children, creativity and romance are all in the same house. That's not the marriage house, it's the 5th house. Pluto just crossed the cusp of your 5th house one degree, and Jupiter will be there in just a few days. You are going to have two planets in your house of creativity and self-expression, so there's a lot of activity there for some new avenues of creativity and self-expression and definitely some discipline with your weight problem and looking at your father complex. You're just right on schedule.

Notes to Myself:

Beth: OK, you've given me a lot to think about by telling me about this father complex, the father figure within myself. I never really viewed it that way, that we have inner masculine aspects. As I view authoritarian males as irrational or whatever, that's actually perhaps the part in myself that I need to address.

Rebeca: Yes, because it's negative only because you don't know about it. Talking to you has been so valuable to me. Do you mind if I transcribe our session and use some of the material we have talked about in my book?

Beth: By all means, go ahead. You are taping this, right?

Rebeca: Yes, I am. So I'll make a copy of the tape, and then I'll mail it to you.

Beth: Wonderful. We talked about so much that I need to hear it again and pore over it, but this has been very helpful for me.

Rebeca: I've been working on this book for five years. I've had so many things come up in my life that have stopped me from finishing, but I am finally moving into the part where I am talking about our mother and our father because I think we marry our mother and our father. If we can embrace those parts of ourselves, then that can be a much healthier expression of who we actually are. People tend to put whatever is in their Shadow in their Marriage house. They make their partner into their parent, even a father who was missing. You know, when a father is missing, you can idealize that father and you have no idea who that father is because they weren't there. So you actually have to father yourself; you have to develop that father part of you.

Beth: As a matter of fact, the reason I went into the Air Force was because my father was in the Air Force. I even said back then I did it because that was always my ideal. That was what he did. That's interesting. Yeah, I hear what you're saying.

Rebeca: I would like to recommend one book. It's called *Astrology for the Soul,* and it's on the North Node.

Beth: Yes, I don't understand the North Node.

Rebeca: Well, this book will help explain it, and the author, Jan Spiller, devotes about 25 pages per Node, and it's fabulous. I've given it to therapists, and they use it in their practice, and they don't have to be astrologers to understand it. It's the one book on my recommended reading list that I recommend to everyone.

****

Notes to Myself:

CHRIS
Wednesday, February 26, 1969
3:17:00 AM EST
Sillery, Quebec
Tropical   Placidus True Node

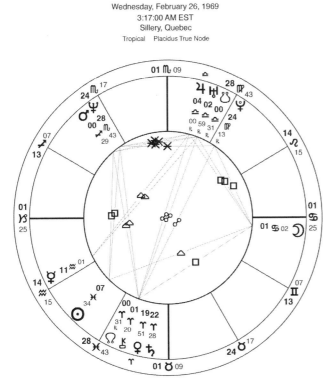

Example 3: Chris - Taking Back His Power by Owning His Shadow in Relationships

Rebeca: I've looked at your chart and your relationship issues, and my first question to ask you is have you ever had a reading?

Chris: Oh, yes, about 10.

Rebeca: Can you tell me a little bit about some of the challenges you've experienced, or do you want me to just tell you what I see and then we talk about it?

Chris: Let's go that way.

Rebeca: OK, well, looking at your chart, there are three major things that would happen in your relationships. The first one that probably is the most important is that the South Node in the chart is in Libra. Are you familiar with the South Node?

Chris: No.

Rebeca: The meaning of it is that if we understand past lives, which astrology is based on, but even if you don't believe in past lives, if you just understand that we have inherited predisposed patterns of character that we are born with, one thing that a person with South Node in Libra would overdo is revolving around a partner, like losing yourself to the needs of that person. Getting involved with someone who is selfish, (he laughs) dominating, abusive, angry, kind of bossy, wants their own way a lot without really wanting to compromise or take care of any of your needs. The challenge is that you would be more conciliatory than you should be.

Chris: Yes.

Rebeca: You would be more accommodating, and you would have to dance faster to get that person to be in the relationship, because they have a tendency to not really need anybody. That's one aspect. Then the other one. You almost have a split Anima, having two different kinds of people you would be attracted to because the Moon is the ruler of your marriage house and your Moon is in Cancer. Depending on how much you own your own Moon, having the Moon in Cancer for a man is being very sensitive, very emotional. Being a Pisces Sun, you would be very compassionate and might have a difficult time setting boundaries. But having the Moon ruling that house, you would find that people will be moody, very changeable, that you would have to parent (he laughs), that you would have to be the father figure for them. Maybe you pay for too much or you give too much. They are showing you a technicolor picture of what you are needing to learn, which is to be more selfish yourself...

Chris: ...yes...

Rebeca: ...to take care of yourself and to ask for your needs to be met. Describe what would emotionally gratify you and then if that person is unwilling to compromise, making an effort to sit down with that person and insist on compromise or going your own way.

Chris: ...yes...

Rebeca: ...because you are too accommodating. You have a tendency to give in too easily for the sake of the relationship. Your North Node is in Aries, and so Aries would be an energy and an archetype that you would need to embrace more fully. That's very difficult when you have Mars, the ruler of Aries conjunct Neptune, which is the ruler of Pisces. Neptune is very diffuse, very soft. It's creative, imaginative. It's poetic and selfless. So there is a tremendous amount of this energy of being "TOO NICE" (he laughs). I don't know how else to say it. Too nice.
Just very very kind. Your friends, and your family, if you have children, probably love that about you because you are so nice and so giving and so generous-hearted. So the Shadow side of you would be the exact opposite!

Chris: Yes, right.

Rebeca: The Shadow side of you is willful, dominating, controlling and doesn't give anything unless you're getting something from it. The Shadow side of you is the exact opposite of everything that you believe about yourself. And the way that you would see your Shadow would be to be fascinated by people who display openly, unashamedly the opposite extremes.

Chris: Exactly.

Rebeca: The Shadow side of you is begging for acceptance, and once you start living out those energies yourself, then you don't have to attract people who are doing it to an extreme.

Chris: Right...

Rebeca: ...because you are willing to say, "No, this is what I want, this is where I am going. This is what I am going to do. You wanna go with me, great — if you don't, I'll see you later!" Develop some of that independence, some of that, "I-don't-need-you attitude."

Chris: Yes.

Rebeca: The fathering role that you take on so easily is because of the fear of vulnerability. It's the fear that if I open up and I'm emotional, I will just be so emotional, it will be too embarrassing.

Chris: Uh-huh!

Rebeca: Because I am very emotional (he laughs) and I am soft and I am sensitive and when I get hurt, I clam up and I go into my shell (Moon in Cancer). Then I start telling myself what I should logically be feeling instead of what I'm actually feeling, because my Mercury is very logical and wants things to be orderly, make sense, and be fair and everything isn't fair.

Chris: Right. Excellent.

Rebeca: Then Venus conjunct Saturn is another aspect. Venus is how we love and receive love. With Venus conjunct Saturn — Saturn is the planet of restriction, responsibility, heavy karma; it's the place where we feel burdened, where we feel we don't measure up, that other people are better at it than we are. So Venus and Saturn in Aries says, "I am afraid to take on that energy, that leadership role, that capacity to be more self-centered, more self-focused." Then there are times when you actually do display those characteristics, and other people see it, but you don't.

Chris: Right, yes, that makes sense.

Rebeca: Part of the karma of Venus conjunct Saturn is a heavy fear of vulnerability. It's a fear of abandonment. A fear of not being good enough. "I don't know how to do relationships. They don't work for me. I give up before I've even begun." The antidote

Notes to Myself:

to that energy is to take your time before you give your all to anyone. Really evaluate that person almost like an interview. Let's watch this person and wait and see what happens before I start bending over backwards and let them kick me.

Chris: Yes.

Rebeca: If you are pursuing someone, notice if it's not an equal give and take. There is no equality. I suggest to people that you turn around and walk away as if their life depended on it. Once you walk away, the energy shifts because you are giving to you. You're taking care of you. If that person comes back after you or gives you a call and starts making compromises, then they are back in the game. They are back in the ball park. But if they are not and you keep pursuing them, it's like saying, "Kick me again."

Chris: Umm. Uh-huh.

Rebeca: It's kind of like saying, "I don't deserve to be treated with respect." It's a tough one because it doesn't really happen until later in life that we develop the capacity to be patient, to wait, to set the seeds out, to put the seeds out for that person to see if they will bring some of their own energy to the table and be a little more giving, and see if they are interested enough — I mean in this day and age, women call, too.

Chris: Absolutely.

Rebeca: They absolutely do. A guy doesn't have to take on the entire burden of being the one to call. If he makes an effort and she doesn't make any effort whatsoever, then chances are you are beating a dead horse. She's not that interested.

Chris: Yes. Yes.

Rebeca: Now, what I would like for you to do is tell me your story.

Chris: Wow, my story. Well, this is fascinating in this very short time that we have talked. My story is one of transition right now. Many of the things you are talking about in terms of what would be more the light side of me, the more obvious side of relationships and the Shadow side, they are getting blended in my life these days.

Rebeca: Good.

Chris: I left an 18-year relationship last year. I have three children. Yeah, I left. I had a whole lot of transformation going on. I changed my name. I took my first name. I am 39 years old, as you know by my chart, and the last year and a half have been a radical transformation time that has been a challenge in many ways. A lot of those areas of relationship that you are talking about were what I used to be — the way I'd operate in the world.

Now I am struggling with this new way of wanting to be and not feeling totally comfortable with it yet. As if I'm still looking for an external approval to say, "Yeah, it's OK for you to want what you want. It's OK in relationship for you to want the type of partner that is about equality, is going to service your needs as well as you servicing hers." That got really exhausting after 18 years.

Rebeca: Oh, yeah. I can just imagine.

Chris: And it's not just in that area, Rebeca, it's all through the family. You know I sort of played a little bit of the black sheep In my family for years. I have one sister, and my parents are still alive. It's that same sort of dynamic. We will take as much from you as you can give. Please make us feel good about ourselves, and what you really, really want, we're not that interested because it kind of scares us. We're not really comfortable with your power, let's say.

Rebeca: Your intensity.

Chris: My vision, whatever it is. Yes, my intensity. Exactly. We'd rather just coast through life, make our critical judgments and tell you that you should be doing x, y and z, that sort of thing. So, that's a bit of my story. It's a total redo right now, a rebirth.

Rebeca: And it's going to continue because the planet Pluto, which is about death and rebirth, is coming over your ascendant, and your ascendant is your 1st house. It's your rising sign. The 1st house is our personality. It's our mask. It's how we approach life, so you are coming into your own. You're coming into your own power. You're facing your own demons, and so you are willing to recognize your Shadow as Pluto moves through that house. It's been going back and forth in Sag, and you have 1° Capricorn rising.

Chris: That's right.

Rebeca: And Pluto is back at 28° Sag now, but it's going to come back because it's retrograding. It's going to come back to that 1° Capricorn again probably by Christmas, and then it's not ever going to go back into Sagittarius again. It's going to go straight into your 1st house.

Chris: Wow!

Rebeca: That Pluto energy — you will absolutely love reading all the books on the dark side. You will feel like, "Oh, my God, where was this all my life?"

Chris: What do you mean by that? What books?

Rebeca: Well, I'll recommend some. *Evil, the Shadow Side of Reality* by John Sanford. That book is awesome. He talks about Jesus and St. Paul — how Jesus had a Shadow and how he dealt with it. And

Notes to Myself:

how St. Paul tried to eliminate the Shadow from Christianity by saying, "Do good, do good all the time," and divorced us from a very natural, instinctive way of being.

Chris: Oh, yes.

Rebeca: Because of Christianity — well not just because of Christianity — because of a lot of the major religions, we have all these polarizations going on all over the world. The more of us who integrate our Shadow, the better off our entire planet will be.

Chris: Oh, absolutely.

Rebeca: There's also a DVD that I know you would love watching. It's called *A Matter of Heart*. It's based on Jung and his life and all these analysts that were his analysands, but they became analysts themselves. So they interview him, and he's talking live and they interviewed all these people and it's about relationships. You can get it at the Jung Center. Where are you? In Quebec?

Chris: I'm in Alberta.

Rebeca: Well if you can't get it, I'll get it for you and charge your card and mail it to you.

Chris: I have some friends that are near a Jung Center so maybe they can get it for me, but I'll let you know. It's funny, because I've been studying a little bit of Jung for about five or six years. So I had this kind of awakening about six years ago. A light went on like, "Woooh, oooh!"

Rebeca: That's what helped you get out of your marriage.

Chris: Oh, it totally did. It was so funny, too, Rebeca, because within a month of that I was saying, "Oh, geez, I am going to be leaving Marian." She was my wife, and it took me five years, five long... well, four years... to really protest that. "Oh, my goodness, she's not going on this journey with me." It was really painful, but it was necessary. I had this whole shamanic thing happen, like the Universe, sort of collective-consciousness stuff, a very powerful opening of the shamanic, which still continues to this day, but it's in a different form. I studied a lot of alternative medicine and all that sort of jazz. It was kind of like being a student of myself. Now I'm getting into returning to something that I loved as a kid, which was soccer, falling into the role of coach, to the level of having an international coaching license.

Rebeca: Awesome.

Chris: And I'm starting a company in coaching for kids, and it's all fairly radical, sort of next-generation stuff. It's something that over the next 6-12 months... it's something that's going to shift more dramatically around because I'm still working through these areas of "Well, how is this going to be accepted?"

Rebeca: If it's something you want to do, then it doesn't matter what anybody else wants. That's your North Node. It's kind of like, "OK, this is what I'm going to do, and if they don't all agree with me, that's OK. I want to do it because it gives me pleasure and I want to be with children and whatever."

Chris: Oh, yeah, exactly, and I'm with people that get pleasure out of doing it, too.

Rebeca: And you have the Sun in the Money house in Pisces, so being your own boss, owning your own company is right on. Jupiter by transit is in your 1st house right now. I'm not a predictive astrologer, but to tell you a little bit about what that means... it just means you would be feeling a bit more optimistic, that you would be feeling more hopeful about everything you're envisioning. Saturn just left your Marriage house. Saturn was in your Marriage house for two years, and that's when you started. Well, four years ago it was on your Moon first, and then it approached your marriage house. Astrology is like clockwork.

Chris: Oh, totally.

Rebeca: Saturn was on your Moon, so you got real depressed. (He laughs.) You realized then, "My needs are not being met here, so what am I doing? Beating my head up against a dead wall."

Chris: Oh, gosh, yeah...

Rebeca: Then for two years as Saturn transited your Marriage house, knowing you, you tried to get a reconciliation. You tried to make things work, but you really didn't get anywhere.

Chris: Yeah...

Rebeca: So then it went into the 8th house, and the 8th house is about sharing resources with a partner, so you had to become your own resource because the resource was no longer there. So you're right on, like clockwork.

Chris: That's so cool. It's so funny, too, because we went and took this program called "Children of Divorce." It was a full-week program that I did with my kids, and she was there, too, but in a different group. It was really healthy. I met somebody in the group, and we became friends, and she called me. We sort of had a bit of a fling through the early part of this year. I started thinking I want to do some Shadow work now. Let's go. She has literally, within the last couple of hours, dropped me an email. "I want these books back now please," and I thought, "Wow! This is fantastic." I am so done with that relationship. It was really weird, like trying-to-please-my-father stuff again. Well, anyway...

Rebeca: Well, the other part of you is very fatherly, so you would attract people who need an inordinate amount of understanding.

Notes to Myself:

223

Chris: Ohhhh... yeah...

Rebeca: "You're abandoning me." They would be just like emotional sponges. It's like a bucket that can't be filled.

Chris: Yeah. I would tell her, "I want to be with the adult side of you, but this little girl part..." She'd look at me with these eyes like she was five years old. Whoa! I've got my own kids, thank you very much!

Rebeca: OK, (I laugh)... now let's look at the Shadow part of that.

Chris: (laughing) Yeah, OK.

Rebeca: OK, because that's the whole point. We look in the mirror, and that's what we see. We see that person, and they are kind of childish. So our own child is screaming out to us. This is the neat thing about astrology. We all have lots of different people in us.

Chris: Oh, yeah...

Rebeca: We're the fatherly role. We're the child. We're the aggressor. We're the dreamy, spiritual person. We all have these character parts, and they all have to be lived out. In terms of when someone is needy, I would recommend another really great book called *Between People: Communicating One-to-One.* It's a great book on relationship by John A. Sanford. He talks about how relationships break down because one person expresses need and the other person doesn't hear them.

Chris: Wow!

Rebeca: Or one person is vulnerable, and the other person refuses to be vulnerable. So the person who is being vulnerable becomes overly vulnerable because they are compensating because the other person isn't willing to express their need, and it kind of just keeps mushrooming when nobody is being real. It's hard to be vulnerable when you just met someone. I highly recommend that people wait six months before they get sexually involved.

Chris: Oh, yeah.

Rebeca: That is a long time, and in those six months, if people could do that, I genuinely feel you can get to know each other without that extreme vulnerability, because once you're having sex — "You belong to me and I belong to you." From a guy's perspective, OK, I'm going to do whatever you want so we can continue to have sex. (He laughs out loud.) From the woman's perspective, "I'm going to give you sex because I want to be in a relationship, but the truth is I'm afraid of you now because you could leave me at any time. You could abandon me." Neither person is willing to be real anymore because they've reverted back to being a child. Each person reverts to wanting their parents' approval because they are too vulnerable. We're vulnerable when we start having sex prematurely, and we ruin intimacy, because intimacy is "in-to-me-see."

Chris: Oh, I agree.

Rebeca: "Look at my Shadow stuff. Look at my nastiness. Look at how pleasant I can be. Look at how generous I am. Look at how selfish I can be. Whatever. I'm all the different parts, but I'm your friend." You know how with our friends we accept everything about our friends. Our friends can be jerks. We say, "Oh, they're just being a jerk today. That's only one part of them." They are not always like that, and we forget about it. We forgive them. But with someone we are sleeping with, it becomes a mountain. It is no longer a little mole hill. It becomes a huge mountain. And all the emotions and all the feelings come up. There's a saying in the *Course in Miracles* that says everything, unlike love, comes up because that is what's down there.

Chris: (He laughs.) Yeah.

Rebeca: So it behooves us when we have Saturn conjunct Venus or Saturn ruling or in the Marriage house or Saturn in Libra — Saturn actually rules your rising sign to learn to wait. When you've developed so much along the father role, you know you're a father, you have three kids. When you've developed so much along the father role, then your other side is begging for acceptance. Your other side is beckoning...

Chris: Right.

Rebeca: ...for you to embrace her, which is the feminine side, the feminine side which says, "I'm gonna take care of me. You're not going to take care of me. I'm gonna do it first." When you're mirroring back to me that you're taking care of me and I'm mirroring to you that I'm taking care of you, then we're really wanting to be together. From the fact that we have things in common, we enjoy each other's company, and we can get past some hard things. We communicate. We're friends. We're moving into the age of Aquarius. This is not about sacrificing and being martyrs anymore. This is not about codependence anymore. This is about friendship.

Chris: Absolutely. Absolutely.

Rebeca: And if that person is not our friend from the get go, we don't need them! Whenever you notice that you are being selfish, do you put yourself down?

Chris: Oh, I have a major guilt complex. That would be like a critical parent or a judging parent. You are not allowed to do that. You have to think of everybody else.

Rebeca: Because I see that really strong in your chart.

Chris: Yeah, that comes up particularly with anything that has to do with sex. There's some strange stuff that happens, and I don't quite understand it. I've done a lot of personal development work, and I don't understand. It comes up with money. I'm not really supposed to spend money on myself. When I do, I like it, but I feel guilty liking it. Yeah. Although you know, like I said at the beginning, it's changing because of what you are talking about — the Age of Aquarius. I do a lot of work with the Kabbalah. I do a lot of work with Feng Shui in terms of personal visioning. And when I write stuff about the partner or the feminine energy that I am interested in getting into union with, it's all about those types of things that you're talking about. It's all about equality, where there's acceptance, where there's nurturing. I know that those are the parts of myself that I have to give to myself.

Rebeca: Right. First.

Chris: So that's what's happening right now. It's like unscrewing a cork bottle. In some ways it feels like I'm going into my ancestry and uncorking my spine.

Rebeca: Wow!

Chris: I was all twisted up, and it's like... "Whoah... you're not allowed to leave a wife. You have to get a Joe job and be responsible financially. Your dreams are secondary to my needs." That would be my parents or my previous partner. It even sometimes comes out with my kids. I can almost get a little too much of being the martyr with my kids. It's very easy for my ex-partner to guilt trip me, and I can easily be manipulated. I am learning the art of not letting that happen, saying, "No, tonight's my night. End of story." To say, "It's not acceptable," but it's tough.

Rebeca: Yeah, it is because you are practicing your whole other side, which is what they've overdone. All these people that we draw into our lives, they overdo all that.

Chris: Oh, totally. Yeah, you're very on, because my previous mate was chronically late. Sometimes hours. I would wait and wait and wait. Now I don't tolerate that. I don't wait. I'm dropping the kids off, and this is the time. This is the way I run my life.

Rebeca: It probably shocks her.

Chris: Oh, it totally shocks her because she got into a new relationship two weeks after I left, and the same patterns are continuing, of course. I am so not interested in that. I'm going back to when I was a kid. My favourite girlfriend of my entire life was when I was five years old. I was in love with her, but we would play together and run around, and she was my best friend. We discovered the world together. It was just so sweet. Not that I want to be five years old, but I do long for that type of equality in relationship. We were friends, and this is what I want to do.

Rebeca: "We're best friends" is the goal.

Chris: Yeah, we're best friends.

Rebeca: We like each other. We don't have to ask each other when it's your turn to give or your turn to help. It's your turn to do. Your turn to give in.

Chris: Oh…. yeah.

Rebeca: We just do it.

Chris: Absolutely.

Rebeca: It's almost as if when you have the North Node in Aries like you do and Venus and Saturn in Aries. It's almost as if you have to take the opposite extreme for a while so that you can get used to that.

Chris: Right.

Rebeca: You have to be more selfish for a while just to get used to it before you can kind of come back to the middle, because if we don't know how to do something, we're just going to slip back into the other.

Chris: Yeah, right, right so that's the period of time right now where even though I had a bit of a fling, it just got drawn out into a longer-term friendship. We were kind of helping each other out therapeutically through the ending of a relationship. It got to a point where I said to myself, "What? I am not ready." I let her know right away I'm not really available. I'm here for my kids, and I'm getting my business going, and that's really my stage of life. Yet there's a part of me that longs for a partner, longs for intimacy. I'm also not going to be available to do the work energetically. The patience that you talked about earlier is certainly tugging me around these days.

Rebeca: Also, the patience of waiting until relationship has matured or developed or gone past the point of the infatuation because the infatuation is physical. It's sexual attraction. It's mostly physical. It's a chemistry, but it doesn't necessarily mean that there's stability or harmony or even things in common. It doesn't even mean that. You can be madly in love with somebody and not even like them. (He laughs out loud.) Yeah, been there, done that.

Chris: Exactly. Been there, done that.

Rebeca: But another interesting thing, too, is because friendship

Notes to Myself:

227

Notes to Myself:

is something that develops slowly, you can grow to love somebody that's a friend. Even though at first it was just a friendship, it can grow to "being in love." Some people say that's not possible, but I've done it, so I know it is. You know where you grew to love that person. You see all of that person — their warts — everything. You start to develop a genuine caring for the person because they're so there for you. You start giving back, and it becomes reciprocal, so it is amazing. We're moving into a different kind of relationships. I think it's the fact that men and women have to become masculine and feminine. Men can't just take on the "I'm the daddy, I'm the father, I'm the protector, and you're the weak person. You're the one that needs looking after. I have

to be so understanding, blah, blah, blah, because you're so emotional." What happens with the man's Anima, his feminine side? If she's hurt, if she's slighted, if she's rejected, he'll get really moody. He'll go inside himself and become kind of carping and critical even.

Chris: Yep.

Rebeca: The reason for that is because his feelings have been hurt and he has not expressed it. So men are having to learn how to express their real feelings. And women are having to learn how to take charge and learn how to be focused — make their way in the world and not be so dependent, because codependent relationships are out of balance.

Chris: Yes, they very much are, and it seems like on the way that next sort of stage, all these extreme things that are occurring.

Rebeca: For everybody. We're all going through this right now. It's a major shifting that's taking place, and I think it's going to take years because, for one thing, we have to get rid of our romantic delusions. (He laughs.) The main one is that if you physically and sexually have a lot of chemistry with somebody, that they are actually going to be a good partner. They may not be a good partner at all. They may not even be your friend.

Chris: (He laughs.) Yes, I get that. Wow! Thanks, Rebeca.

* * * * * * * * * *

REGINA

Saturday, December 7, 1968
12:18:00 AM CST
Houston, Texas
Tropical   Placidus   True Node

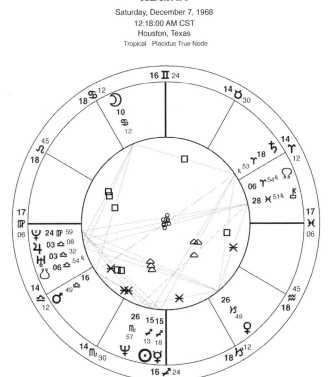

Example 4: Regina - The Case of Restrained Emotional Expression

Rebeca: The first thing I'd like to describe is your rising sign because that is what people first see about us when they meet us. Astrology is so helpful because it shows that we have a lot of different characters, and each one of them can have a different agenda. Sometimes people meet us, and when they see our outer mask, they think this is who we are, but it's only one part of us. Your rising sign is Virgo, and Virgo is very detail-oriented, pretty meticulous, kind of quiet and shy, unobtrusive, always looking to improve yourself, a bit self-critical, very high standards. You really like neatness in your environment, and it's important. There are a lot of planets in your 1st house, so there are a lot of different parts of you that show up right away. The planet Pluto is in Virgo, and it's right on your first house cusp. Pluto is very charismatic; it's powerful, so even though you may be shy and quiet, people sense that there's an intensity about you. You can look straight through them, so you're deep and penetrating. You have a propensity for wanting to probe, wanting to see what's hidden, wanting to see below the surface and very interested in what's taboo and hidden — the Shadow. A person who would be passionate, intense and emotional underneath, a kind of seething, it's kind of underneath, it's not expressed, a seething that people can feel. When you are really upset, you clam up, but that doesn't mean that all the moods and the feelings and the intensity go away, it's all still there.

The second thing that's very important is the Moon. The Sun, the Moon and the rising sign are very descriptive of our personality, and then the rest of the planets are additions that color who we are. And of course your Sun is in Sagittarius, but you know that. Moon in Cancer is pretty emotional. Cancer is a sensitive sign. It's mothering, it enjoys mothering others, but also being taken care of yourself. The Moon in Cancer is very sensitive to people's feelings. You can tell if people are hurting, and you want to reach out. Now, when it comes to expressing your own feelings, you hold back. That's because there is an influence to the Moon from Saturn. Saturn is the planet of restriction, responsibility. Saturn is the part of us where we feel the most fear. And wherever our Saturn is and how it aspects other planets tells us a little bit about what restricts us, what keeps us from expressing our nature fully and where we have to work at it. So Saturn squares the Moon. That would make you cautious and lack trust. It takes a while for you to trust. You don't just all of a sudden express your deep feelings. Now, the Sun in Sagittarius is blunt, honest, more direct about other things going on in the environment. When I talk about your feelings, I mean this is where you're really sensitive. For instance, if somebody approaches you in an aggressive or coarse way, you just cringe.

Regina: Yes.

Rebeca: You go inside, instead of directly confronting them. The Sun in Sagittarius is another part of you. It's the adventurous part. It's a risk taker, it's a gambler, an explorer, independent, freedom-loving, restless, loves travel, loves change, meeting new people, with a very strong need for freedom. That freedom has to do with philosophies, being open-minded, wanting to learn about all the different religions. So that part of you is more outgoing and the rising sign is a little more subdued, so it just depends on where you are. You have Sun conjunct Mercury in Sagittarius, and Mercury is how we think, how we communicate, how we express ourselves, and it's how we learn, so sometimes you may not even realize you've hurt somebody by being blunt. But you love teaching and sharing ideas. Communication is like food to you. You are probably a writer.

Regina: Yes. (She laughs.)

Rebeca: You would be a very deep writer, very thorough. You would analyze things thoroughly before you would trust. You can also be very willful, fanatical, intense about getting your desires met.

Regina: Yes. (She laughs.)

Rebeca: You see how all of these are contradictory?

Regina: Yes.

Rebeca: Well, the reason they are so contradictory is there is so much different energy in you that you are very well rounded in the sense that you have Earth, Air, Fire and Water in equal amounts. That makes you a unique person in that you can be very practical and reliable, which is Earth. You can be very adventurous, intuitive and spontaneous, which is Fire. You can be very sensitive to feelings, which is Water, and you can be Air. You can also be a very deep thinker because thinking and communicating are strong. Each one of these is almost or nearly equal. None of them dominates the other. When I look at the Sun in the 3rd house, I would specifically say that communication is important to you. What do you do?

Regina: I'm a technical writer.

Rebeca: OK, technical having that Pluto in the 1st house squaring Mercury and the Sun. Pluto being thorough, analytical, loving research and very interested in depth psychology.

Regina: Oh, yeah.

Rebeca: I may have already mentioned this before, but you're interested in what is taboo. Where other people may be afraid, you're not in the least bit. You want to learn about it before you decide whether you are going to be afraid of it. So you're very willing to probe anything that's different. Other people might say, "Oh, I'm afraid of that; that's too scary." So you have a strong aptitude for being a researcher, an investigator, a reporter, a forceful and convincing speaker and a writer. I would even say a teacher, and a very thorough teacher at that.

Regina: Oh, OK.

Rebeca: You also have Jupiter in the 1st house. The 1st house is your persona, so Jupiter there would make you very jovial, generous, outgoing, spontaneous, risk-taking. Then there's another planet there, too, which is Uranus. And Uranus is the planet of iconoclasm, uniqueness, independence, where we beat to our own drum. Because the South Node is conjunct Pluto, Jupiter and Uranus, you overdo the need for freedom, you overdo optimism where it might bite you in the butt because you weren't cautious. You might be overly impulsive when it comes to relationships and maybe need to be a little more cautious.

Regina: OK.

Rebeca: But this is where it's complicated for you, because Saturn is squaring your Venus and it's squaring the Moon. The Saturn part of you is cautious, has tremendous fear of abandonment and has a fear of getting close because you might lose your freedom. So there is a push-pull. Part of you wants intimacy, and part of

Notes to Myself:

231

you wants freedom, and both of those are very equal in your chart. Let's see what else... I would say that you would be a person who wouldn't wear your heart on your sleeve, would be much more self-protective. Venus is in Capricorn, and Capricorn is ruled by Saturn, so you are attracted to much older people, wiser people...

Regina: Yes.

Rebeca: ...people who are reliable, who can provide security for you. You're attracted to somebody who's established, who has made a name for themselves in the business world, who has position and stature. That's one aspect of what you are attracted to, but then there is another part. The other part is the planet Neptune that rules your Marriage house, and the planet Neptune is about dreamy, spacy, idealism, and it can bring confusion, wanting to save people, finding wounded people that you can fix. You're the one that comes in and orders their life and gets everything working for them because they are not doing it. And then yet there is that other part of you that's attracted to people who are more established, more conservative, conventional, people who are older and wiser. They can still be older and wiser, but they could also be creative, maybe into photography, dance or music, or even healers like doctors or nurses. Neptune also rules the ocean, so it can be (chuckle) a sailor, somebody who is very spiritual or has the exact opposite problem, an escapist, an alcoholic, a drug addict... where you think, "If I just work a little harder on them, they'll get it." But they are not even open to doing that.

Regina: Wow!

Rebeca: That person needs to save themselves, and there's that strong tendency within you to want to save or heal or fix and to be understanding... mainly because you want to be in control because you are the one who's more giving. So you might attract people to you that are confused, unreliable, unpredictable.

Regina: Yes... yes.

Rebeca: The South Node in Libra is also in the 1st house, so there is also this tendency that when you do get involved with somebody, and it takes you a long time to even get involved with anybody, but when you do, you can revolve your whole self around that person. You have two different distinct patterns. One is impulsive: it's quick and it's over. And another one is you take your time, but once you do actually get involved, you've lost yourself and you have to be more direct with that person. You have to express what your needs are. You have to learn the art of compromise and ask for your needs to be met. There's a part of you, Mars squares the Moon that can be unpredictable yourself. It can clam up because it's so sensitive, gets angry and is moody and you would go into your shell. Depending on the situation, sometimes maybe at work, you can be impatient, irritable, bad-tempered... need to exercise, and that's a better use of that energy. Find outlets where you are physical.

Regina: OK.

Rebeca: The need for excitement and change and freedom and no restriction is one strong aspect. A second strong aspect is the fear of closeness, and the third strongest is the wanting to heal, wanting to save.

Regina: And they've all played a critical part in my life.

Rebeca: OK, tell me about it.

Regina: My ex-girlfriend and I had been on-again, off-again for 12 years. She was an alcoholic, and I thought that I could save her. I wanted to help her. When I did that, we got close. But every time we got too close, she'd leave or end the relationship. I finally got to the point where I couldn't keep getting close and then separating. So we no longer speak. I'm sad about it, but I see the part I played in all of this, the enabling part.

Rebeca: I would say it's the fear of being out of control.

Regina: Oh, OK.

Rebeca: Because Saturn, which is where we feel fear, is in the 8th house of resources, so the Shadow side of that would be being deeply afraid of merging, that you're deeply afraid of sharing your resources with somebody totally... money. So it might look like she's the one who's doing all this, and it's kind of a convenient scapegoat for you to say she's all of that. The Shadow side is you would also have a deep fear of closeness, a deep fear of losing your independence, but you're not an alcoholic.

Regina: No.

Rebeca: You're too self-preserving for that. You're too responsible, and you're too self-critical. If you would start doing anything like that, you would start harping on yourself.

Regina: Yes, my body is like my temple. I have to preserve it. We were brought into each other's life for a reason. I showed her some things, and she showed me some things. What was I afraid of? Yes. Those types of things. Deep things that I wasn't willing to acknowledge when we first met. Yeah, what you said is true. A little fear of getting too close, sharing an apartment, money, and car. Whoo! Gosh!

Rebeca: And being afraid of being burned.

Regina: Yes, but I've done all of that a number of times with her.

233

I've gone back over and over and over again, but this time I don't want to do that anymore.

Rebeca: Well, you're probably moving into a time... let me look at what's going on with your transits real quick. Oh!... the planet Uranus is on your Marriage house cusp, which means that there's separation. Uranus rules separation and division. What happens is both people become more objective because they separate. It's a requirement. Ideally, you would be willing to have a relationship with somebody new and you would start as a friend, that you would not jump into anything too quickly. Kind of experiment. Meet new people. Start out as friends instead of putting out, "Oh, this person's perfect for me," before you've even gotten to know them. Give yourself that time to establish trust, whether they can take care of themselves, because you're not the big healer. If you're trying to heal somebody, often the person you're trying to heal is you. They're the mirror to show you where you're wounded, but it looks like it's them. So we get to say to ourselves, "I'm so good. I'm so generous. I'm so loving. If I could just love this person enough, they'll heal," but the truth is, if you were healed, would you be messing with them? So it's a mirror.

Regina: Wow!

Rebeca: Yeah, it is a mirror, and it's so hard to see it because it looks like it's somebody else and you don't identify with any of it. But here's the interesting thing about the Shadow. Our Shadow is the exact opposite of everything we identify with very strongly. So if we identify very strongly that we've got it all under control, we're good, we're good to go; underneath, we're not.

Regina: (She laughs.)

Rebeca: So it's better to have some doubt. It's better to have some confidence and some doubt and to have a balance between my needs and their needs. There's a need for intimacy and reliability, safety and security. And there's also such a strong need for freedom. So to me, when you have that in such a juxtaposition, then you have to establish relationships with people who are trustworthy, number one, because that's Saturn, that's reliability, trustworthiness, and trust takes time.

Regina: Yes.

Rebeca: And if you're putting out there to somebody "This is who I am. This is what I need. This is where I am going," and that person says, "Well, that's good. This is who I am, what I need and where I am going." And there's a balance between giving and taking, sharing expenses, sharing responsibilities. The only way to do the 7th house in a healthy way is where you are doing a dance. It's never one person's way or the other person's way. And whenever you notice that you are getting out of balance with anybody, because we all get out of balance, we all do, we have to pull back. We have to stop, sit down with our partner and express ourselves. This is something you're really good at work, but you're horrible at when it comes to love.

Regina: Yes, and I caught that a few years ago. I thought, "How come I can do this at work, but I can't do it at home?" I can't figure it out.

Rebeca: Because you're real sensitive. You're afraid of being hurt, afraid of not being appreciated. You're also very sympathetic, so there's a duel. You know, it's not that you are just sensitive only for yourself. If that person's hurting, you're sensitive and sympathetic to them, too, but that sensitivity has to be brought out into the open, even if it might come out at the beginning in fits and starts. At the beginning, when we're afraid to show our feelings, it kind of comes out in an infantile way. It sounds demanding.

Regina: OK.

Rebeca: It sounds needy, and that's the biggest fear. It's very difficult to express need. I think everybody has difficulty with it, but especially if you have Moon in Cancer and all these aspects to your Saturn and your Venus. There's a sensitivity and an awkwardness about expressing need because you're supposed to be — with that Virgo rising — very analytical and together.

Regina: Uh-huh.

Rebeca: And expressing need has to happen in the moment, and you have a very strong need to be fair, but you also need to be fair to you. You can be too accommodating. Too compromising. Just for the sake of the companionship.

Regina: YES!!!

Rebeca: It's a very Libran quality to be too accommodating and then the exact opposite, like totally selfish, without even thinking of the other person, and when you are accused of being selfish, indignantly saying, "I am not! I am always thinking of you." Yet there is a paradox, because there are two sides to you. There's a real restless, independent "I'm going to do my own thing," and then there's this real sensitive part. So in order to balance all of this paradoxical energy, you have to do some of it sometimes and do the other sometimes and to REALLY COMMUNICATE! I think that when people can't communicate, they should write things down, not just write things down, and give that person the letter because you're a letter writer.

Regina: (She laughs.)

Rebeca: The 3rd house is the house of writing letters, so you're a journaler and a letter writer, and when you're upset, you write the letter. Well, write the letter, but sit down with the person face

Notes to Myself:

235

to face. "I can be really clear about what I want to convey from a calm space, and I want to talk about it." So talking, communicating, expressing need — all of that — has to start happening slowly where you see if this person is going to hear you. What if you express need? What if you say "Don't say you're going to call me if you're not going to call me."

Regina: Yes, I hate that.

Rebeca: And then they say, "OK, I'll call you. Have I been doing that?" Then the next time they do it again, and they do it again and you think, "Well, why even communicate with this person? They don't hear me." Then trust is shattered because each person is not really hearing. Say it happens once and then it happens again and then you blow it off. Well, if you really want that relationship to be healthy and you want it to have passion, passion requires authenticity between partners. You can have a false harmony if you want, or you can have passion, which means that at all times, each person is being authentic.

Regina: The real thing.

Rebeca: Yeah, because otherwise you have a harmony, but nothing is really being communicated, so there's a lot of confusion, there's a lot of doubt, there's are a lot of mixed messages and hurt feelings that don't get spoken between both people because, I guarantee you, you hurt her as much as she hurts you and partly from holding back.

Regina: From both people?

Rebeca: Well, I don't know her, but I know you, and you hold back your real feelings. You need to be more direct and ask for what you want, and then you also have to learn to listen. And if it's too hard to discuss it, write it down and take turns in the sense of "Let's do this exercise together. Let's improve the quality of our communication," and as John Sanford says, "Communication is like a ball."[2] You throw the ball at that person, and then they throw it back, and then you throw the ball at them, and they throw it back again. There's nothing more irritating than sending an email to somebody that has a communication, not just a joke or cute thing, it's an actual communication, and nothing comes back from them.

Regina: Yeah!

Rebeca: And you think, "Weird." You wonder if that person even got it, and you would think that most people know this stuff, but they don't. I have heard so many people complain to me, "Oh, I write to him or I write to her, and she never responds. Well, she or he is not in the relationship as much as I am," and it could very well be that they are completely in it, they just don't realize what's important to you.

Regina: OK.

Rebeca: Because you're a 3rd house Sun. Third house is communications, and you have Sun, Mercury and Neptune there, so you have strong ideals about communication, but you're not communicating when it comes to relationships. You're a great communicator when it comes to your work. What kind of technical writing do you do?

Regina: I write detailed instructions on how to install software on government systems. I love that. It's very detailed. It's specific. "Do this. Do this and do that." What else do I do? I do a lot of proofreading and editing.

Rebeca: Awesome. And what do you do for adventure?

Regina: Well, I've been working out. I also do some spiritual things. I like to travel.

Rebeca: So would you be willing to disclose some of the complaints that your partner had?

Regina: Things she said to me?

Rebeca: Uh-hmm.

Regina: She said that I didn't tell her things. One night in 2003, some sexual things happened that really hurt me. Afterward, I didn't mention the pain because I thought that she'd get mad. At that time, I had a really hard time speaking up or addressing problems. In 2005, I told her how the night in 2003 had hurt me. We talked about it and my difficulty in speaking up at the time. Things seemed OK. In 2007 (after she'd had a few drinks) she brought up that 2003 incident and accused me of "choosing not to tell her things." I tried to explain that I didn't "choose" to do that. I told her how difficult it was to address problems then, but she kept repeating that I "chose" not to tell her.

Rebeca: So did you all go back and forth, back and forth?

Regina: Well, yes, we went back and forth. Then we stopped all communication on New Year's Eve. She just wanted to be friends and tell me who she was dating. I told her that that wasn't acceptable to me. I'm not going to hurt myself like that. Neither one of us said that we were not talking anymore, but it pretty much became clear on January 1, 2008, that we weren't talking any more. We haven't spoken since.

Rebeca: Well, having Uranus coming over your Marriage-house cusp, it was inevitable that there would be a separation. That helps both people so that both people can get a better perspective of what they are doing. Sometimes people come back together even when Uranus is there, or maybe they just start travelling apart more. One way or another, there is some kind of a separation. The real

Notes to Myself:

meaning is for you to look at what your real needs are in relationship and wanting you to choose something different for yourself. Whenever we're stuck in a pattern, whatever the pattern is, Uranus comes in there and says, "You have to do something different now. You can't keep doing the same thing and expecting a different result. You have to learn how to dance."

Regina: Well, I finally learned how to dance in August. I finally learned how to say what I think or what I feel, not in a mean way, but be OK with that and not worry that somebody's not going to like me because of it. That's one of the things I've learned.

Rebeca: Another thing that may be going on inside of you is maybe recognizing how some of your relationship patterns have to do with your upbringing and your family.

Regina: (She laughs.) It's like you're in the house with me, because I've been going through that. I've been backtracking and looking at my family and how things turned out this way.

Rebeca: Well, the planet Pluto, which is about transformation and healing and going into the unconscious, is in the 4th house of Home and Family by transit. The 4th and 10th symbolize mother and father, and they affect us so much in who we choose to be in relationship with. Until we recognize there's a pattern there that has to do with our parents, we can't really change it.

Regina: Yes. I know I've been chasing my mom. "See me. See me." I recognize it now, including previous relationships, not just her. I went through the same thing. I felt neglected, but I kept pursuing that person because I thought they would see me and love me.

Rebeca: Right... and having Moon-Saturn means a difficult relationship with our mother, and then there's Venus. The Moon and Venus are the two feminine parts of our psyche, so astrology is not based on the planets out there doing something to us. The planets are reflecting inner states. There's the alchemical dictum of "as above so below; as within, so without." So what's inside us is outside. So we may only notice when our mother is cool, aloof, not there for us and distant. We may pull it out of her. She might be totally different with one of our other siblings. It's really remarkable. When I started studying astrology, I was just amazed, because I have five siblings. Our parents were different, and they were in different stages of their life, of course, because there's a span of 20 years between the youngest and the oldest. You can see in yourself that you're growing and changing, and who you are now is not the person you were five years ago, and, having Pluto in the 1st house, you're kind of like a snake that sheds skin. Every five to seven years you have a different personality.

Regina: (She laughs.)

Rebeca: Or there's a major shift in who you think of as yourself.

Regina: I like that.

Rebeca: You have a real tendency to probe beneath your own surface. You want to plumb your depths; you want to know what's hidden inside you. You're not a superficial person. You might for the sake of companionship be a people pleaser, but that's really not your nature. Your inherent nature is deep. It's very motivated toward self-knowledge, wants to explore... How does this relate to me? What did I do to deserve this? What is this about? What am I supposed to be learning here? Sagittarius is a teacher and they're a student. They have a tendency to bounce back from disappointment by being optimistic and having faith that something else will happen, but they can ignore what's real. What's reality and the reality function for you is the feminine side. That side of you wants practicality, wants things to be tangible — "Prove it. Prove it to me." The Sun side is the male side of you and the Mars side. Your Mars is in Libra, and you have a sextile between the Sun and Mars, so the male side of you is outgoing, it's direct, it's confronting. It's challenging, but the male side is where we take off after our goals.

Regina: Oh, OK.

Rebeca: It's how we apply ourself in our work, how we go after getting our car fixed, whatever it is that we have to take charge of and go handle. We don't have any problem with that.

Regina: No, uh-uh!

Rebeca: But the female side of you is real sensitive. The Venus part is the Aphrodite that wants to be affectionate, told that they are beautiful, wants to be treated like a Queen. The female side, the Venus side, is the Aphrodite in us, and it's fickle. The Moon side is the nurturing, motherly, sensitive, caring, side. Your Moon in hard aspect to Saturn says to me that you hold back your emotional feelings.

Regina: Ohhhhh!

Rebeca: You have a deep fear of being hurt, being rejected, so instead of expressing need, you end up doing exactly what is going to happen to you because you've done it to them. You have not expressed need. You have not expressed emotion, so you end up being abandoned because the other person felt abandoned, too. Does that make sense?

Regina: It does. I understood it on a deep level, and I know exactly what you're talking about. It's like a reflection.

Rebeca: Yeah, it is. It's a reflection. There's no accident who we get involved with. None whatsoever. It's actually remarkable.

Regina: The universe is an amazing thing.

Rebeca: It is.

Regina: I'm fascinated every day. I mean these bodies, the plants, the animals, the stars...

Rebeca: When I first got into astrology, I really thought, "My God! This is so real. This is the planets. They're doing it to us. We don't have any free will." Well, our free will is how we respond to all of this. The more we know about ourselves, the more self-knowledge we have, we can choose. If we don't know about something, then we can't choose. So self-awareness is essential to me for growth. Self-awareness, reflecting on patterns and seeing why these people are here and, you know, whenever we get an "AHA," we're contributing to the cosmos. We are. We're all connected. The planets aren't any different than the rocks and the trees and the animals. They're all part of nature, and we are also

a part of nature. We are spiritual, but we are also human and animal. We're not just spiritual beings. We're human beings. So it's like we connect to everything in the universe and everything in the universe is connected to each other and it's moving, it's evolving, it's changing. As the planets move... as we're changing, it looks like, well, let's say OK, Mars comes along. It's in Libra right now, and it's about to conjunct your South Node, and it just conjuncted your Uranus. The Uranus part of you is the independent, freedom-seeking person. Mars sitting there on that Uranus and Jupiter would make you feel impulsive. Did you just do something impulsive?

Regina: Yes.

Rebeca: And what happened?

Regina: I felt great. I am going to go to this party, and I'm not a party person, and I was OK with that.

Rebeca: Great!

Regina: And you know other things as well, doing more social events, because I know that I am very reserved, but I am going to go and try something different, and I've been happy with that.

Rebeca: Well, that's super! Well, Uranus in your Marriage-house and opposing your 1st house gives you that sense of being ready to change. I want something different, so I have to be different.

Regina: I do want the real thing even though we'll always get reflections...

Rebeca: Well, every single time it gets better.

Regina: Oh, OK...

Rebeca: Every single time you get into a relationship, it gets better because you're different, because you've learned something from the one previously. And each person, because they are unique, brings you a different aspect of yourself. Whatever part of you is ready to develop, that's the next person that you meet.

Regina: I like that, Rebeca! Ok... basically you're ready for the next lesson.

Rebeca: Yes, if we can look at our past relationships like that. They were learning experiences. Then we can maybe not take it so personally that we're destroyed or devastated. We can bounce back from disappointment and have a little more philosophical outlook and not take it so deeply like, "Something is wrong with me." There's a tendency in your chart to say, "I'm the one who's at fault. I'm unworthy. I can't have what I want." Well, if you're true to yourself, if you're patient with yourself. if you're generous to yourself, if you take care of yourself, you will see it reflected back to you. If you're overdoing, overgiving, overextending at your expense, then that's what you get to see mirrored back.

Regina: OK!

Rebeca: It doesn't work the other way around. It works from the inside out. I've been learning about the Shadow since 1990, learning through relationships. It was my fate to go through relationships, some very, very difficult challenging ones, but every single time it's gotten better. And I directly relate it to the more I'm willing to take care of myself and the more I'm willing to ask and communicate, the better things will be. You know friends. Think about it: your heart strings are not tied to that friend. They can leave, and it's no big deal. You're not emotionally invested. If they do something you don't like, chances are you're going to tell them. But when it comes to somebody that we're intimate with, we're afraid because they could leave us. But see, if we are afraid that somebody can leave us, we've put our parents on them, our rejecting parents. Then we revert to being a little child, the little child in us that was abandoned, abused, neglected or whatever. We'll perpetuate that with another person until we start being our own parent. When we start being our own parent, then we're going to protect ourselves.

And it might come out a bit needy at first. It might sound impulsive and needy, and we might drink a little before we can even say anything because we're not used to it. BUT with time, with patience, with clarity, we start to take care of ourselves, and we start to see it mirrored back. The best place to do this exercise is with our friends. Establish really good friendships. That can be male or female. I have friends of both sexes. I have male friends that I've had for 20 years. They are like brothers. They would do

Notes to Myself:

anything for me. One of them has a key to my house, and if I needed anything, I could call him and vice versa. It works both ways. It's a two-way street.

Regina: You're there for each other, a good friend. That's all right.

Rebeca: And I have another friend who's had a real difficult time with drinking, and I tried to help him, tried to talk to him, tried to give him tapes and books, steer him in a different direction. He came over one day and we were going to go walking, and he was so smashed that it was uncomfortable walking the park with him. I told him, "I don't want you to come over anymore if you're drinking. Just don't come, because you just keep repeating yourself over and over. It's real uncomfortable. You get real belligerent. You're not making sense, and I have to listen to it, and I don't want to."

Regina: You don't have to. (She laughs.)

Rebeca: Yes. I don't have to, and at first he was offended. He said, "Well, I don't need you. I'm not going to bend over backwards to be your friend. Blah, blah, blah, blah." I said, "I'm not asking you to bend over backwards. I'm asking you to be present. I want you to be present when you're with me. I'm giving you my presence."

Regina: Right. That's so right.

Rebeca: So, he went off, and he had years... several years... that he's had to struggle with this, but I never forgot him. I'd always either call to see how he was doing and talk on the phone, or send him an email here and there, or whatever, but I refused to even invite him to my parties anymore because he would disrupt them. But I never let him go. I never abandoned him totally, but I wanted to take care of me. Well, he's changing. He's quit drinking. He recently called and said he's joined AA. He wanted to go walking with me again. I welcome it completely and totally, but, see, I never let him go. I never ever forgot him because there were many years before he started drinking that he was really there for me. He was a good friend. He has always been a good friend. So when we establish friendships with people, we have to be willing to be real. If they are doing something that doesn't serve us, we have to be willing to tell them.

Regina: Right.

Rebeca: If we don't tell them, then what are we doing? We're hurting ourselves.

Regina: Right. That was something I could never really do with her because sometimes I was scared to speak up. Maybe she was mad and that made me more fearful. I just couldn't get the words out. I don't know. I don't know if we'll ever speak again.

I don't know that. I mean, I still think of her and still dream of her. I see what she's shown me and the things that I've shown her.

Rebeca: Well, that's a start. As you move forward in life and you take your time, things will change because you're going through some big changes. Pluto going through the 4th house of Home and Family means major changes. It's bringing all the stuff up from our childhood and looking at it and seeing how we might be contributing to what we get. I honestly believe that we are to be our own parent instead of wanting somebody to parent us. I remember you said earlier, "I've been chasing my mother."

Regina: Yes.

Rebeca: I've been wanting my mom to look at me. "Look at me. Pay attention to me."

Regina: Yes.

Rebeca: When you start paying attention to you and you make it really clear this is who I am. This is where I'm going. This is what I need, and I'm real open to who are you, "Where are you going? Let's talk about it. I'll compromise with you, but you have to compromise with me."

Regina: Right.

Rebeca: Because of that authenticity, neither person has control. Both people have to be authentic with each other, and therefore it's always shifting, it's always changing, it's always dynamic, and there's always passion. Passion goes away when nothing real is being said.

Regina: I like that. I like that saying.

Rebeca: If we're authentic and we're real with people, they could leave us. We have to be willing to face that risk, that they're going to leave us. Then if they really need to go, well then OK, see you later. We have to be willing to walk away as if our life depended on it. I think it's really important before we let them walk away that we tell them the truth, that we're honest and not from a place of a baby, or pointing or blaming or shaming or destroying the person, but from a place of an adult. "This hurt me. This didn't work. This is how I experienced your energy and what you were doing in our relationship. Now would you please tell me what you experienced because I want to know?"

Regina: Yes.

Rebeca: I want to know if I hurt you. I want to know if I wasn't accommodating enough. I want to know if I was being selfish, and you didn't know how to accommodate me. I want to know what you felt.

Notes to Myself:

243

Notes to Myself:

Regina: That's what I want, honesty and communication with people.

Rebeca: That's your life's work.

Regina: That is what I want, and I've been working on that, just talking to people, looking them in the eye, telling them my true feelings, saying, "How do you feel about this?" And they tell me what they feel about it, just really having a genuine conversation. I would love for that to translate into...

Rebeca: ...a relationship.

Regina: Yes.

Rebeca: Well, you're going to have opportunities to meet a lot of different people right now. And I think it's really wise what you're doing — going out and making friends — making friends from different types of groups. Do things you've never done before. You have an opportunity right now with Uranus coming through the 7th to meet a lot of interesting people and date. Everybody you date doesn't have to be a marriage partner.

Regina: (She laughs.) OK.

Rebeca: When you have the South Node in Libra or five planets in Libra like me, there's a tendency to evaluate a person right away ... "Is this a partner for me?" instead of "I think I would like to get to know this person; they look interesting." So kind of throw that out that they're too old, they're too young, they're too fat, they're too skinny, whatever. Yes, we have to have an attraction. I don't think we can date somebody if there is no physical attraction or where we see somebody and they are 50 pounds overweight and we're not. It's not appealing. Or we might be the one that's 50 pounds overweight. I'm not saying that that's bad. I'm just saying that most of the time people have to be equal in a lot of different areas and have some things in common — have things in common to stimulate their interest, to make their relationship interesting. If you have nothing in common with that person — that's my first marriage. Bless his heart, he's a genuinely good person, a very giving, genuinely caring person, but we had absolutely nothing in common. We could not talk because, no matter what I would say, I was wrong. We saw things differently. He knew better, and he was 11 years older than me. OK, he was the parent, and I was the child. I married my father and my mother, both of them. Jungian psychology stresses that we do that. I've read several books that say we marry our parents, and from what I've seen doing astrology readings for people and watching people that get divorced and get married again, it's true. I'm 56 years old.

Regina: Really?

Rebeca: Yeah.

Regina: I would've never guessed. Oh, my gosh, because I looked at your picture on your Web site, and I thought she may be early 40s. OK...

Rebeca: I look like I'm 45 because I take care of my body. I'm very Libra. We're ruled by Venus. I'm very vain. I exercise. I eat healthy. I'm very good at how I eat.

Regina: I wouldn't have guessed. I mean not that 56 has a certain look, but...

Rebeca: I know. I get told that all the time. "You don't look a day over 40," and I have guys come on to me that are 15-17 years younger than me. And I had this habit of dating people that right away, if they weren't a marriage partner, I wasn't interested, but I've changed my mind. I am making an effort to change in that regard. I want to know what kind of person they are, not just what they look like or how much money they have. The last guy I dated seriously didn't have any money, but he's one of the neatest people I've ever met.

Regina: Aaaah! I want that. To be loved.

Rebeca: Well, we all want that. We all want to be loved, and I think we all want to give love. We don't just want to be loved. We want to give it. Love is what makes the world go round, so the bottom line is we've got to love ourselves first.

Regina: Yes.

Rebeca: Because if we love ourselves first, then we're going to see it mirrored back.

Regina: Yes.

Rebeca: Then when we have another chance at love, because it doesn't come around that often, the older you get, (the fewer people you'll be attracted to), but the next time it comes around, think about some of the things you learned from the person before. Make a list of some of the things we talked about today. Let's talk. Let's write things down if we're not communicating. If my feelings are being hurt, I need to say so. If at first our feelings come out childish, it's because we're not used to expressing our feelings. We're used to being the one in control. Pluto rising has a horrible habit of wanting to be in control. Therefore I'm going to tell you what I'm thinking, but I'm not going to tell you what I'm feeling. It's a lot easier to tell you what I'm thinking.

Regina: OK. Very good. Very good.

Rebeca: When we meet water people, they can be too feeling-oriented for us since we have so much Air and Fire. What kind

Notes to Myself:

of Sun sign was your partner? Not that the Sun sign is everything, because it's not.

Regina: Aquarius, and I thought, oh, water...

Rebeca: No, Aquarius is an air sign. Aquarius is a detached, aloof, beat-to-their-own-drum, iconoclastic, freedom-oriented person. That's what she was mirroring to you. But then that can be an Aquarius with the Moon in Scorpio. You don't know until you've looked at the whole chart. I recently met this new guy who is a supplier for me. I'm a graphic artist, and we're working together. Uranus is in the same place where it is for you on his Marriage house cusp. He met me and took me to lunch, and I was telling him all about astrology, and he was so interested, and he was 30, really young. I said, "I'll run out your report for you," and I gave it to him. Well, several months, two months went by. We decided to start meeting for lunch every month just to talk. I just liked him so much I decided, "Yeah, I'm willing to do that." So I did. I don't do that that often because, for me, people find out you're an astrologer and think they can just pour out all their energy onto me to solve their problems. That's not how he exchanged with me. It's so balanced, and he's become a good friend, referring business to me, etc. So one day he came for lunch, and he said, "You're not going to believe what happened. We looked at my report that you gave me. We read it. She read it out loud. It was like she finally understood me. It was so accurate, Rebeca." I said, "I know. I've been studying this for 20 years." So in my book, I talk about that. If you know your astrology and they know your astrology and you know theirs and you both sit and talk about it, it helps you understand that person. They're not going to be who you want them to be. They are going to be themselves.

Regina: Yes.

Rebeca: And if they do need freedom, and they do need to be a little bit unpredictable, and you need safety and security, both need to be respected. You need for them to call you and say, "I'm going to do this instead of what I planned to do with you." They are breaking their plans with you, and you're willing for that to happen as long as they communicate and not one hour — or worse, five minutes — before you're supposed to get together.

Regina: Yeah, as that might be a problem.

Rebeca: Not even the same day. Ideally — I know that not everything is an ideal and there have to be exceptions — but they should call you the day before so that you can make plans to do something else or so that you don't expect them. Giving that person their freedom means they can think however they want to think. You don't tell them how to think. You don't tell them how to dress. You don't tell them who to have as friends. You're really open to their being a free bird, but you're willing to be committed, and you're in a partnership. IF both people are communicating, then it's cool.

Regina: Yes. I can see that.

Rebeca: That is how trust is established by authentic communication and really hearing what the other person says to you. Yes. Trust is earned. It's not had as a gift.

Regina: Wow! You've given me a lot to think about. Thank you so much.

* * * * * * * * * *

NOTES PART FIVE:

1) Richard Idemon, *Through the Looking Glass, a Search for the Self in the Mirror of Relationships,* Edited by Howard Sasportas, *Seminars in Psychological Astrology, Volume 5,* Samuel Weiser, Inc., York Beach, Maine, 1992, pg 12

2) John A. Sanford, *Between People: Communicating One-To-One,* Paulist Press, New York/Ramsey, 1982, pg 1

**To schedule a Consultation
with Rebeca Eigen, call 281-799-2900.**

shadowdance.com

Astrologically, as we have said, this process corresponds to an ascent through the planets from the dark, cold, distant Saturn to the sun. To the alchemists the connection between individual temperament and the positions of the planets was self-evident, for these elementary astrological considerations were the common property of any educated person in the Middle Ages as well as in antiquity.[1]

CARL GUSTAV JUNG

*W*e must still be exceedingly careful not to project our own shadows too shamelessly; we are still swamped with projected illusions. If you imagine someone who is brave enough to withdraw all his projections, then you get an individual who is conscious of a pretty thick shadow. Such a man has saddled himself with new problems and conflicts. He has become a serious problem to himself, as he is now unable to say that *they* do this or that, *they* are wrong, and *they* must be fought against. He lives in the "House of the Gathering." Such a man knows that whatever is wrong in the world is in himself, and if he only learns to deal with his own shadow he has done something real for the world. He has succeeded in shouldering at least an infinitesimal part of the gigantic, unsolved social problems of our day. These problems are mostly so difficult because they are poisoned by mutual projections. How can anyone see straight when he does not even see himself and the darkness he unconsciously carries with him into all his dealings?[2]

NOTES FOR THIS PAGE:

1)   C.G. Jung, CW 14 - *Mysterium Coniunctionis,* Princeton University Press, Bollingen, 1963, par 308, pg 230

2)   C.G. Jung, CW 11 - *Psychology and Religion: West and East,* Princeton University Press, Bollingen,1958, par 140, pg 83

RECOMMENDED READING TO LEARN MORE ABOUT C.G. JUNG, DREAMS and ASTROLOGY:

* Highly recommended

The Undiscovered Self, *AION,* *Memories, Dreams, Reflections,* *Answer to Job,* *Psychology and Alchemy,* *Alchemical Studies,* *The Psychology of the Transference,* *Mysterium Coniunctionis,* *Symbols of Transformation,* *Two Essays on Analytical Psychology,* *Modern Man in Search of a Soul,* *The Psychology of the Transference,* *Civilization in Transition, The Archetypes and the Collective Unconscious, The Development of the Personality, Psychology and Religion: West and East, The Structure and Dynamics of the Psyche, The Tavistock Lectures* *which are contained in Vol. 18, The Symbolic Life* - Dr. Carl Gustav Jung

The Kingdom Within, *Between People: Communicating One-To-One,* *EVIL: the Shadow Side of Reality,* *Invisible Partners,* *Dreams, God's Forgotten Language,* *Dreams and Healing* * - John A. Sanford

The Psyche as Sacrament, Christianity, the Illness That We Are, *Love, Celibacy and the Inner Marriage* - John P. Dourley

Ego and Archetype, The Science of the Soul, *Transformation of the God Image, The Mystery of the Coniunctio,* *Creation of Consciousness, The Mysterium Lectures, The Aion Lectures, The New God Image,* *The Psyche on Stage, Anatomy of the Psyche, Transformation of Libido, The Christian Archetype, A Jungian Commentary on the Life of Christ, Melville's Moby-Dick (Studies in Jungian Psychology by Jungian Analysts), The Archetype of the Apocalypse: Divine Vengeance, Terrorism, and the End of the World, Encounter With the Self: A Jungian Commentary on William Blake's Illustrations of the Book of Job, Eternal Drama: The Inner Meaning of Greek Mythology* - Edward F. Edinger

The Invisible Church, Finding Spirituality Where You Are * - J. Pittman McGehee, D.D. and Damon J. Thomas

The Paradox of Love, a Jungian Look at the Dynamics of Life's Greatest Mystery * - J. Pittman McGehee, D.D.

The Symbolic Quest *, Dreams, A Portal to the Source,* *Psyche and Substance: Essays on Homeopathy in the Light of Jungian Psychology, The Alchemy of Healing: Psyche and Soma* - Edward C. Whitmont

The Middle Passage: From Misery to Meaning in Midlife, Under Saturn's Shadow: The Healing and Wounding of Men, *The Eden Project: In Search of the Magical Other* * - James Hollis

Understanding Jung, Understanding Yourself, *Dreams and the Search for Meaning* * - Peter O'Connor

Your Shadow, Beginner's Guide to Jungian Psychology - Robert Robertson

We: Understanding the Psychology of Romantic Love, *Balancing Heaven and Earth, He, She, Transformation, Owning Your Own Shadow* * - Robert Johnson

Living Your Unlived Life, Coping with Unrealized Dreams and Fulfilling Your Purpose in the Second Half of Life, Robert A. Johnson and Jerry M. Ruhl, Ph.D.

Meeting the Shadow - The Hidden Power of the Dark Side of Human Nature * - Edited by Connie Zweig and Jeremiah Abrams

Your Golden Shadow, Make Friends with Your Shadow - William A. Miller

Avalanche, Heretical Reflections of the Dark and the Light * - W. Brugh Joy, M.D.

Getting to Know You, *Digesting Jung, Food for the Journey* * - Daryl Sharp

The Shadow in America, Reclaiming the Soul of a Nation - Edited by Jeremiah Abrams

Coming Together, Coming Apart — The Union of Opposites in Love Relationships * - John A. Desteian

A Little Book on the Human Shadow - Robert Bly

Jung on Evil, edited by Murray Stein

Shadow and Evil in Fairy Tales, Alchemy * - Marie-Louise von Franz

Embracing Our Selves, *Embracing Each Other,* *Embracing the Inner Critic* * - Hal and Sidra Stone, Ph.D.

The Road Less Traveled,* A Different Drum, Community Making and Peace,* People of the Lie* - Scott Peck

Knowing Woman* - Irene Claremont de Castillejo

C.G. Jung, The Fundamentals of Theory and Practice* - Elie Humbert

A Primer of Jungian Psychology - Calvin S. Hall & Vernon J. Norby

A Critical Dictionary of Jungian Analysis - Andrew Samuels, Bani Shorter and Fred Plaut

The Wounded Woman: Healing the Father-Daughter Relationship* - Linda Leonard

Jung and Reich: the Body as Shadow - John P. Conger

The Way of Individuation, The Psychology of C.G. Jung - Jolande Jacobi

Psyche's Seeds* - Jacquelyn Small

The Meaning in Dreams and Dreaming* - Maria F. Mahoney

The Mystical Magical Marvelous World of Dreams* - Wilda B. Tanner

Love, An Inner Connection - Carol K. Anthony

Journey of the Heart - A Conscious Path to Love* - John Welwood

What Men Really Want, the Definitive Guide to Love and Intimacy in the 1990s - Herb Goldberg, Ph.D.

The Ability to Love - Allan Fromme

Astrology for the Soul*, Cosmic Love* - Jan Spiller

RELATING: An Astrological Guide to Living with Others on a Small Planet,* Saturn, A New Look at an Old Devil,* Star Signs for Lovers,* Neptune - The Quest for Redemption, The Astrology of Fate - Liz Greene

The Dynamics of the Unconscious,* The Development of the Personality, The Luminaries, The Inner Planets - Liz Greene and Howard Sasportas

The Gods of Change,* The Twelve Houses* - Howard Sasportas

Psychological Astrology - Theory and Practice* - Dr. Glenn Perry

Your Secret Self: Illuminating the Mysteries of the 12th House,* The Astrology of Self Discovery* - Tracy Marks

Healing Pluto Problems,* Moon Signs, An Astrological Guide to Self Awareness - Donna Cunningham

Love and Sexuality, An Exploration of Venus & Mars - Babs Kirby and Janey Stubbs

Aspects in Astrology, A Comprehensive Guide to Interpretation - Sue Tompkins

Made in Heaven, Sun Shines* - Michael Lutin

The Inner Sky, The Dynamic New Astrology for Everyone,* The Changing Sky, Skymates, The Book of Pluto,* - Steven Forest

Astrology, Karma and Transformation* Stephen Arroyo

The Astrology of Karma* - Pauline Stone

Planets in Transit* - Rob Hand

Psychological Horoscope Analysis
for individuals - $65.00 + $8. P&H
★ **Psychological Horoscope Analysis** — Liz Greene's unique interpretation of the birth chart focuses on the strengths and weaknesses of your psychological type. She discusses the conscious and unconscious aspects of your personality including a description of your shadow, the psychological atmosphere during your childhood, typical patterns in your relationships and the best way towards integration and development. The text is lively, thought-provoking, psychologically deep and free of "astrologese." The analysis is a serious discussion of an adult person's problems in life and, therefore, is not offered for children under 14. *18-25 pages. Specify gender, birth date, time and place.*

Career and Vocational Horoscope - $65.00 + $8. P&H
★ **Career and Vocational Horoscope** — has generated considerable interest, because finding and pursuing a career path that is right for you and uses your talents leads personal success, material rewards, recognition and achievement. Liz has written an analysis that deals with the fundamental issue of our role in the mundane world. It considers key questions like what potential and specific talents can you bring into your working life? What difficulties and limitations hold you back either in real terms or simply blocks that can be overcome? All manner of angles are considered in relation to the question of what is your calling or ideal vocation.

Liz writes in her unique style — where each time you read it, new dimensions and avenues to explore are revealed. Not only is there the pleasure and rewards of self-discovery as in other reports by Liz Greene, but there is a real possibility that the insights can translate into personal success outside your inner personal world. *Specify gender, birth date, time and place.*

Relationship Horoscope - $75.00 + $8. P&H
★ **Relationship Horoscope** — Liz Greene relationship analysis for any two adults over 18 who are having a love relationship. The report analyzes what brings you together, the essence of the relationship and the deeper issues activated inside you as a result of the relationship. *20-25 pages. Specify gender, birth date, time and place of both partners.* You can also order a second report written from the other partner's point of view for - **$40.00.** + $7.

Yearly Horoscope Analysis - $65.00 + $8. P&H (12 mo) ★
Yearly Horoscope Analysis — "The Meaning of the Time" uses selected transits and progressions to explore the year's main themes as well as outlining the prevalent themes for each month. She also discusses the trends in each sphere of life: emotional, mental, physical and spiritual. The text focuses primarily on the inner developments, conflicts, changes and realizations which reflect the real meaning of time. *40-50 pages. Specify gender, birth date, time and place.*

Child's Horoscope - $65.00 + $8. P&H
★ **Child's Horoscope** — Liz Greene uses her deep understanding of astrology and psychology to give parents her special insight into their child's personality. Discover a child's psychological type, talents, needs and anxieties enabling him/her to find and follow the right path. *20-25 pages. Specify gender, birth date, time and place.*

Long Term Perspectives for Individuals - $75. + $8. P&H

★ **Long-Term Perspectives - 6 Year Horoscope** —Astrological cycles do not take human calendars into account. The movement of the planets have their own logic and timing. The long-term horoscope for 6 years starting from the beginning of the current year, allows you to look into the long-ranging and complex processes of your psyche. Your inner development, which is reflected by transits of the slower-moving planets and progressions, is usually not in a hurry and gives your personality time to integrate the new. It is helpful, though, to know these new developments in advance and Liz Greene provides some insights.

Besides your own personal themes, Liz Greene analyzes the collective constellations of the new millennium, and how they influence your individual horoscope. *Approximately 50 pages. Specify gender, birth date, time and place.* **251**

People often ask me, "Rebeca, are we compatible?" And I say, "What's inside is outside. Look at the mirror."

Rebeca Eigen's consultations take you into your unconscious to empower you and bring forth your Gold.

Have you ever wondered why a situation or a particular type of person continues to appear in your life? Why do certain patterns or events happen in your relationships? Do you want to understand these situations, recognize when they are upon you, grow thru them and change?

YOUR unique birth chart (based on accurate time, date and place) shows that what is inside will show up in your Outer world experiences as if by coincidence, but it is actually synchronicity.

Whatever sign *(archetype)* is on your 7th house cusp which is also called the *descendent*, whatever planets reside therein, are a detailed picture of what you will develop in this Lifetime *with or without your intention or consent.*

So you might as well learn about this part of you and make a decision to develop it because you can then experience the more productive aspects of that particular energy – **TOGETHER!**

Rebeca Eigen will listen to your story and then using your birth chart, she will help you see where blind spots could be happening that keep you stuck. Rebeca's expertise is in facilitating you to discover your own Shadow, a concept of Carl G. Jung. As you learn to embrace your unlived life, you will love your whole Self and this self-knowledge will empower you as you make a conscious effort to *rewrite your story.*

7th House Astrology Consultations & Shadow Work for Relationships

For Individuals and Couples. Visit **shadowdance.com** to review the different **Astrological Reports** and see all consultations available including prepaid **4 or 6 Week Commitments of Shadow Work** utilizing your birth chart. Check out my **YouTube channel** to see the series called **YOU & Astrology,** *Astrology = Archetypes* and subscribe. To participate, email me at *rebecae@shadowdance.com.*

SCHEDULE MORE THAN ONE APPOINTMENT & SAVE

Rebeca Eigen - 7th House Astrologer *& Relationship Alchemist* **281.799.2900**

SHADOW WORK with Rebeca Eigen will help *all of your relationships, not just your romantic ones!*

CONSULTATIONS AVAILABLE

By taking a look at your Astrological 7th House energy from a Jungian perspective, Rebeca will help you find the hidden treasures in your chart and will reveal the hardwired relationship requirements that your soul designed for this lifetime.

VENUS and YOUR 7th HOUSE Planets, Ruler and Aspects and Intro to SHADOW WORK

Like diamonds, we have so many different facets – some are easier to identify than others. Some we project onto our partners. This works fine for a time, but a major reason we are drawn to a particular individual through love or hate is to see ourselves in the mirror they are holding up for us, although often to us it looks like it's them. This is when understanding both your 7th House and Venus, really becomes instrumental to your ability to create and sustain relationships. With this knowledge, you are now capable of recognizing and taking back the pieces of yourselves that they had to carry for you. Knowing about your Shadow is life-changing.

YOUR SATURN Sign and House: Where We All Feel Inferior

The planet Saturn is symbolic of your limitations, your greatest fears and can become your Achilles heel in the sense that it is difficult to express this energy constructively at first. Traditionally, Saturn has been described as how we hold ourselves back, where we feel awkward and self-conscious, and it seems that these fears we feel internally are caused by factors that are external or happening "to us." In this consultation, Rebeca will help you see that your Saturn sign, placement, and aspects will show you a way to see Saturn as a place of strength. With self-awareness, personal integrity, and appreciating the need for becoming grounded, each delay or restriction can be viewed as an area where taking responsibility instead of blaming fate will lead to mastery.

The NODES of the MOON in Our RELATIONSHIPS

This consultation will lead you to a valuable understanding of your karmic intentions for this lifetime. Knowing our nodes (which are considered to be karmically ingrained characteristics we've repeated over many lifetimes) also gives us even more detailed information about our relationship patterns. The Jungian word compensation comes into focus here as we see that what we overdo in our life will be compensated for in our unconscious and now will become fodder for projection. The habitual and ingrained tendencies described by our South Node are out of balance and require conscious intention to grow towards what will round us out, best described by our North Node. The nodal axis often will be something that, once we are aware, can show us what our soul is really striving for in this lifetime as our life's purpose.

COUPLES CONSULTATIONS — Defining What Our Relationship Needs Are — TOGETHER

The benefit of a Couples Consultation is to help you understand yourself, your partner, and the complex relationship situations your partner has come into your life to help you both integrate within yourselves. Your will find that your relationship is not an accident, and that you can learn to meet each other halfway when you understand the complexity of your energy (archetypes). Who you are as a couple is a combination of the hidden aspects of yourselves that you are in the process of developing, as well as the conscious energies you share. You can become a GIFT to each other's spiritual and psychological growth. *This work requires 3 separate sessions. I work with couples one-time individually first, and then together.*

MORE SHADOW WORK

As you begin to go into your unconscious more and more will come up and/or something happens in a relationship in your environment and you just need help understanding why this particular person or situation and how can that be about you, you wonder. I will listen and then look at your chart and point out where the blind spot could be happening. It can also be coming from the other person or something you will have to develop to stop a certain behavior or pattern. So if you need more help, integrating your shadow, that's my specialty is helping you discover and embrace your unlived life and rewrite your story. *What you will find out is the Universe had your back all along — you just didn't know it.*

- TESTIMONIALS -

"Thank you for introducing me to shadow work several years ago. I don't know where I would be right now if it were not for meeting you during that crazy time in my life."

Michelle R., Bossier City, LA

"I had often wondered how I could begin to unlock the secrets of my subconscious mind, why I had made some of the choices I'd made and why I had chosen some of the relationships I had chosen. At last, Rebeca Eigen's teachings have offered me that key.

Ruth Ann P., Houston, TX

HOUSE/SIGN	PLANET
1 ♈ *Aries (Mar 21 - Apr 20)*	♂ MARS
2 ♉ *Taurus (Apr 21 - May 21)*	♀ VENUS
3 ♊ *Gemini (May 22 - Jun 21)*	☿ MERCURY
4 ♋ *Cancer (Jun 22 - Jul 22)*	☽ MOON
5 ♌ *Leo (Jul 23 - Aug 23)*	☉ SUN
6 ♍ *Virgo (Aug 24 - Sep 22)*	☿ MERCURY
7 ♎ *Libra (Sep 23 - Oct 23)*	♀ VENUS
8 ♏ *Scorpio (Oct 24 - Nov 22)*	♇ PLUTO
9 ♐ *Sagittarius (Nov 23 - Dec 21)*	♃ JUPITER
10 ♑ *Capricorn (Dec 22 - Jan 20)*	♄ SATURN
11 ♒ *Aquarius (Jan 21 - Feb 18)*	♅ URANUS
12 ♓ *Pisces (Feb 19 - Mar 20)*	♆ NEPTUNE

Made in United States
North Haven, CT
03 June 2022